# It's Never Too Late To Plant A Tree

## Your Guide To Never Retiring

Jeanne Haseley

Lutha Haseley

*To Paul Schmitthousen*
*Best wishes*
*[signature]*
*3/1/04*

# It's Never Too Late
# To Plant
# A Tree

## Your Guide To Never Retiring

## Mel Helitzer and Morrie Helitzer

*To Paul.*
*Ray Skinner*

U S P

## University Sports Press
### Athens, Ohio

ISBN 0-9630387-45

Library of Congress Cataloging-in-Publication Data
2003096658

To
*Irene Helitzer*
*and*
*Linea Warmke*

in love and appreciation

Design and composition: Froma Bessel
Photo editor: Lyntha Eiler
Cover: Patrice Kroutel

# It's Never Too Late To Plant a Tree

## Community Projects

## Creative Arts & Communication

## Education

# Entertainment

# Health

# Helping Kids

# Humor

# A World Without Boundaries

# Never Too Old

# New Business

# Seniors To The Front

# Yes, You Can
# Retire to Something

When asked to write a Foreword for this book, I hesitated. I could almost hear the inevitable reaction:

"Edgar Bronfman? What does Edgar Bronfman know about ordinary people? He writes a book about reinventing yourself after retirement, but who's he talking to? Jimmy Carter, Everett Koop, Walter Cronkite, Kitty Carlisle. What has that got to do with me, somebody who never made the front page of a newspaper and never will, somebody ordinary?"

My short answer is that the women and men profiled in *It's Never Too Late To Plant A Tree* are **not** ordinary. Yes, some of them are off on extraordinary missions such as Ed Artis, bringing food, medicine and help to the people of Iraq and Afghanistan; or E.J. McClendon on his worldwide campaign to eradicate polio. But many of those profiled you'll recognize as not too different than people you know, maybe yourself. The difference, if you will, is that they're cultivating their own backyards, teaching and learning, and in the process, they're making a difference. Let me give you a few examples.

Frances Petit helped clean drug dealers and prostitutes out of her neighborhood in Saskatoon, Canada, and she's 90. Mary and Bob Longacre are helping hard of hearing kids participate in activities for which their

> **What troubles me is the attitude, "I'm too old to learn about computers and stuff like that."**

schools have no budget. Burrell Ross goes to the hospital, cuddles and rocks babies whose mothers can't or won't. Elise Mitchell Sanford uses her photographic skills to help those diagnosed with disabling mental illnesses.

What Petit, the Longacres, Ross and Sanford and so many others in this book have in common with the "famous people" about whom I wrote, is a determination *to retire to something*, not simply to retire, period. What I stressed in *The Third Act*, and want to reinforce here, is that there are widely available opportunities to help make possible a rewarding Third Act in your lives.

To begin with, there are resources galore. Here are some that I list in my book:

 **My father, "Mr. Sam," as he was known, did many and generous deeds in his lifetime, but releasing iron-fisted control of the company he had built wasn't one of them.**

The AARP, the nation's leading organization for people 50 and over; Access America for Seniors, offering a whole range of government services and benefits for seniors; Alliance for Retired Americans, created to protect the health and economic security of seniors; Gray Panthers, intergenerational advocacy organization dedicated to social change; Habitat for Humanity International, a nonprofit, ecumenical Christian housing ministry that welcomes volunteers of all faiths who are committed to Habitat's goal of eliminating poverty housing; International Executive Service Corps pairs professionals with businesses, nonprofits and government in some 120 countries; National Executive Service Corps sets up consultancies tailored to the specific needs of the small to medium business and the skills of senior-level business executive volunteers; New Directions guides senior executives and professionals into new full-time and part-time opportunities, business ventures, board directorships, consulting, humanitarian pursuits and active retirement; Peace Corps fights hunger, disease and opportunity around the globe and welcomes older applicants; Retired and Senior Volunteer Program matches people age 55 and older with local groups in need; Service Corps of Retired Executives (SCORE) enables retired business owners and executives to share their real-world knowledge with aspiring entrepreneurs; Senior Job Bank, (Job Links for Seniors) offers government and nonprofit sites for seniors; SPRY Foundation, a national nonproit whose mission is to help adults plan for a healthy and financially secure future; Tech Corps links technical experts with schools for the purpose of training the workforce of the future.

You can get more detailed information on each or all of the above by going to a search engine on your computer. And if you tell me that you don't use the computer, stand back, because you just opened the door for another lecture.

Nobody expects you to be a computer whiz. I'm not, and I don't pretend to be, but even if you don't own or have access to a computer, your local library does. What troubles me is the attitude, "I'm too old to learn about stuff like that." No you're not. Except in your own mind. You're not being asked to take up skydiving, although Bud Reid did at age 93. What's truly astonishing is that seven years before, he was bed-ridden with Guillain-Barré syndrome, (GBS). Now, Reid intends to keep going until he's at least 100. Mind you, I'm not going to start skydiving, and I'm not challenging you to do so. What I'm saying is find those things that work for you. And do them!

The "I'm too old to change…" is a sure signal that you're shutting down your engines or already have. The good news is that you can At

Hillel Leadership Conference
©1995, Mark Finkenstaedt

turn them back on, if you choose to. Better yet, as you move towards retirement, plan ahead. Yes, I'll play my theme song again. Retire to something!

As for fear of failing by trying something new, the artist, Georgia O'Keeffe, who lived and worked well into her 90's once said, " I've been absolutely terrified every moment of my life, and I've never let it keep me from doing a single thing I've wanted to do."

I hit on the title *The Third Act* as more than an attention-getter. It's a description of the roundness of life and the value of recognizing that Act Three is not meant to be a stress-free slide towards Eternal Rest, after Act One of Learning and Act Two of Working.

Before you can move onto The Third Act, you have to be able to let go of The Second Act. I don't have to look any further than my own father, the late Samuel Bronfman, for an example of someone who couldn't or wouldn't let go. "Mr. Sam," as he was known, did many good and generous deeds in his lifetime, but  releasing iron-fisted control of the company he had built wasn't one of them. The company suffered, and so did he. He had prostate cancer the last two years of his life, and still he would not let go. In the end he ruled by veto, not by imagination. I was always determined that I would not be like my father in that respect, and I believe I've succeeded.

On the opposite side of the coin, as a model for letting go, there's Rabbi W. Gunther Plaut, widely regarded as the leading historian, scholar and **I'll play my theme song again. Retire to something!**  representative of the Jewish Reform Movement. He arrived in this country penniless, a refugee from Germany in the 1930's. In the years that followed, he proceeded to build a worldwide reputation in religious circles. At age 65, he voluntarily retired as spiritual leader of the largest Reform Congregation in Toronto. In *The Price and Privilege of Growing Old* (CCAR Press) Rabbi Plaut describes what happened:

"The spring festival of Shavuot (Pentecost) had passed, and the anticipation of leisure was beckoning. Except this time, I felt none of the relief I had hoped for. Instead of becoming carefree I was suddenly wondering how, come fall, I would handle the workload. Rather than feeling librated I felt depressed—not clinically, but enough to worry me. Obviously something had changed. The first signs of aging had set in, and I became aware of it on that spring day in 1976. I was not quite 64 years old."

The following year Rabbi Plaut retired. But has he stopped working? Far from it.

Now in his 90's he has gone on as a writer, lecturer and scholar. In *The Price and Privilege of Growing Old*, one of more than two dozen books to his credit (which, incidentally, he composed in 2000 on his computer) he writes about his post-retirement experience:

"When people had greeted me on occasion by saying, 'I'm so honored you came,' my wife had often reminded me: 'Don't let it go to your head, it's the office that honors them, not you.' She was right, and retirement only underlined the truth of it. The whole identity shift didn't happen all at once; it just built up (or rather down) with a kind of slow inevitability."

Rabbi Plaut personifies the importance of what might be called the "AA's," Attitude and Activity, exemplified by people who continue to strive and thrive. As for Rabbi Plaut, his mother left him an extraordinary legacy. At age 88 she started going to the university. At 100 she got her B.A.

The beauty of the stories in this book is that in every case a determined effort was put forth. And the fact that a dream is deferred doesn't mean that in the end it is denied. Fifty years after he first entered the seminary, Father Tom Farley celebrated his first Mass in Ellsworth, Maine. Louisa Groce at 81 became the oldest person to be ordained in The Evangelical Lutheran Church in America. In a different vein, Emily Kimball turned an avocational interest into a successful business venture. She calls herself "The Aging Adventurer." So did Harriet Lewis, a housewife, who, inspired by her daughters, became an adventurer later in life and offers slide shows on her experiences. Ray Thomas retired from a successful retail lumber and construction business and organized a county community foundation. A master craftsman, Thomas makes fine inlay tables that sell for as high as $16,500 each at auctions. The proceeds go to the foundation's many community support programs. Thomas refuses to sell any of his works for personal profit, and they've become collector items. Finally, while I'm not sure of what "ordinary" is supposed to mean, Gillie Stalder, who ran a printing press during his working life, used his culinary talents to develop "Gillie's Noodles," which are sold in supermarkets.

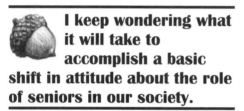 **I keep wondering what it will take to accomplish a basic shift in attitude about the role of seniors in our society.**

Still, I keep wondering what it will take to accomplish a basic shift in attitude about the role of seniors in our society. So much of the discussion, the debate if you will, centers on what this aging population will mean in terms of **costs and burdens**: Social Security, Medicare, the need for some to keep working, thereby squeezing out younger people, a more heavily loaded tax base to meet expanded senior needs. Yet how often do we hear about the **benefits** that can flow from this amazing resource of experienced, capable citizens, a substantial number in good health and perfectly willing?

Jess Bell recognized what it meant by establishing senior production lines at his cosmetics packaging firm in Ohio. I believe what Bell did is a model that can be replicated elsewhere in the country to the benefit of all. Oh for the day when "Ageism" will give way to "Capability Plus" in viewing the neglected productivity of men and women in their 60's, 70's, 80's and 90's.

Perhaps we should leave the last word to 90-year-plus Rabbi Plaut, who concludes *The Price and Privilege of Growing Old* this way:

"Language is a powerful instrument for change. We who are old deserve to be seen for who we are: individuals who do not want to spend the rest of their days as society's offal, discarded and delegitimated. Most of us still have much to give; rescuing our potential from thoughtless waste and making it available to all will be a common benefit. The young will learn from the exercise and the old will acquire self-respect. It is a win-win project.

"When that happens, the biblical saying, presently unpopular, may gain new currency: 'Grey hair is a crown of glory.' That would herald another 'new age.'"

Speaking personally, I'm lucky, blessed with genes of longevity and a spirit of optimism. It hasn't made me immune from sadness and disappointment, but I'm still buoyed by a sense that when we reach out, we can touch the lives of others for the good. In turn, those touched are likely to respond; if not directly to us, so what? As long as their deeds of kindness and help flow to others, it can have a great multiplier effect. What an opportunity. What a blessing. And what this book proves time and time again, it is there for us to do.

Edgar M. Bronfman

---

Edgar M. Bronfman retired as CEO of Seagram's at the age of 65. He is president of the World Jewish Congress and the World Jewish Restitution Organization, and chairman of the Governing Board of Hillel. He is the author of *The Third Act: Reinventing Yourself After Retirement, The Making of a Jew* and *Good Spirits: The Making of a Businessman.*

# Why This Book?

Do we really need one more book on Retirement?

No comment, because....

*It's Never Too Late To Plant A Tree* is **not** another book on retirement. It's *Your Guide To Never Retiring*. And that's more than a catchy phrase.

In the pages that follow you'll read of women and men in their 60's, 70's, 80's, who just keep going. Ten are already in their 90's.

"Wait a minute," says the gentleman in the front row, "I'm retired and I love it. Are you trying to make me feel guilty?

Absolutely not. We have a friend in his 70's, who's a great Mr. Fix-It. He enjoyed a successful career in the construction business, and to this day, his motto is, "Hand me the wrench and move over." Does he have any regrets that he retired? "Listen, I'm so busy with all my projects, I need an assistant."

More power to him, and those like him.

But we're addressing millions of men and women who find retirement less than fulfilling, and millions more who approach retirement with concern.

Who hasn't read about the "graying of America," and what it means in terms of Social Security, Medicare, 401(k)'s and retiree benefits? A complex subject that's not going to vanish. We don't have a global solution, but we're convinced that part of the local, state and national answer lies in utilizing a great resource that is sometimes comfortably dismissed as "The Golden Agers."

We hear a good deal about sexism, racism and a variety of other "isms," but not much about "Ageism." Ageism is defined as "prejudice or discrimination against a particular age-group and especially the elderly." It made it into Merriam-Webster in 1969, and Ageism has wastefully fenced off a valuable and growing segment of our society from making much-needed contributions to it and being rewarded accordingly.

A survey by the AARP found that nearly 70% of people over 45 plans to continue working after 65. And look at these statistics:

By 2050, there will be more then 2-million Americans 100 years and older. Two-thirds of all people who ever lived past the age of 65 are alive today. One of three girl infants born in the United States in 2003 will live to be 90.

The times are a-changing and *It's Never Too Late To Plant A Tree* provides constructive examples of how Ageism is being countered. A fringe benefit, we trust, will be a more realistic treatment in television programs of the 65+ generation, not as a bunch of amiable codgers or slightly befuddled buffoons, but as productive, seasoned veterans with much to offer.

To set the record straight, this book is not a "12-Step Approach", nor a "How To...", nor "33 Things They Never Told You About Retirement." The advice we offer is advice by example, the examples of those who are profiled here.

Read about seniors who:

> • Work on production lines and allow a business to thrive
>
> • Form Virtual Retirement Communities so those over 65 need not relocate if they do not choose to do so.
>
> • Advocate on their own behalf.

We'll tell you about freshly minted writers, artists, musicians, entertainers, educators, business entrepreneurs, humorists, lecturers and crafts people. And some who've come back to long nurtured dreams.

Truly, age is no barrier. Louisa Groce became the oldest ordained minister in The Lutheran Evangelical Church at the age of 81. Tom Farley picked up where he'd left off 50 years previous to say his first mass in Ellsworth, Maine.

Above all, you'll find it's possible to do good in your own backyard, or to move into A World Without Boundaries. We have accounts of more than a half dozen community projects and examples of those who've mounted campaigns miles and miles from home: Food for the hungry. Tackling the ravages of polio. Fighting child abuse in the workplace.

If none of the above rings a bell, don't be discouraged. Here's a list of benefits we've run across that are bound to be useful.

## *Benefits of Planting*

1. Staying productive.
2. Fulfilling a dream.
3. Enhancing and enriching your life.
4. Giving back to society by ascertaining some genuine need that's not being met.
5. Providing extra income.
6. Bringing family closer.
7. Making new friends.
8. Improving your health. Activity builds endorphins that fight disease. ("If you don't want to grow old, then don't stop growing").
9. Becoming important to your community.
10. Gratification in supporting a cause you value.
11. Discovering new talents.

## *Why You Should Get Started Now*

1. Tomorrow may come sooner than you think. Or, if you procrastinate, it may never come.

2. Start researching your options and interests. Now. "Stop living at work and start working at living"

3. Specialize. "If you scatter yourself, you end up being concerned about everything and make no changes. If you concentrate on one thing, you can make a difference."

Read on. If you don't find at least one example, one person, one adventure that triggers an opportunity or a possibility, we'll be surprised. And if you have a better idea, let us know. We're busy digging away on our next plot of land. And we're receptive to helping hands.

# Two Presidents Who Never Retired

On a cloudy March day in 1933, a solemn-faced Herbert Hoover left the Presidency of the United States. A master at making things work, "The Great Engineer" had failed to rescue the nation from a deepening Depression, despite his best efforts. Still full of energy and dreams, his three decades of distinguished public services were seemingly forgotten. The cheers that swirled about him were for his confident, photogenic successor, Franklin D. Roosevelt. "The only thing we have to fear is fear itself," FDR declared. Hoover was 58.

January 20, 1981. Thirty-eight years have passed and Inauguration Day has moved up from March 4th to January 20th. Another engineer, President Jimmy Carter, watches his confident, photogenic successor take the oath of office.

*President Carter shaking hands with an Ethiopian child.*
©1997 The Carter Center/Robert Grossman

The voters had rejected him, as they had, for different reasons, rejected Hoover. Carter was 56.

Separated by 60 years in age, the two men shared bonds of common experiences, beliefs and commitments, perhaps more significant than their differing political allegiances. Both had grown up on farms: Hoover, in Iowa and Oregon; Carter, in Georgia. Hoover was a practicing Quaker; Carter, a serious, church-going Baptist. Central to their lives were concepts of public service, humanitarianism and "doing the right thing."

**"When I left the White House, I was a fairly young man and I realized I maybe have 25 more years of 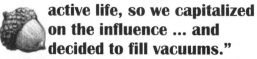 active life, so we capitalized on the influence ... and decided to fill vacuums."**

No blueprint exists for what former presidents can or should do once out of office. Nor is the circumstance of their departure a clear indicator of what will become of them, subsequently. Some have left office wealthy and acclaimed; others, on the edge of bankruptcy and in disrepute. John Adams for years was lost in the shadow of Washington and Jefferson. He waited two centuries for proper recognition of his accomplishments; yet he alone, among former presidents, went to the U.S. House of Representatives, where he served for 17 years. A singular act.

In the cases of Herbert Hoover and Jimmy Carter, disheartened though they may have been, each accepted the cards dealt him and moved forward.

Jimmy Carter's unflagging determination to reach for new horizons is well known. His winning the Nobel Peace Prize in 2002 was clearly a sign of vindication. In announcing the award, the five-member Norwegian Nobel Committee praised Carter's decades of "untiring effort to find peaceful solutions to international conflicts, to advance democracy and human rights, and to promote economic and social development."

In acknowledging his selection, the former president said that his greatest legacy was The Carter Center, an Atlanta, Georgia-based, non-governmental organization devoted to global peace and social justice, established in 1982 by Carter and his wife, Rosalynn.

"When I left the White House," he said, "I was a fairly young man and I realized I maybe have 25 more years of active life, so we capitalized on the influence that I had as a former president of the greatest nation in the world and decided to fill vacuums."

On a recent trip to Africa, the former president saw a toddler about the same age as his youngest grandson, and he quickly thought how different the quality of each child's life would be. One would lack adequate food, medical care, and the right to live in freedom.

"The destiny of the young African boy is much bleaker than that of a child in a developed country," Carter says. "There is no doubt that the most serious challenge to the world today is the growing chasm between rich people and poor people."

"Most of us never visit places where people really have nothing," Mrs. Carter says. "We wanted to use our influence to make a difference and decided to build The Carter Center, at first to resolve conflicts. But we soon realized you cannot have peace when stomachs are empty, children suffer from easily preventable diseases, and people have no say in determining their own futures. The Center helps people acquire knowledge and tools to improve their own lives, so changes will be permanent."

To date, with a staff of 150, the Center has made a difference in more than 65 nations:

- Observing 45 multiparty elections;
- Reducing Guinea worm disease by 98 percent worldwide;
- Creating new avenues for peace in Sudan, Uganda, the Korean Peninsula, Haiti, Liberia, and Ethiopia;
- Helping 4 million farmers in Africa to double or triple grain crops;
- Building coalitions to improve mental health care policies;
- Working to prevent and correct human rights violations.

"Our definition of human rights is very broad," says President Carter.

"It involves not only civil and political rights, but rights to adequate food, shelter, education, health care, and economic opportunity. These are all interrelated, and you cannot have permanent peace without addressing them all."

**"But we soon realized you cannot have peace when stomachs are empty, children suffer from easily preventable diseases, and people have no say in determining their own futures."**

Today, the Center has eight health programs and four peace programs. Recent projects have included resolving conflict between the government and opposition in Venezuela, observing elections in Kenya and Jamaica, bringing mental health professionals together to examine the psychological aftermath of September 11, and working to eradicate river blindness in the Americas.

"One example of why we work in both peace and health is that of Sudan," Carter says. "The Center has led the effort to make Guinea worm disease the next disease to be eradicated. Sudan has more cases than any country, but without an end to the civil war there, we cannot get access to key areas to prevent it. So our conflict resolution experts have worked to help the Sudanese government and rebels seek an end to the fighting."

The Center has been established as a permanent legacy to the vision of Carter and his wife, a vision of what it takes to create a world where everyone can live in peace, explains Center Executive Director John Hardman.

"The Carters have built a strong international institution that will continue to implement their vision. We have a superb staff of experts and a strong partnership with Emory University, and we are creating an endowment to continue the work of the Center indefinitely," says Dr. Hardman. "Most of all, there is a 20-year track record of achievement inspired by the Carters' vision. For more information, you can visit: www.cartercenter.org."

Says Nobel Laureate Carter, "Peace is more than just the absence of war. There is an inner peace that comes from a mother knowing that she can raise her children with adequate food, education, and health care, that they will grow with dignity and self-respect, and have hope for a better future."

As part of its outreach program, more than 100 undergraduate and graduate students work as interns with Center programs for academic credit or practical experience each year. Approximately 130 volunteers donate an average of one day of their time each week to the Center. They work with program staff, assist with special events, and conduct select private tours. Internship information is available at this site. For information on volunteering at The Carter Center, contact the volunteer office by emailing carterweb@emory.edu or by calling 404-420-5104.

Domestically, a good deal of attention has focused on President Carter's work and support for Habitat for Humanity, a nonprofit, ecumenical Christian housing ministry dedicated to eliminating substandard housing and making decent shelter a matter of conscience and action.

In a well-publicized event, Carter strapped on a tool belt in 1984 and led a work group to New York City to help renovate a six-story building for 19 families in need of decent, affordable housing. His goal was to build homes and awareness of the critical need for affordable housing.

"We have become small players in an exciting global effort to alleviate the curse of homelessness," Carter said.

While Jimmy Carter is alive, well and very much with us today, Hoover, on the other hand is more distant in time. Consequently, his post-White House achievements are less in the public consciousness. In a lifetime that spanned 90 years, he gained prominence in four major careers: engineering, international relief work, government and politics, and reform of governmental bureaucracy. Ironically, the high point of his public career, the presidency, was dominated by the Depression and proved a bitter disappointment.

Out of office, Hoover and his wife, Lou, went back to live in the house they had built at Stanford in California. Hoover became chairman of the board of Boys' Clubs of America, reflecting a life-long concern for the children of the world with a special interest in boys of the city streets. A shy man, for many years little was heard of him. Finally, when he returned to public view, he built quickly and efficiently on lessons learned and practiced decades earlier. Because

*President Hoover surrounded by Polish war orphans during his famine-relief survey of Warsaw, April 2, 1946.*                    ©1946 International Newsreel

the past was very much a prelude to Hoover's post-retirement years, a few words about his early years are in order.

Orphaned at age 9, young "Bert" was raised by a maternal uncle, Dr. Henry John Minthorn, a physician in Oregon. Although his adoptive parents wanted him to attend a Quaker college, Hoover, with a gift for mathematics, enrolled at newly opened Stanford University in California, the first step in becoming an internationally renowned mining engineer. His engineering and business skills made him a world traveler, taking him to China in 1898. Less than two years after arriving, Hoover, together with his new bride and hundreds of foreign families was trapped in a Tientsin compound, when the fiercely anti-foreign Boxer Rebellion erupted. Hoover sprang into action. He directed the building of barricades and the provisioning of food and water to 600 anti-Boxer Chinese who had taken refuge in the compound.

Ever on the move—between 1902 and 1907 Hoover and his family circled the globe five times—Hoover was in England at the outbreak of World War One in 1914. Thousands of American tourists flooded into London trying to book passage back to the states. The U.S. Embassy asked Hoover to help and named him head of the Committee of American Residents in London for Assistance to American Travelers. The committee accommodated over 120,000 Americans.

Shortly thereafter, with the German invasion of Belgium, 10 million Belgians, under sea blockade by the British, were in

**Hoover in 50 years never accepted for his private use any payment he received for public service.**

danger of starvation. As head of the Committee for Relief of Belgium, Hoover negotiated for the supply of food through the British blockade with guarantees by the Germans that the food would reach its destination. To achieve this monumental task, Hoover relied on his three greatest strengths: technical ability, practicality and morality.

**During World War I, the American ambassador to England described Hoover as a "simple, modest, energetic little man who began his career in California and will end it in Heaven, and he doesn't want anyone's thanks."**

In a message to President Woodrow Wilson, Walter Hines Page, the American ambassador to England, described Herbert Hoover as a "simple, modest, energetic little man who began his career in California and will end it in Heaven, and he doesn't want anyone's thanks." More specifically, Hoover in 50 years never accepted for his private use any payment he received for public service.

When America declared war on Germany on April 6, 1917, President Wilson called Hoover home to take charge of food organization in America as U.S. Food Administrator. America had to provide food for her own armies and the other Allies, for the Allied peoples and for the American people at home. The Great Engineer did the job.

A scant 20 years later, World War Two broke out in Europe and put Hoover back on the public stage. FDR had rejected Hoover's offer of assistance, so as a private citizen, Hoover established the Polish Relief Commission. For two years the Commission fed 300,000 children in the German-occupied territory of Poland until the war stopped the private effort. For the duration of the Second World War, Hoover and his relief committee fed the small democracies: Belgium, Holland, Finland, and Poland.

War's end did not solve the problems of need and starvation.

In 1946 post-war famine threatened Europe again. President Harry Truman, who had succeeded Roosevelt, asked Hoover to head the Famine Emergency Commission. The former president, now in his 60's, traveled 500 miles through 25 countries in 57 days. He organized the food of the world to sustain several hundred million people until the next harvest. He was once again working at a task at which he was expert.

That task done, in the spring of 1947, Congress turned to Hoover to undertake a study of how to reorganize the executive branch of the federal government: to improve economy and efficiency of federal agencies; to get rid of overlapping bureaus and services; and to define the executive functions, services, and activities.

The Hoover Commission spent 15 months in research and offered 280 detailed recommendations for change, many of which were implemented. By then President Eisenhower had assumed office and he promptly appointed Hoover to undertake a second Commission, this time to consider what the Federal Government should and should not do. He did the job.

Late in life, Hoover wrote, "Being a politician is a poor profession. Being a public servant is a noble one."

That principle guided two great planters, Presidents Herbert Hoover and Jimmy Carter, with remarkable results.

# Community Projects

"Cultivate your own garden" is the celebrated conclusion of Voltaire's novel, "Candide." Voltaire's hero, after traveling the world, returns home, realizing that he need search no further, that the tasks at hand are ones to which he can turn most productively.

Some of the heroines and heroes profiled here did travel the world before returning home; others never strayed that far. But all of them found tasks where they lived to devote their energies and talents.

Gifford Doxsee invested himself in Rural Action, an organization devoted to reverse the decline of southern Ohio and lift it back by its bootstraps.

Clifford Fahrer rejuvenated a Victorian theater in Wilmington, Ohio, once a vaudeville house and opera house, that had fallen into disrepair. Now it is home to more than 12 live theatrical production a year, a community center for a number of the town's social organizations and a source of pleasure to thousands of residents.

Frances Petit is 90 and lives in Saskatoon, Canada, above Montana. A successful entrepreneur and businesswoman, she saw her neighborhood slide downhill, as drug dealers, pimps and prostitutes moved in. But she fought back and succeeded, refusing to shrug and turn away. Read her story.

Ray Thomas makes fine inlaid pieces of furniture that can bring in excess of $16,000 a piece. Except they're not for private sale. Thomas's masterpieces are auctioned to support the Muskingum County Community Foundation in Ohio.

For you veterans of World War Two, remember "Wild Bill" Donovan, the man who founded the OSS? His deputy was Ned Putzell, a name less familiar perhaps, but someone who's still around—a man who became mayor of Naples, Florida and has kept going since then, beautifying his community.

And finally, Irving Silverman, who pays little heed to his legal blindness and hearing disability. He organized a memorial grove for 141 inhabitants of Tremont, Maine, who lost their lives at sea. He pushed and wheedled the Fire Department in Tucson, Arizona to reduce the teeth-rattling speed bumps. And he's not finished.

Are these unusual men and women? Yes. Are they doing what is beyond the reach of the rest of us? No. Look in our own backyards. Seek out local resources for ideas and assistance. Senior citizen centers. Churches and synagogues. Rotary Clubs. The American Legion. Kiwanis.

Cultivate your own garden. Watch it flourish and grow for the benefit of others and for your personal satisfaction.

# Preserving Rural America

Hundreds of small towns in America are on their deathbeds. Sickened by the exodus of economic bases from rural communities to urban cities, these towns exhibit an illness of national concern, since many believe that society's moral values are eroding rapidly.

The opinion of many of America's environmental opinion leaders is that, "Small towns are the foundation of our country. They are the last bastion of our country's wholesome values of family, community and democracy. And as they die, the future of our country is in jeopardy. We need to find leadership to stem a decline that has no short-term answers and seems overwhelming; moreover, there may be few monetary rewards for those who serve as leaders. Yet the challenge must be undertaken."

A small cadre of altruists is heeding the call. One of them is Gifford Doxsee, professor emeritus of history, who retired from Ohio University in 1994.

Before and since his retirement, Doxsee has been actively involved in Rural Action, an organization whose purpose is to reverse the decline of southeastern Ohio and lift it back by its bootstraps.

This is no easy task.

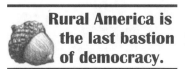

**Rural America is the last bastion of democracy.**

Dependent on natural resources such as coalmines since its colonization, the area slid off its economic plateau when world energy consumers switched to oil and gas. Coal-mine employment dwindled along with outmoded strip mines, farms consolidated and what little industry remained found it difficult to replace young employees who were moving to better-paying jobs in metropolitan areas. Within a few years, southeastern Ohio became a verifiable poverty area.

One community attempt to reverse the decline is Rural Action. Carol and Bruce Kuhre founded the nonprofit community-development organization in 1994 to promote economic, social and environmental justice in Appalachian Ohio. Rural Action serves as a catalyst to bring other recognized organizations into its cooperative programs. By guidance, encouragement and some financial support, it aims to promote self-esteem and sustainable quality of life.

Rural Action solicits its funds from church and fraternal organizations. And that's how the Kuhres met Doxsee. He was asked by his Episcopal Church of the Good Shepherd to be the liaison for its sponsorship and support of the Rural Action committee. It wasn't long before the community-outreach program so interested him that soon after he retired from the university he became a Rural Action board member and two years later its board president

Rural Action has undertaken a score of projects in its first decade. One of its most successful has been the plan to make the area a tourist attraction, because of its picturesque hilly geography,

©2003, Terry E. Eiler

*It's Never Too Late to Plant a Tree*

numerous lakes, beautiful forests, fishing streams and rivers. But tourism couldn't be enhanced before the region's rivers and wells were purged from the run-off of polluted water that seeped from abandoned coalmines.

In 1998, Rural Action encouraged local organizations to intensify a program of purification of area streams. Within five years, one mining creek, called Monday Creek, was successfully purified. The fish returned and spawned, sports fisherman grew in number and the program's success inspired environmentalists to plan to cleanse other area creeks whose run-off feed into the Hocking River, the main water artery,

**"It may take several generations, but it must be started and sustained now."**

"It may take several generations," says Doxsee, "but it must be started and sustained now. That's why we exemplify "It's Never Too Late to Plant a Tree.""

Modesty fits Doxsee's personality, but not his accomplishments. As a GI in World War II, Doxsee was captured during the Battle of the Bulge and spent five months in a German POW camp in Dresden with Kurt Vonnegut, whose famous novel *Slaughter-House Five* was based upon their common experiences.

Besides being a war hero, Doxsee is an authority on European history, the history of world oil, and the benefits of upgrading the environment. As a result, he is a frequent guest speaker at schools and community groups. Rural Action is just one of Doxsee's retirement pursuits. He is or has been a president or board member of a dozen statewide and area organizations from his church to the arts.

"Collectively," he admits, "they keep me busy as well as mentally and physically active. All retirees need to roll up their sleeves and take on constructive projects. I feel strongly it prolongs our lives."

E-mail: doxsee@ohio.edu

# He Brightens Your Life

Clifford Fahrer is a role model to thousands of retirees who volunteer for community service. Thanks to him they recharged their professional skills by helping local public service organizations accomplish goals that otherwise would have been left undone.

©2003, Bruce Strong/Light Chasers

*It's Never Too Late to Plant a Tree*

They make up for the lack of financial rewards by public appreciation. "A guy who becomes Mr. Fixit in a small town is more popular and trusted than the mayor. "

Fahrer got his reputation in the fifth grade when he was severely reprimanded by his teacher. Instead of doing his lessons in class, Clifford was taking apart watches to see what makes them tick. The teacher was especially upset because it was his watch.

Since then, Fahrer has never stopped tinkering.

Today, after retiring as chief engineer from Milacron Corporation, a machine tool manufacturer he served with for 33 years, Fahrer devotes his free time as head of lighting projects for his hometown's historic Murphy Theater. Completed in 1916 by Charlie Murphy, former owner of the Chicago Cubs, the Victorian theater in Wilmington, Ohio was constructed to be both a vaudeville house and an opera house. Now it is home to more than 12 live theatrical productions a year and also serves as a community center for a number of the town's and county's organizations.

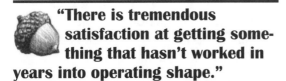 **"There is tremendous satisfaction at getting something that hasn't worked in years into operating shape."**

When he first took on the assignment, Fahrer had to deal with a rheostat light control board that was built in 1918. Patching it every time he turned it on, the board often shot off sparks and unwelcome flashing lights. "Often," said Fahrer, "there was a better show going on backstage."

With the lighting board so antiquated, Fahrer was once asked if he had trouble with the fire marshal. He said, "He was part of the tech crew working backstage."

He helped modernize the house and stage lighting systems, a project that took over two years. To save money, he even designed his own light sockets for the house lighting. "There is tremendous satisfaction at getting something that hasn't worked in years into operating shape."

Now the theater, although in constant need of rehabilitation funds for such major projects as air conditioning and handicapped seating, caters to national touring companies.

 **"We never have enough volunteers, because only one in 50 sticks it out."** Fahrer has worked with such celebrities as Pat Boone, the Oak Ridge Boys, Brenda Lee and Glenn Campbell. When TV star John Ritter married a hometown girl, Amy Yasbeck, the couple used the lovely theater as a wedding chapel and put Fahrer in charge of the lighting arrangements.

Working backstage is a wonderful retirement project. The busier you stay, the younger you are.

When there is a show to mount, Fahrer works along with a group of volunteers who build sets, set lights, work on the sound system and revamp the seating for 10-to-12 hours a day, four to five days a week. "We never have enough volunteers, because only one in 50 sticks it out," he admits sadly.

"They don't know what they're missing. Show business is hard work, but fun. There is tremendous satisfaction in backstage tech production, there is great camaraderie between cast and crew. There is no end of important things to do on cue."

When he's not at the theater, Fahrer likes doing restoration work on antique cars and motorcycles. His dream is to be in the pit crew of a motorcycle racing team, and he has a 65-year-old friend who joined a drag racing team.

"If you're involved in motorcycle racing, you're always moving," he said, "and just remember a moving target is harder to hit."

E-mail: cdfahrer@earthlink.net

# On Night Patrol
# With A 90-Year-Old

Your neighborhood is running down. You're well past retirement age with two small pensions and a little money in the bank. The climate is cold. Sounds like it's time to move on.

Not if you've been toughing it out since you were a teenager on a farm, who quit school to help support her family. Not someone like 90-year-old Frances Petit.

> **"I've got nothing against the prostitutes, if they weren't so noisy and shouting and drinking."**

"When I moved to this part of Saskatoon 30 years ago," she says, "it was a nice area. But about five years ago, a couple of blocks from where we live, prostitutes, drug dealers and unruly kids overran the neighborhood. My daughter, Alice, and I decided we had to do something."

They started writing letters to the newspapers. They arranged Town Hall meetings, where they spoke to seniors of affected communities. They talked on the phone, on radio programs and began appearing on TV. They protested to the City Council, telling them how difficult this was making life, especially for seniors.

For a time, Petit felt that she was up against an immovable object. "The City Council just wouldn't respond. They were in a state of denial that there are neighborhoods like this in Saskatoon. But there are, and we're beginning to make some progress."

It wasn't immediate. The next step for Petit and her daughter was to organize nighttime patrols, reporting on what was happening, particularly with men cruising in cars for prostitutes. She went out on a number of patrols herself.

"Mind you, we're not vigilantes," she says. "Our job is to report what we find to the police, so they can take action."

Prostitution is not illegal in Saskatoon, the largest city in Saskatchewan, which sits north of Montana. Soliciting is.

"I've got nothing against the prostitutes," she says, "if they weren't so noisy and shouting and drinking. But wherever there are prostitutes, there are criminals of all kinds, drug

> **Organizing and being militant is not new territory for Petit. "I've been an activist since I was 18."**

dealers and drug addicts. But, it's the 'johns,' the men who go looking for them; those are the ones we focus on. We have a street in my neighborhood that we call 'The Stroll.' The traffic on that street was unbelievable. One resident reported that 230 cars passed his house at 1:00 A.M.

"So what we did was to take the license plates of those cruising cars and turned them over to the police. The police would then call on the man and warn him. If the 'john' was caught with a prostitute in his car, the police could impound his car. If he appeared in court and was found guilty he could lose his car and pay a heavy fine. He could choose not to go to court, but pay $500 and go to 'john school,' where he was told of the injury his actions caused the community. If he got caught a second time, he could be in real trouble."

In the meantime, Petit continued working in the cutlery import business she and her husband started more than 30 years ago. She and her daughter run the business, and at 90 she continues to do all the paperwork for Atlas Cutlery & Butcher Supplies, Ltd.

Still she found time to push ahead on her cleanup project. The drug houses became a target for "Renewing Our Communities Committee," as Petit's group is known. "We made a fuss and called the landlords, reporting what was going on in their houses and what this was doing to the neighborhood. Little by little, we were able to get rid of some of the drug houses," she says.

*It's Never Too Late to Plant a Tree*

Organizing and being militant is not new territory for Petit.

"I've been an activist since I was 18. I fought for the poor and underprivileged during the '30's. I organized for the Farmers Union to help get better conditions for our farmers and for the Canadian Commonwealth Federation (C.C.F.) before it became the National Democratic Party, because I believe in its social aims. Remember, I was a farm girl, who dropped out of school at 15 to work. I know what the lives of poor people are like, but I don't believe that if you start out poor, you can't better your life.

"For example with those mobs of kids, most of them come from poor families, which is all the more reason for them to have an education. When we reported them, and the authorities looked into it, they found that something like 3,000 school-aged kids weren't even registered at schools. We've been pushing for a curfew like other cities have and finally have a Council member from our district who's putting pressure on for action.

*Community Projects*

"Some people didn't like what we were doing or how we're doing it, but you know, many more people are behind us. They just don't speak up. After I began to appear on television, strangers would come up to me in the Mall, and say, 'I saw you on TV and I'm with you.' I don't expect everyone to agree with us. I just want them to get thinking about what's going on, not pretending that problems don't exist."

After her husband's death in 1982, Petit let the cutlery business languish for a few years, then decided to go forward with her daughter, who was interested in smokehouses. Most smokehouses, at the time, were imported from Germany or the United States and were very expensive. Her daughter began building moderately priced smokehouses for butchers. Today, the smokehouses are a substantial part of the business. More recently, Petit's granddaughter set up the main retail outlet for Atlas Cutlery & Butcher Supplies, Ltd. in Alberta. They even have a website, www.atlascutlery.com.

# Not Cockeyed, Just an Optimist

What do you do for an encore, when you've been Executive Officer to General "Wild Bill" Donovan of the OSS during World War Two, a senior executive at Monsanto Chemicals for 30 years, and mayor of Naples, Florida?

"Why you just keep going," says Edwin "Ned" Putzell, Jr., now in his 90th year. "The idea of sitting around or playing golf never

©2003, David Ahntholz

appealed to me, and there's so much out there that needs to be done."

Formal retirement more than 25 years ago hasn't made much difference in the way Putzell responds to problems. Whether it's being in the right place at the right time or responding to opportunity quicker than the next person, he keeps finding the necessary connections and solutions.

"It was 1937. I was getting ready for my last year at Harvard Law School, and wanted to be a law clerk the summer before. The secretary of the school, who was a prominent Wall Street attorney, told me to forget it. 'This is still the Depression,' he said. There were no jobs and no one would hire me. 'I'll bet you the best meal in any restaurant in Boston that I can find a job on Wall Street,' I told him.

"I'd never been to Wall Street, and I really didn't know what I was talking about. But I took the train down to New York and I walked my legs off all Friday and all Saturday. I'm not even sure of where I was walking. By the time I was finished, I had five job offers. One was from Bill Donovan, a former Assistant US Attorney General, Congressional Medal of Honor winner, and senior partner of a big law firm. That's the one I took.

"After I graduated, Donovan hired me again. Pretty soon things got hot internationally, and President Roosevelt asked Donovan to come to Washington to work in a basement room

**"There's not another fool in town who'd give eight hours a day, five days a week as a volunteer without pay."**

in the White House as Coordinator of Information. Donovan took me with him. Later Roosevelt re-named it the Office of Strategic Services. With the war on, Donovan went into a general's uniform. With his help I entered the Navy and was assigned to the OSS, even though the Navy had turned me down twice before Pearl Harbor because of my eyesight. In time, I became the general's Executive Officer."

*It's Never Too Late to Plant a Tree*

**"I believe so heavily in community activity for everybody who can make or find the time."**

Putzell's next opportunity break came on his way to California to consult with Movie Director John Ford on making a film about the OSS. Putzell had stopped in St. Louis with an introduction to Edgar Monsanto Queeny, CEO of Monsanto Chemical. They hit it off so well, Queeny asked Putzell to fill the Treasurer's position, which had become vacant.

"I told him I wasn't a finance guy, but I took the job for a year and a half before I became General Counsel. I stayed with that for 30 years until I retired in 1976. I hadn't thought much about where we would go after St. Louis, but my wife had been spending winters in Naples on Florida's West Coast, and kept urging me to take a look.

"I told her Florida wasn't for me, but finally I visited Naples. Within 24 hours, we bought a lot and a half and went on to build a house on it. That started a roll. One day I was playing bridge and one of the players, who was on the City Council, said the Airport Authority needed a chairman. Would I take the job? I did and served four years then, and a decade later another four years. In between, I became a chairman of the board of Provincetown-Boston Airline, the chief tenant of Naples Airport."

With a strong interest in nature and the environment, Putzell found himself heavily involved with The Conservancy of Southwest Florida. He was CEO for five years at the end of which, he told the Board, "There's not another fool in town who'd give eight hours a day, five days a week as a volunteer without pay. You've got to hire someone. They finally did with money from a benefactor. With that out of the way, I was talked into running for mayor. Which I did and became mayor in 1986."

"I believe so heavily in community activity for everybody who can make or find the time. That's my soapbox. I've been able to apply my experience working with people. You see, I'm a perennial optimist. My wife can verify that. Relating to people is easy, if you just meet them halfway. Don't expect them to come to you. The challenge is relating to people who are difficult to deal with. You just have to work with it. Usually they come around, if you meet them halfway.

"I think my experience in OSS was unique and creative. It taught me how to relate to others, whether it was in Congress or in the military. It's had an influence on me ever since, and I'm grateful for it."

> **"I think my experience in OSS was unique and creative. It taught me how to relate to others. It's had an influence on me ever since."**

When asked for a creative experience that stands out in his "retirement" life, Putzell's example is practical, down-to-earth.

"When I was mayor, I decided we had to landscape the medians of this town. They were just weeds and grass growing in them, right in the main drag of the town and elsewhere. I was told you can't raise taxes, so I got on the hustings and told the public what the need was. It worked and we raised the property tax two percent for two years, got $800,000 with which we landscaped the medians. They're there today, and I tell you I'm proud of it.

# An Unlikely Don Quixote

Irving Silverman sits in his private lighthouse in Bernard, Maine looking across to Cadillac Mountain and the waters of Bass Harbor towards Europe where his parents were born in the 19th century. But he is not thinking of decades past. His eyes are fixed on the future, wondering when the next call will come for him to mount up and right some wrong.

Five feet, five-and-one half inches tall, 171 pounds ("too heavy"), Silverman, at 83, is an improbable Don Quixote. But he is, nevertheless, undeterred by being legally blind since birth and hearing impaired for many years.

A half-mile from the lighthouse, which he uses for ecumenical Sabbath prayer services, is a memorial grove for the Town of

©2003, Rich-Joseph Facun

Tremont's 141 inhabitants, who were lost at sea, a Silverman inspiration.

> **"The height of the speed bumps in my community could shake out your insides and break your car's axle."**

"It occurred to me one day," he says, "that there was no tribute to the fishermen and their families who had died at sea. So, I went to my 'kitchen cabinet,' a network of people I know, and asked them to start doing research on names, dates, etc. When it was completed, I started a fund-raising effort in the town. We found a 2-1/2 ton natural stone, had it hauled to the site, then had a bronze tablet affixed to the stone. A local landscaper cleared the area to make it a quiet place to reflect and contemplate. For the dedication, we invited clergy from the surrounding area to participate in a service, which was attended by more than 250 people. That was in 2001. Since then it's become a place of comfort, where you can place flowers or just sit and look out at the waters."

The death the following year of Silverman's wife, Nancy, after 43 years of marriage, has added an even more personal note to the memorial area for him.

"If it affects me," he says, "it might be affecting someone else. If other people are being ignored, if there's a need to be filled, or something unfair that can be set right, why shouldn't I try to do something about it?

"Living in a small town with compassionate residents, there are frequent occasions when emergency financial aid is necessary. So Nancy and I created the Southwest Harbor/Tremont Medical Needs Fund, a few years ago, which has provided more than $100,000 in benefits to individuals needing help for a variety of health purposes."

Neither is geography a limitation. In Tucson, Arizona, where he lives during the winter, he befriended the dean of the Eller Business College at the University of Arizona.

"I was auditing some business courses and realized that there was a need for a course in Social Entrepreneurship. Yes, making a living, earning money is important, and I've been successful as an entrepreneur, so making more is not a concern at this point. But there has to be something else. More than 30 students enrolled in the course. Now it's being continued. Best of all, other universities are adopting the program."

Some problems Silverman encounters are more down to earth. Literally.

"The community in Tucson where I live is private and responsible for its own road maintenance. Fifteen years ago, when the area was

**"Finding allies, developing a network came to me early and has worked for me to this day."**

developed, someone decided to put in speed bumps as a safety measure. Well, that was a good idea. The height of the bumps wasn't. They were much higher than the standards set by the City of Tucson. Not only could they shake out your insides, they could break you car's axle."

The Homeowners Association was not sympathetic to reducing the height of the bumps. So, Silverman went to the local Fire & Ambulance Rescue Company. They agreed that the high bumps were an obstacle, when responding to emergencies. With their support, Silverman made a presentation at the Homeowners membership meeting. Most of the homeowners agreed. The bumps have been reduced.

Using his wits to gain his goals is not a recently acquired talent. When he graduated from the Sight Conservation class of his elementary school, he was consigned to a vocational, rather than an academic high school, because of his vision. A compassionate principal and nurse insisted that he could attend academic high school and arranged for his admission.

"Finding allies, developing a network came to me early and has worked for me to this day," Silverman says.

From college, he went to work for the Knitting Industry's trade association, where he was responsible for the business side of their publications. All went well, but by the 1980's, foreign imports were cutting seriously into the industry's business and the advertising revenues of their publications.

"I saw the handwriting on the wall," he says. "I knew we needed an alternative to make up for lost advertising revenue."

That kind of forward vision, visual impairment notwithstanding, came easily to Silverman. He suggested creating trade expositions. The expositions were a hit from the start, and upon his retirement in 1985, Silverman and his wife launched a highly successful exposition business of their own. In time, however, further visual deterioration forced Silverman to sell his business.

Old entrepreneurs may not die; they just fade away (to borrow from General MacArthur's farewell address). This old entrepreneur did not fade away. For over 60 years he had been collecting antique wood type, which had grown to over three million letters including more than 600 complete fonts of fancy and Gothic design. At his wife's urging, Silverman began to create new uses for artifacts for people interested in purchasing type, and he named the business "Nancy Neale Typecraft" in her honor.

In addition, as a reflection of the Silvermans' interest in preservation, they helped established The Hamilton Wood Type Museum in Two Rivers, Wisconsin and have donated half their collection as the core of the Museum.

Has Don Quixote retired? Not at all. With his thinning white hair, frizzled beard and broad-brimmed, straw Southwest sombrero, Silverman is just in hiatus, trying to adjust to the loss of his wife.

"I've been attending some of the Bereavement Support groups," he says. "There's a lot to be done to improve the way they operate. And I have some ideas."

How else could it be?

E-mail: typenancy@aol.com

# He Doesn't Need a Jab to Get Him Started

Stephen Guthrie isn't around to explain why he slept with a pitchfork and two guns at the head of his bed, but there is an explanation.

To find out, you can visit the Putnam Underground Railroad Education Center (PURE) in the Putnam Historic District of Zanesville, Ohio. It's located at 522 Woodlawn Avenue in a pre-Civil War building next to Stephen Guthrie's House.

 **Abolitionist Stephen Guthrie slept with a pitchfork and two guns at the head of his bed.**

Stephen Guthrie slept (probably restlessly), guns and pitchfork at the ready, because he and his two brothers were abolitionists under attack from southern (pro-slavery) sympathizers who came from Virginia to settle Zanesville, across the river from Putnam.

The George Guthrie house, a documented stop on the Underground Railroad that took African-Americans from slavery in the South to freedom, is directly across the street from PURE. The home of A. A. Guthrie, president of the Ohio Abolitionist Society, is up the street at 405 Woodlawn.

As for the house at 522 Woodlawn, by the time Dick and Brad Johnson deeded it to the Putnam Restoration Fund of the Muskingum County Community Foundation (MCCF) in December, 1998 it had fallen into serious disrepair.

Enter Ray Thomas, the founder of the MCCF. A life-long Zanesville resident, he had retired from the retail lumber and construction business that he started after returning from World War Two and turned it over to his two sons and grandson.

*It's Never Too Late to Plant a Tree*

"I built it into a pretty good business," says Thomas, now in his 80s, "but I was so busy all my life, I didn't have time to do enough for the community. So, once I retired I decided now was the time. Yes, I organized the Muskingum County Community Foundation. There are community foundations all over the country, and I figured we ought to have one."

"One of the things the Community Foundation did was to help organize the PURE Center board. Under the leadership of Kathy Rowan Brantley an inter-racial group of influential Zanesvillians got the Putnam Underground Railroad out of the station.

They wanted to preserve some of their local history, which went back some 150 years, and they got me involved.

> **"My pieces have brought as much as $16,500. I give them to charity auctions. I vowed I'd never sell one."**

My job," says Thomas, "was to be the superintendent and building coordinator for restoring this old house. It needed a complete restoration, and since I was familiar with the building trades, that was my job, and I did it."

The PURE Center is located in an area loaded with history. Among the Stephen, George, and A. A. Guthrie houses is the Putnam Presbyterian Church where the Reverend William Beecher (brother of *Uncle Tom's Cabin* author Harriet Beecher Stowe) preached anti-slavery sermons.

Under Thomas's supervision, the job entailed restoring many features of a single-family home of the 1830s to 522 Woodlawn. And then to prepare it to include a fifteen-station state-of-the-art computer lab to facilitate learning about the Underground Railroad for visiting schoolchildren.

The stated goal of the PURE Center is "to promote digital literacy for schoolchildren with state-of-the-art technology and telecommunications and to provide them with a positive learning environment that promotes harmony among diverse groups."

David Mitzel, Executive Director of the Muskingum County Community Foundation, praises members of the PURE Center Board who are assembling artifacts from Africa, as well as from pre-Civil War and post-Civil War Zanesville, and will create a library on the Underground Railroad and the Abolitionist movement.

Children who visit from the surrounding areas will be able to experience a video produced locally and shown on public television as well as live presentations related to the Underground Railroad. In the summer, there is a plan for choral groups to present programs from the second-story porch to audiences assembled on the lawn below.

PURE will also share resources and will network with other freedom centers, museums, and libraries across the state and nation.

Thomas is proud of the Foundation's many activities.

"We do lots of good work, contributing to many different worthwhile causes. You can take a look at our website, www.mccf.org, but don't ask for my e-mail, because I don't have one. The Foundation has given away millions of dollars in the last 15 years. People can mark their contribution for beautification, local nonprofits, youth organizations, school projects, scholarships, or any worthwhile community project for a better way of life. You name it.

"To find out more about community foundations you can look at a book that Dave Mitzel and I put together about the foundation. It is titled *Artistry, Community, Legacy.* It's a beautiful hardcover book. We printed 1,500 copies and all of Zanesville's service clubs are selling them for $40 a book that will go to support the rebirth of downtown and of Putnam."

Thomas has another powerful, if unusual fund-raising tool.

"I do real fine inlay work in nice Federal style tables that I build. I turn plates of exotic woods on my lathe and inlay them in a unique way. My pieces have brought as much as $16,500. I give them to charity auctions. I vowed I'd never sell one. They're collector items because I refuse to sell them – never sold one of them. The only way somebody can get one is to buy it at an auction to benefit charity. Yes, the Foundation keeps me pretty busy."

Thomas doesn't talk about getting finished. He's satisfied that his many projects will continue to bear fruit after he's gone. He points to the slogan of the Muskingum County Community Foundation:

> "Man has made at least a start on
> discovering the meaning of human life
> when he plants shade trees under which he
> knows full well he will never sit."
>
> —Elton Trueblood

*Artistry, Community, and Legacy*
By Raymond W. Thomas and David P. Mitzel
©2002, The Muskingum County Community Foundation Press
Zanesville, Ohio 43701

# Creative Arts and Communication

Fifteen minutes of fame may be a goal for some; not long enough for others; and of no consequence to still others. If it's not fame, but creativity, that inspires you, then you'll want to know more about some of our artists and artisans who are profiled here.

Ora Anderson was a newspaperman and lobbyist before he retired and converted a longtime hobby of bird carving into a successful business. Now in his 90's, he has a year's backlog of orders. His only promise, "I'll carve a bird next week."

Grief, inexplicable and implacable, overwhelmed Saul Bennett when his eldest child died of a brain aneurysm. Without ever having written a line of verse before, turned to poetry for relief, restoration and a new lease on life.

Alicia C. Fink left her native Ecuador when she was 18, but Ecuador never left her. A love of ethnic art moved her to translate an attraction to the culture of the Indians of Ecuador into a burgeoning career as a maker of precious metal clay jewelry.

Not many of us are going to find our faces on a U.S. postage stamp. The great jazz artist Billie Holiday didn't live to see it happen, but Bill Gottlieb, the man who took the photo that appears on the stamp, did. It's part of a collection that he exhibits and sells worldwide.

Elise Mitchell Sanford has turned her photographic skills into a vehicle for bringing those diagnosed with disabling mental illnesses into a world of socialization and communication. Now in her 70s, Sanford essentially does her job single-handedly working with students from 17 to 55. The Athens Photographic Project is a model for replication elsewhere.

On an impulse, Tom Tuley joined a class in painting after he retired, although he didn't think he had much talent. His sales since then have proven him wrong. Looking back, he can't believe that he spent 38 years putting on a business suit, shirt and tie each working day of the year.

Some of you may remember, as a kid, seeing a Civil War veteran, marching in a Memorial Day parade. Probably in a wheelchair, not actually marching. Keep an eye out for Ray Skinner. He shows up in a full Civil War uniform and reads to school kids from diaries and letters that date back to that era.

# Free As A Bird

"When you're still carving birds at my age, you want to be careful about how many back orders you have. It seems every day somebody calls with another order. I just got two yesterday. Game birds, songbirds, decoys, I make them all. Right now I've got 50 commissions waiting. If I carve one bird a week, which is what I do, that's about a year's worth. Can't get too far ahead. When someone puts an order in my hand these days, I say, 'Don't count on it. I'll carve the next bird next week, but that's about as far as I'm going to promise.'"

Ora Anderson, at age 91, is still selling his wood carved birds all over the world.

Anderson's interest in birds goes back to his boyhood in Kentucky. "That's when I started loving birds," he says, "and I've traveled all over the world bird watching. Anderson carved his first bird in

©2003, Terry E. Eiler

1947, not waiting for retirement to get started. At the time, he was editing a successful regional farm newspaper, *Farm & Dairy*, one of many career shifts he's made during his lifetime.

"Writing was something I always wanted to do. While I was still in high school, I was interested in typing and in literature. Later I hung out at a little newspaper, *The Jackson (Ohio) Herald*, and when I graduated from high school, that was 1929, they hired me. Next year they made me editor," he says. "Not that I was all that good. It was the Depression, and I was what they could afford. I was there for seven years. The paper's still in existence."

---

**You can find Anderson's carved birds in France, Japan, Hong Kong, Canada and throughout the United States. He's done 3,000 of them since he started.**

---

"One job led to another. I went from *The Herald* to *Farm & Dairy* in Samel, Ohio, and spent four years with them. Next I moved to a Dairy Farmers Milk Marketing Cooperative, headquartered in Pittsburgh. I must have been sharp enough negotiating with the dealers, because the dealers turned around and hired me to run their state association in Ohio. It was really a lobbying job, and I did that for four years. Next thing the Ohio Bankers Association hired me away, and that's where I stayed for 20 years until 1973.

"I retired from The Bankers Association in 1973, as soon as I was eligible for my pension. I was 62 years old, and there were just so many things I wanted to do. So my wife, Harriet, and I bought this little, old, worn-out hill-farm just outside of Athens, Ohio, 98 acres. Harriet was an artist and a very successful one, a helluva salesperson. She specialized in art of the 1950's, 60's and 70's, big acrylics that were very fashionable. She died 23 years ago, too soon."

The out of doors has been a lifelong passion of Anderson's. He's a past president and a lifetime board member of the Nature Conservancy of Ohio. "With the farm," he says, "I started out from day one to plant trees, tear out interior fences, build trails, all that

good stuff. And, because of my interest in nature conservancy, I've converted that farm into one of the most amazing natural preserves in southern Ohio. I've got seven farm ponds full of fish, frogs and birds. Got everything. I'm so proud of it, I just go around grinning."

Anderson's bird carving began at the end of a family vacation in the Northeast, when he bought a hand carved bird in Long Cove, Maine. He decided to start whittling, and not long afterwards, he ran into an old decoy carver in Delaware County, Ohio.

"He was a marvelous man, a real character," he says. "His advice was to go to bird shows. In the early '50's there were only four in

*Creative Arts & Communication*                                                     *57*

the United States. First one I went to was on the south shore of Long Island. Well, I just fell in love with what I saw and started entering shows myself. Pretty soon, I won a few ribbons and that inspired me to keep going. Today, there are 40 or 50 woodcarving shows in the country and thousands of woodcarvers. I try to make my birds as realistic as possible, and I'm just amazed at the detail and accuracy of some of these carvers. No, I don't compete any more, but I just love going."

You can find Anderson's carved birds in France, Japan, Hong Kong, Canada and throughout the United States. He's

**"I'd say sixty percent of the people in this world are good, interesting folks, doing things they enjoy. Ten percent are mean and rotten. Stay away from them."**

done 3,000 of them since he started, and has no intention of stopping. He works with basswood, also known as linden, water tupelo and white cedar. " Early on I planted 500 basswood trees on my farm, and now they're big enough for me to cut and use."

Asked about the differences in the kinds of people he's met in his varied pursuits, he says, "I'm a people person. I'd say sixty percent of the people in this world are good, interesting folks, doing things they enjoy. Another thirty percent are all right. Don't excite you very much. Maybe play golf four days a week. The other ten percent are mean and rotten. Just stay away from them."

As for his energy, "Of course it's not what it used to be. I tire more easily, but that doesn't stop me from enjoying the things I do. And, even at my age, I just love to hug women, and believe me there are a lot of huggable women who like being hugged. And I'm more aware of tiny tots. Got four great-grandchildren of my own. When I'm in a store and see one of those little ones riding in a shopping cart, I just have to stop and get down and grin at them, and have them grin back at me.

"The more interests you can develop, the more interesting you're going to be, and the more happiness you're going to bring to yourself and to others."

# Poetry Helped to Heal Him

Saul Bennett never planned to be a poet. Approaching his 60th birthday, he had never written a line of verse. Then, a tragic twist of fate changed his life. Forever.

The story is best told in Bennett's own words:

"Following a lengthy career in business, culminating in my appointment as president of a Madison Avenue PR group, I am devoted to poetry. I turned to poetry in 1995 to tackle the furies of my grief following the sudden death of our eldest of three children, Sara, 24, from a brain aneurysm.

"Sara was a journalist, as I had been at the start of my career after graduating from Ohio University. Looking for a way to deal with the boundless grief I felt, I began writing poems about Sara's death—and her life. I had never written poetry before, but the poems just flooded out of me, like an eruptive volcano. I was looking at a snapshot of our family taken 12 days before she died. I took out a magnifying glass. I held it over the photo, making Sara's image grow larger and smaller, and from that came 'Measurements.'

> "...Sara, her mother, sister
> I; looking pleased
> in quickfreeze-pose
> seconds before our Taps..."

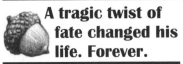
**A tragic twist of fate changed his life. Forever.**

Sara's death also triggered Bennett's resignation from the PR agency in 1996. Two years later, the family moved to Woodstock in upstate New York. "It was time," he said. "As I wrote in one of my poems, 'We fled the density.'"

Bennett works in a small shed behind their country house in Woodstock. "It is totally devoid of furnishings, so to bring in anything seemed intrusive. I describe the shack in a poem called 'Nothing.' I think the 'spartan-ness' of the surroundings in the shack takes on a sort of religious quality."

*Resuscitation* is a typical "Sara poem" taken from "Jesus Matinees and Other Poems."

*Whenever without warning*
*her name preceding*
*the last of another*

*appears below before me*
*in a black daylily field*
*of print I press opposing*

*thumbs hard and flat applying*
*utmost pressure against*
*the page obliterating*

*all in the rigid row save*
*Sara thus restoring to my eye's*
*heart my daughter's beat.*

While some of Bennett's poems are still dedicated to Sara, he has moved on—or back—to childhood memories. "At first," he says, "all the poems were 'Sara' poems; that is, addressing the death of our child. Gradually I found myself reflecting on my own childhood, at first with regard to Sara's death, then 'free-standing' reverie poems. All were emotional. And, yes, I'm still writing both. My new collection, 'Sea Dust,' now being assembled and due to be published in about a year, contains many poems on both themes."

"I do poetry readings frequently before various groups—general audiences, bereavement organizations, college students (including an invitation from Sara's

**"I turned to poetry in 1995 to tackle the furies of my grief following the sudden death of my eldest child."**

alma mater, Skidmore College), and even conduct walking tours, under the auspices of the 92nd Street Y in New York City, to the site of many of the poems in *Harpo Marx* that 'locate' childhood experiences."

Describing one of those walking tours, as reported in *The New York Times*, Bennett says, "What strikes me is how little the neighborhood has changed...The faces are different; the Irish, German and Italian immigrants who lived there have been mostly replaced by East Europeans, South Americans, Koreans and

Indians. Some of the stores have changed hands. The old A&P is a Rite Aid, Al's Candy Store on 43$^{rd}$ Avenue is a Middle Eastern grocery. ('It was run by an old woman, but the place was called Al's so we called her Al and she never blinked.')" But the "feel" of the old neighborhood remains, he concludes.

*Harpo Marx at Prayer* is set at Sunnyside Jewish Center and takes its name from Bennett's recollection, when he was six years old, of a mute boy praying at the Center. A poem from *Harpo Marx* evokes old memories:

*"From their back room*
    *they sold you*
*If they knew you*
*And you called ahead*
*To this one family Auto*
    *Supply*
*Gefillte fish they worked up*
    *themselves*
*In big pots on a stove behind*
    *a curtain*
*Like Prohibition.*
*My mother*
*for the holidays would go*
    *there around*
*The corner across under the*
    *El from Sunnyside*
    *Gardens*
*Where my father took me to*
    *the fights*

*Fifty for the winner, a watch to the*
    *loser*
*Their recipe was so delicious*
*The mothers said*
*Big carp*
*And pike boulders spiked*
*With carrot pebbles*
    *shuddering*
*In a pond of pale yellow jelly*
*They sold on the sly smelling*
*Against the front-of-the-store*
*New rubber and sunny*
    *precious*
*Oils enough to grease*
*Every Polo Grounds seat.*
*When mothers asked for it*
*they winked*
*But never gave away*
*Their recipe*

Bennett has also returned to public relations with the formation of The Bennett Group, http://bennettgroup.net., working from his base in Woodstock. "The accession from Marston to The Bennett Group was a natural," he says, "except I do it all myself, with no staff. It's still public relations counseling."

"Today, poetry has become, to a large degree, my *raison d'etre*, and I have been fortunate in the recognition I've received," he says. "My first collection, *New Fields and Other Stones/On a Child's Death* was chosen to launch a new publishing imprint, Archer

©2003, Lee Ferris

Books, in 1998, and subsequently received the Benjamin Franklin Silver Award. My second collection, *Harpo Marx at Prayer* (Archer Books 2000), was submitted by the publisher for Pulitzer Prize consideration and was the subject of a news feature in *The New York Times*. Also, I would be remiss in not mentioning Michael J. Bugeja, an Ohio University professor of journalism and ethics and a widely-published poet, who helped me immeasurably in getting started."

As for where he will go next with his poetry, he answers:

"Wherever it takes me. Not surprisingly—and this is so with many poets, I think—to a degree I write the 'same' poems year after year. Which is to say, poems on the themes closest to me. An interviewer recently wrote that I am a poet of 'loss'—of life, of childhood, of a degree of innocence. And, if you add to my poems about Sara, and my childhood, the poems I continue to write about the Holocaust, for example, the poems are 'recurring.' This should not suggest that all my poems are solemn, for they are not. Quite a number are, I think, humorous and self-chiding."

E-mail: saulben@aol.com

# Back To Her Roots

It was 1959 and Alicia C. Fink was all of 18 years old, when she moved from her native Quito to the United States. She attended college, married, became an American citizen, raised a family and taught high school Spanish for 28 years. But in all those years Ecuador never left her.

For Fink becoming a jewelry-maker was a second career waiting to happen. It started with a childhood fascination with Ecuadorian folk art that blossomed, when she retired in 1999 from Hilton High School in upstate New York. Off she went to travel and do some of the things she'd planned to do "once I have the time." That lasted about one year, before she found herself restless. Her husband is a professor at the State University of New York, Brockport, and they were not about to uproot.

What to do? The solution came via a catalog offering a three session, six hour course at the nearby Rochester Museum and Science Center, "Making Your Own Jewelry: Precious Metal Clay."

**"I didn't have an art background, but members of my family are very artistic."**

"I jumped at it," she says. "I didn't have an art background, but members of my family are very artistic. I have an extensive collection of folk art, love my ethnic wardrobe and have always been attracted to the culture of Indians in Ecuador. Also, I wear a lot of silver from my time in the Southwest United States."

"Getting started with precious metal clay wasn't all that complicated," she explains. "You take a lump of clay and mold it to the shape you want. When it dries, you fire it in a kiln at 1650 degrees. All the natural materials, other than the silver burn off, leaving fine silver. By the time I finished the course at the Rochester Museum, I was enchanted and ready to go to work.

*It's Never Too Late to Plant a Tree*

"First, I needed some equipment; to begin with, a studio. Goodbye, TV room. Hello, studio. A table. That was easy. I found a strong old door, finished it, put it on a couple of saw horses, and presto, I had a table. A kiln for firing my clay required an investment of five hundred dollars. Done. If I couldn't make jewelry that I liked, I could always sell the kiln for half what I had paid.

"It was easy for me to go back to work. I made earrings and pins for myself and for my sisters. Before long, I

**"My jewelry making is not a hobby, usually four hours after breakfast, then another three hours later in the day."**

found that not only did I like what I was making; apparently other people did, too. In fact, they liked it enough to buy some of my pieces. I decided to take the plunge and hold a show in my house. I sent a mailing to my high school colleagues and some friends. The turnout was pretty good, and encouraged me to take the next step.

"Teaching and learning is in the blood, I guess. Both my parents were teachers, and because I had taught for so many years, it was a matter of finding the right subject. The Precious Metal Clay (PMC) Guild was the answer. The Guild offers certification and after an intensive three-day test, I had my certificate. Now I teach, as well as work. I can tell you, my jewelry making is not a hobby, usually four hours after breakfast, then another three hours later in the day.

"In May of 2001, I exhibited at a show in Albuquerque. I got a lot of attention and one of the exhibiting artists said, 'You don't belong at a show like this. You want to be in an art gallery.' With the encouragement of friends and others at PMC Guild, I was able to place at the Rochester Memorial Art Gallery a series of jewelry pieces based on petroglyphs I saw in New Mexico. Petroglyphs are paintings or carvings on rocks, often prehistoric in origin. They are similar to the Paleolithic cave paintings in France or Spain, depicting shapes of animals and people and hunting scenes."

Fink also has a collection of silver necklaces, pendants, bracelets, pins and rings, often combined with semi-precious stones, for sale at an upscale boutique in Rochester. If she was concerned about the isolation of working alone, she enjoys encouragement from her husband and two sons, along with a highly supportive community in the PMC Guild and the virtual world of the Internet.

"The PMC has a marvelous website, www.pmcguild.com, and if you e-mail someone a question, generally within 24 hours, often less, you get an answer," she says. "At the first International PMC Conference in Ohio last summer, 45 artists came from Japan, where PMC originated less than 10 years ago. "It's only been in the United States for five years and the Japanese who came are really the gurus. I keep learning so much all of the time."

As for the future, Fink recently did a second show at her home. She sent out 100 invitations and 75 people came. She sees no time cap on how long she can keep working. She just laughs, "Let's just say for another 10 years anyhow."

E-mail: afinkny@yahoo.com

# Billie & Bill—
# A Picture Perfect Team

My teeth hurt, my back aches and my hearing aid isn't working too well. I'm the second half of "Billie and Bill," Bill Gottlieb, William P. Gottlieb in full. "Billie," as every jazz fan knows, is Billie Holiday. She's on a U.S. postage stamp; her likeness is from a photograph I took of her in 1947. I was 30; Billie, "Lady Day," was 32.

That photograph may be the most widely reproduced of any jazz artist. In all my work, I especially tried to capture personality, but it's an elusive quality, and I was successful only part of the time. With that picture of Billie, I believe I hit it on the button. Each time I look at it, I see her voice, filled with anguish. Billie was at her most beautiful then, which was not too long after she had come out of prison on a drug charge. She couldn't get any drugs or alcohol while she was behind bars. She lost weight and came out looking gorgeous, and her voice was, I think, at its peak.

**"With that picture of Billie, I believe I hit it on the button."**

I'm 86 now, busier than ever and having the time of my life. I'm lecturing all over the world, consulting regularly with journalists, book editors, museum curators, artists and producers of multimedia documentaries, showing and selling photographs that I made more than 60 years ago, mostly with a Speed Graphic. It's given me an opportunity to travel to places where I'd never been before, to meet people I might never have met and to meet them, not as a tourist but as an active link with the past.

None of this happened overnight. Between the two bookends of my jazz careers, I spent 30 years in the corporate world, working first for Curriculum Films, an educational filmstrip company, before starting my own filmstrip company, University Films. At University Films, we produced materials for educational and institutional corporations, such as Encyclopedia Britannica Films, D.C. Heath, McGraw-Hill, and Oxford University Press. That led to McGraw-Hill buying my company in 1969 and hiring me as president of a division. I kept that position for ten years before "retiring." During that time, University Films produced some 1,400 filmstrips, 400 of which I wrote. I also wrote 16 books, mostly stories for children (including several Golden Books) with others in science for older readers. Worldwide sales of my books total about five million to date.

My career as a jazz photographer and journalist can be divided into three periods: a stint as "Mr. Jazz" in Washington, D.C., before I went into the Army Air Corps in 1943; a post-war position as assistant editor of *Down Beat*; and my "retirement" in 1979 from the corporate world, which is when I made another career—I think this will be last one—out of my earlier jazz photos.

©2003, Thomas Hart Shelby

Having said that, I don't recommend getting started writing and photographing the jazz greats, the way I did. It resulted from food poisoning. The day before the end of my sophomore year at Lehigh University, I got trichinosis from a serving of undercooked pork. While bedridden over the summer, "Doc" Bartle, a classical pianist, an ardent jazz fan and a good high school buddy, visited me frequently. Bartle collected international music magazines, which said that jazz was America's greatest contribution to the arts. He shared his interest with me, often bringing along Louis Armstrong and Duke Ellington records when he visited. I was quickly transformed from a Guy Lombardo fan into a jazz buff.

When I graduated from Lehigh in 1938, my first break came with a job at *The Washington Post*, selling advertising. A few months later I

> **"I traded hundreds of 78-rpm records from my collection for a Speed Graphic, the basis for a highly rewarding new career many decades later."**

volunteered to write a weekly jazz column for the Sunday edition. It meant an extra ten dollars a week on top of my base salary of $25. The best part was being able to take photographs, as well. It happened when *The Post* decided it was too expensive for a photographer to accompany me to local nightclubs and theaters. So, I traded hundreds of 78-rpm records from my collection for a Speed Graphic. What I didn't realize was that in the process I was laying the basis for a highly rewarding new career many decades later.

My job at *The Post* opened the door for me to do a half-hour jazz interview show on WRC, the local NBC outlet, and a three-time a week jazz interview show on WINX, a local independent radio station. That gave me entrée to African-American performers, who were really the key people in jazz, as well as to Whites. It gave me a lever to have Bob Crosby's Dixieland ensemble, which was performing at the Earle Theater (White) do a jam session with Count Basie after-hours at the Howard Theatre (African-American). That was no small feat since Washington before World War Two was still severely segregated.

But my luckiest break was to marry Delia Potofsky in 1939, the daughter of Jacob Potofsky, later president of the Amalgamated Clothing Workers of America. And thank goodness for Delia. She handles the business side of our company, William P. Gottlieb, fills in those pesky blanks for me, when I'm *almost* remembering something, and is the invisible pillar that supports the structure.

As for my work, what am I proudest of? That's a tough question, but it might be the 1,600 jazz photos that are now part of a permanent U.S. Library of Congress collection. In addition, I've been exhibited in more than 150 venues in the United States and abroad, including the National Portrait Gallery in Washington, D.C., the United States Information Service, Amerika Haus in Berlin, the Museum of Modern Art in Stockholm, and the Navio Museum of Art in Osaka, Japan. My work has been featured in books and articles, used for more than 250 record album covers, appeared in television documentaries and major motion pictures, and been distributed on posters, postcards, calendars, and T-shirts. In 1994 the United States Postal Service selected my portraits of Billie Holiday, Charlie Parker, Mildred Bailey, and Jimmy Rushing for a series of postage stamps commemorating jazz performers.

If you want to see more, go to my website, www.jazzphotos.com, which is linked to a Library of Congress website.

Yes, it's been a full life with a family that has expanded to four children, five grandchildren and two great-grandchildren. My aches and pains notwithstanding, Delia and I keep moving along, knowing that the show's not over.

# New Voices / New Images/ New Worlds

"The people I deal with have so much intelligence, so much creative ability, and sensitivity that they're a natural for what I teach them," says Elise Mitchell Sanford, director of The Athens Photographic Project.

She must be talking about classes for the gifted, right?

Well, "Yes," and "No." Sanford's pupils, ages 17-55, have been diagnosed with disabling mental illnesses. But she maintains that the foregoing adjectives describe them accurately.

Sanford's job is a full-time one, essentially, one she does single handedly.

"Yes, it's a lot of work," she says with a sigh, then chuckles, "I suddenly realized I'm 73 years old. Once when I complained to one of my photography teachers that I should have started this

©The Athens Photographic Project, 2002                    Janet Doan, Photographer


*Creative Arts & Communication*                                               *71*

(photography) 30 years earlier, he said, 'If you had started this 30 years earlier, you wouldn't have had the outlook you have. It's all the cumulative life experience that counts.' The same is probably true now."

"Those who are mentally ill have been overlooked," she says. "There have been projects for the homeless, for AIDS victims, for the disadvantaged in almost every area, it seems, but not for the mentally ill. My aim is to teach this group of people how to express themselves and to help them reclaim lost identities. When they do that, they are empowered in a milieu of crisis care that has left them wondering who they are, how they fit in and if they want to fit in. They gain a sense of control and their confidence and self esteem increases. I don't tell them to express themselves as a reflection of me, but of themselves. I'm a well-trained photographer with real world experience in the exhibit world. I don't impose my artistic voice on my students. They need to find their own voices."

Sanford's professional evolution took time. She began taking photographs as an editor for Columbia Gas System, but she says, "I never really kept it up until," and she chuckles again, "I had a mid-life crisis at 52." She goes on, more seriously, "It was also when my son, Michael, was exhibiting early symptoms of his illness, which proved to be paranoid schizophrenia, that I began photographing seriously. And photography kept me sane."

**"Nobody has taken the time to consider that they might be bright, and they usually are."**

The combination of events transformed Sanford into an exhibition artist, and in time brought considerable success with shows in New York, San Francisco, Los Angeles and Houston. She won awards and gained top-notch residencies throughout the country. Her special emphasis became aging and being female. "I used faculty and staff members here at Ohio University who were over 50 as models and photographed them as different personae."

Aging female models were photographed as someone they admired or who had affected them as they grew up. They were asked to bring that person to life before the camera. Called *The Stuff of Dreams*, this work has had a lot of exposure. "It, too, was about identity formation," Sanford says.

Her next crossroads came, when she decided that she would not "play the museum game any longer." At about the same time in 1998 her husband died.

"I'd been exhibiting my own work for a long time and getting disenchanted with it, to be honest. Unless you're a top artist you end up subsidizing the system. I realized that I did not want to continue my exhibition career any longer, but did want to use my experience and training as a photographer and visual artist with a BFA and an MFA in art photography.

"More important, my son, Mike, who is now in his thirties, suffers from schizophrenia. He and others in our rural Ohio area have been left without community services that might provide a diversion from illness at a minimum, and perhaps, a way to recovery, at best. Living with mental illness for 18 years makes all of us desperate."

©The Athens Photographic Project, 2002      Barbara Sue Haines, Photographer

©The Athens Photographic Project, 2002          Stephanie Schmidt, Photographer

*It's Never Too Late to Plant a Tree*

"In any case, I found it very difficult to do my own work," she says. "I thought The Athens Photographic Project was a place where I could put my own energy to work. Because of my experience with Mike, I had gained some knowledge that might benefit other people who are ill. Still, it took me a year to organize, to get the money, to figure out how to do it."

> "I've had photographs of trays or bottles of pills, of sites where people have gone feeling suicidal"

The most difficult part of her work, Sanford says, is time. "Teaching is easy for me. I don't have a problem teaching people who are quite ill, but there's only one of me, and there ought to be more classes. After I teach people in beginning classes, they are hungry for more. What I've done in the process is structure their time for them. Structuring time is usually difficult for people who are mentally ill to do for themselves. I do it by giving weekly shooting assignments that require time and thought."

"My students learn about the history of photography and the history of art, and they love it. Nobody has taken the time to consider that they might be bright, and they usually are. The toughest ones are people with dual diagnoses—in this case that means both mental illness and mental retardation. I've managed to teach the operation of a manual camera to a woman in her 50's, who suffers from both."

"My students are so grateful to have someone who spends time with them, who recognizes their talents and who is not always talking about medications or behavior modification. I've told many people, 'I'm not a therapist. I'm an artist, but art often functions as a therapy; because it's a natural form of expression.'"

Students pay no tuition. Sanford receives no pay, nor do any of the other volunteers. Former students have become volunteers in subsequent classes. She receives funding from such groups as local and state chapters of NAMI (the National Alliance for the Mentally Ill), the Ohio Arts Council and the local mental health board as well as "passing the hat," which was what she did to get started. There have been 13 classes, including an extended black and white darkroom class and five traveling exhibitions of student work that have been seen throughout the state of Ohio, in Washington, D.C. and Cincinnati, OH at national NAMI conventions.

"Exhibitions are juried by experienced art photographers and are professionally presented. The presentation gives credibility to the students' work as art. But more importantly, exhibitions are absolutely necessary in order that the student see the progression from concept to art on the wall, which is a valued commodity. Besides that, others who are suffering from depression, bi-polar disorder, schizophrenia, anxiety and all the other biological brain disorders are given hope and provided with a model when they see the work produced by The Athens Photographic Project.

"Students shoot about a hundred 35mm frames a week in the classes and I believe that the more you photograph, the better you get," she says. Assignments are planned for people who have isolated themselves, she explains. "Our system thinks it's done a good job in helping former hospital patients find a place to live. And it has. But what schizophrenics do after they move into an apartment is close the door. And they get really, really isolated. If there's anything to make people really disoriented and paranoid that will do it."

"So I designed assignments to pull them out. I ask them to photograph their favorite person, place or things, so they can do it right there in their own home, if they choose, without confronting the world. They get positive feedback when their images are discussed in a group critique the following Tuesday. This experience of shooting in a safe place is magical.

"I bring them slowly out, 'What is your neighborhood like, immediately, where you live. Show me what that looks like.' 'Neighborhood' can be defined broadly. Next, I'll ask them to photograph people they know well, like families and friends, because it's hard for most of us to photograph strangers. Then they will do a self-portrait, because so many times when patients are discharged from the hospital there's an identity loss that's so real, you can almost feel it. I try to design the assignments around their recovery of identity, of re-claiming themselves."

Sanford's final assignment is to ask students to photograph their own illnesses. "I've had photographs of trays or bottles of pills, of sites where people have gone feeling suicidal. One man took a picture of a long, long, multi-floored stairway, looking down. Another photographed an empty white chair facing the corner of an empty white room with only a pull chain for help. This is very real and when they photograph the scene, it's almost like saying. 'This is behind me. If I can photograph it, it's not real any more.' For many of us, photographing makes it more real, but that doesn't seem to be the way this works. And the images they've done leaves me breathless."

> **"Having to ask them to return their project-loaned cameras at the end of the program almost brings us to tears."**

Sanford offers three programs a year, 10 weeks in length, twice a week, two to three hours each. "Having to ask them to return their project-loaned cameras at the end of the program almost brings us to tears."

Coming up in late 2003 is a two-day overnight photography and camping trip in nearby Adams County on the Ohio River. "The Ohio Arts Council asked the Project to photograph quilt squares being painted on barns," Sanford says. "This will be our first project-oriented commission. We'll get some vans and 10 or 15 of the students will have a professional photographing experience. We can't afford to stay in motels, so we'll be in sleeping bags, cooking and eating out and meeting people. It'll be a great adventure."

And for those who want to help, why not donate the old working manual camera that's sitting on a shelf or buried in your closet? It can make a difference.

E-mail: esanford@frognet.net

# Who Says There Are No More Civil War Soldiers?

Imagine one of your grandchildren coming home from school and telling you, "This really old soldier came to our class today and read from his diaries and letters he wrote during the war. He was even wearing his uniform and showed us this other stuff he used when he was fighting. No fooling."

"Just how old was this soldier?" you might ask. Carefully, of course. "Really old" for a second grader can be 50, maybe younger.

"Well," your grandchild answers, "he told us to do the arithmetic. That he was born in 1842, so that would make him….?"

While he or she is doing the arithmetic, you go on, still being careful, "Which war was this soldier talking about?"

©2003, Bruce Strong/Light Chasers

"Well, the Civil War."

"I see. The Civil War. And the teacher was there?" You manage to keep a straight face.

"Oh sure, the teacher was there! You can even ask her. It was really cool."

Reality TV is one thing, but what's going on here?

What's going on is that Ray Skinner, a retired professor, a.k.a. Sgt. Edwin Glazier of the Union's 53$^{rd}$ Regiment, is making the rounds of Ohio's public schools at the invitation of teachers and administrators. He's been doing it since the late 1980's, and while there've been a few puzzled calls from parents, the overwhelming majority think what Skinner is doing is great.

"Glazier's letters and diaries, for the most part, aren't about fighting and killing and death," Skinner explains. "They're

**"The diaries and letters are about a soldier's day-to-day life; about being lonesome and cold and homesick."**

about a soldier's day-to-day life; about being lonesome and cold and homesick; what the food was like; about his companions and the places they saw. It's life from the viewpoint of an ordinary soldier."

"Not that Glazier didn't see his share of fighting," Skinner continues. "He was with Sherman on his march from Vicksburg to Atlanta to Savannah and the sea. And for the older kids it's a chance to clear up some of the myths about the Civil War. The diaries say that Sherman was blamed for burning Columbia, South Carolina, but it was a bunch of soldiers who got drunk and did it without orders from Sherman or anyone else."

For those kids who ask how come Skinner's still around today, the "old soldier" (he's actually 77) tells them that when he was discharged in 1865, he was so exhausted, he crawled under the platform at the Athens railroad station and went to sleep.

"Well there's a professor at the University. His name is Dr. Serendipity, but they just call him Dr. Dipity for short, and he was always looking for old coins with a metal detector. So one day he came along to the railroad station, and the detector began to beep like crazy. It had detected my musket. Dr. Dipity woke me up, and that's how I happen to be here. I'm a kind of Rip van Winkle."

What Skinner doesn't tell the students is that he is Dr. Dipity.

> **"Dr. Dipity woke me up, and that's how I happen to be here. I'm a kind of Rip van Winkle."**

Skinner came into possession of the diaries and letters through the Athens County Historical Society and Museum, of which he was president for three years in the late 1980's. One day the museum's treasurer brought him a box with the diaries, photographs and letters that had been given to him by a woman named Jessie Owen.

"She was the widow of one of Glazier's two sons. Neither of Glazier's sons or of his one daughter had any children. Ms. Owen was the last survivor and didn't want these records to just pass away, when she did."

Skinner's fascination with the Civil War, as seen through the eyes of Sergeant Glazier, led him to visit the cemetery where Glazier and his family are buried, to get a group of fellow members in the Civil War Round Table to purchase Civil War uniforms and march in 4th of July parades and to organize a Civil War Elderhostel at Ohio University. One of Skinner's fondest memories is when a local participant in the Elderhostel brought her grandson to the Elderhostel. The boy became so fascinated with the Civil War that his grandmother made him a Civil War uniform and reconditioned an authentic Civil War drum. The youngster became Glazier's companion and served as a drummer boy at Elderhostels and other Civil War presentations.

A videotape of Skinner doing his portrayals of Edwin Glazier at a "Senior Beat" meeting at the Athens O'Bleness Hospital has been shown on Public Access Television in Athens.

"I'd like to be able to publish the diaries—actually they're a set of small books, and some of them are missing, although I do have the first and the last—and some of the letters and photographs. One letter is from Edwin's mother, and she describes Edwin's enlistment in the Army, "To be sure it is a great trouble to part with those that are so near and dear to us with the uncertainty of ever meeting again. But then, our country calls and in a just cause, and should he fall in battle you have the consolation that he died no cowardly traitor's death, but fighting in a great and glorious cause—our nation's salvation.""

In "real life" Skinner enlisted in the Army Air Corps in 1944, right out of high school, only to find that they had no need for more pilots. He was discharged six months after V-E Day and resumed his education at Ohio State University, then Kent State where he earned a Ph.D. He joined the faculty of Ohio University in Athens in 1966 as a professor in Curriculum and Development, took early retirement in 1980, but continued part-time for another 17 years, as his Civil War activities took more of his time. In 1997 he took full retirement from OU.

What Skinner finds most rewarding in his current "teaching" is interacting with the students. "I don't lecture them. I read from the diaries and the letters, and the students ask questions. We talk, and that keeps them interested. Best of all, there's no pressure for me to retire. As far as I'm concerned, I'll just keep going along, getting a little older each year. But only if you insist on doing the arithmetic right."

E-mail: Rskinne@columbus.rr.com

# You Don't Have To Be Grandma Moses

What do you do for an encore, after 38 years of newspapering, starting as a 17-year-old part-time sports writer and capping your career with 12 years as Editor and President of *The Evansville Courier* in Indiana?

There's always travel, catching up on that long list of "Once I get the time…" maybe writing your memoirs. (Okay, so you're not Ben Bradlee of *The Washington Post*, but you've got a story to tell.) Or maybe the answer is off to the side, taking a flyer at something you'd thought about, but never tried, because you didn't think you had the right stuff. Like painting.

At age 55, Thomas W. Tuley loved what he'd been doing, but felt that he was running out of steam. Just didn't have the energy and enthusiasm that had carried him to a successful and rewarding life.

©2003, Jeanie Adams-Smith

"I figured that wasn't good for the newspaper and it wasn't good for me," he says.

The realization was not sudden. It had been percolating for three or four years. Still, taking early retirement was a big step. Being a good businessman, one of his responsibilities as president of *The Evansville Courier*, Tuley sat down with an investment adviser. Could he afford to do it? The numbers came out satisfactorily enough, so that at 2 P.M. on December 31, 1995, he walked out of his big-corner office for the last time. By the next morning, he and Barbara, his wife of 32 years, were headed for the Cayman Islands, a chance to unwind, to think about what might come next.

"I've always had to be busy. The idea of sitting on a couch and watching television didn't appeal to me at all," he says.

Not long afterwards, the Tuleys moved to an outlying area of Nashville, Indiana where they built a log cabin on 10 acres of wooded land. It was as different as life could be from Evansville, where they had raised three children, a girl and two boys. "I'd always worked in cities," he says.

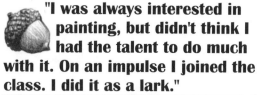
"I was always interested in painting, but didn't think I had the talent to do much with it. On an impulse I joined the class. I did it as a lark."

Their immediate company was each other, their dog, deer, wild turkeys, possums, coyotes and an occasional raccoon. Soon, however, the Tuleys became acquainted with people in their community, and began to do fund raising in a drive to build a new YMCA. He became active in the local Community Foundation and is now raising money to build a new church. Tuley also met a woman who was running a class in Nashville's artists' colony.

"I was always interested in painting, but didn't think I had the talent to do much with it. On an impulse I joined the class. I did it as a lark. I was the token male. I still am. I began to do oils, then watercolors. Landscapes, barns, no abstractions, realism is my style. To my surprise, I wasn't the only one who liked what I was doing. People actually buy what I paint."

©2003, Thomas Tuley

As for what he left behind, Tuley couldn't believe that he'd spent 38 years, putting on a business suit, a shirt and tie each working day and going to his office. "I could never do that again," he says.

"Now, I actually have time to stop and think about what I'm doing. As a newspaperman, the pressure to meet a deadline of one kind or another was always there. I couldn't always make sure the outcome was exactly what I wanted it. When I paint, if it's not just right, I can tinker with it, try it differently, until something clicks and I know what I've got is what I want."

Nor has he given up writing, after so many years at the craft. "Fiction's not for me," he says. " I have two books in the works, both non-fiction. One is about a hurricane."

"A hurricane?"

"One that hit the Outer Banks off North Carolina on August 31, 1993. I saw it up close, because I had a house there. And yes, the house is still standing. A publisher is looking at that book. The second book is a 30-year-old mystery, real life. It's about a man who was declared dead twice. A literary agent is handling that one."

Asked what impact, his work has had on his audiences, Tuley says, "With a newspaper, it might take six months or a year to see any impact, as a result of what you did. With my paintings, it's more immediate and more personal. I like that. I'm never going to be famous. I have a limited amount of time ahead of me. I started painting late in life."

"What about Grandma Moses?"

"She was an exception."

He's not a recluse. "We travel. Australia, Wyoming, Montana, New Mexico, Michigan, other places where I have old colleagues. We've also been to the Caymans twice and Hawaii

> **As for what he left behind, Tuley couldn't believe that he'd spent 38 years, putting on a business suit, a shirt and tie each working day and going to his office.**

twice. My daughter is an attorney, married, three kids. Both my sons are engineers, one mechanical, one civil. They're both unmarried. But I travel less than I thought I would before I retired. I find that I like the quiet here in the woods."

Tuley doesn't live in yesterday's world, exciting as it was. "I miss my old colleagues, but my circle of friends is different now, and that suits me fine."

When prompted, his advice for those nearing retirement or already retired and restless is, "Keep busy. Do what you want to do. Take a chance."

There can be surprise rewards, as well. When Tuley went to find out what his new address in Nashville was, he was told, "4457 Tuley Trace."

4457 is a big number. How many other residents are there on Tuley Trace?

"Two," he says.

# Education

If your grandfather and great-grandfather had been Presidents of the United States, what would your ambition be? No, we're not talking about some future grandchild of George W. Bush, but about Henry Adams of *that* Adams family.

Adams' choice was to become a scholar and a writer, and with the publication of *The Education of Henry Adams*, he became a Pulitzer Prize winner. What Adams wrote is anything but a dry textbook. It recounts his own and his country's education from 1838, the year of his birth, to 1905, incorporating the Civil War, capitalist expansion and the growth of the United States as a world power. Written with immense wit and irony, today it remains one of the most compelling works of American autobiography today.

We do not have a Henry Adams to profile, but the men we do, have one thing in common with Adams. With the exception of Bob Christin, who came from an academic background, but in retirement did an interesting shifting of gears, the others did not train to be educators, but arrived there via their own exposure to the outside world. Herb Kamm was a newspaperman; Dennis Jett, a diplomat; Bill Sams a successful executive in Silicon Valley.

Learning, teaching and education come in many different packages. There was a time when physicians and attorneys, as well as craftsmen, acquired their skills through apprenticeships. And it wasn't the worst system in the world. In medicine, internships and residencies still give evidence of the power of "learning through doing" under the tutelage of the masters.

Our world offers such a wealth of opportunities to learn; the problem can be in making the choice. Community colleges, on-learn learning, semesters at sea—the list goes on.

As for those who teach, there's a richness of opportunity. Yes, there's the rigor of higher education that produces the majority of our teachers and professors. But in the pages that follow you'll discover some unexpected routes that have succeeded.

# A World Full of Students

You can take the teacher out of the classroom, but you can't take the classroom out of the teacher. It's a variation on a familiar quote, and it certainly applies to Robert Christin.

"I loved teaching for 35 years as Professor of English at three universities," says Christin, "and when I retired, I looked forward to a new career. While teaching, I had done some creative writing, acted in plays and a documentary, but that was only part time. Now, I figured I could write every day, act and still do a lot of reading."

©2003, Helen Jones

*Education*

All of which Christin did. Still, something was missing.

"One day I complained to my wife," he recalls. "When I was teaching and came to a passage I particularly liked," I said, "I could read it to my class and maybe spark one or two of the students to read the book. I miss that."

"My wife was a very practical woman. 'Create your own classroom,' she said. 'Go to the library and ask if they'd like you to teach a course on how to read and enjoy modern poetry.'"

Mrs. Christin was on track. The head librarian agreed and set up a seven-week evening program. Posters were made; radio stations were informed. The first night, to Christin's pleasant surprise, 50 people showed up for the course. The local newspaper wrote up the event, and Old Dominion University's Retirement Center in Norfolk, Va., invited him to teach the same course. Later, he offered two writing courses, "Writing Memoirs" and "Writing Poetry."

Christin's new career gained momentum. After three years at Old Dominion, he started to teach "Creative Writing" and "Writing Memoirs" at the local Adult Learning Center—an extension of the public school system. Later he added "Writing Poetry."

"The courses were filled by the first week, often by the first day of registration," says Christin with a touch of pride. "Most of the students continued to sign up to repeat the course. You don't learn to write creatively in one short course, and they recognized that. They were eager to learn, wrote something each week, read it and heard comments from other students and from me. I must say these students became the best I had ever taught."

From a sizable inventory of writing episodes involving his students, Christin offers a sampling of memorable events

"A retired Navy flyer enrolled in my "Writing Memoirs" course. After some initial hesitancy—'I can't do that kind of writing'—he described life growing up with his parents and a crippled brother; a summer after high school spent on a ranch in the West where he rode horses, learned to care for them and groom them. He wrote about the death of a close friend who died trying to land his plane on the carrier deck. This flyer, tough as he needed to be, was soft and gentle when he spoke of the joys of growing up, the joys of life and love in the Navy, and the appreciation for his wife and three children. Yet he thought he couldn't write his memoirs.

**"My wife was a very practical woman. 'Create your own classroom,' she said."**

"A middle-aged woman in the "Creative Writing" course detailed her life in a 'toxic home' with an abusive husband and her experience of the death of her child. At the end of the semester she wrote me a letter of thanks. She had signed up for my course, she said, on the advice of her therapist, after having been discharged from a psychiatric institution. The woman claimed the course had helped her adjust back to normal living. I had not known of her illness until then.

"Another woman in her fifties read her first essay in a "Memoirs" class. When she finished, everyone clapped. After class I told her the students had never clapped before. A few weeks later, with tears running down her cheeks, she told me how wonderful it felt to be able to open up and write about topics of which she had never spoken, for fear that she would be laughed at. She said after that first class, her entire life had been changed."

"What a bonus this has been for me," says Christin, now 81."The interaction with those students keeps me feeling younger than ever, and my ego, if it needed a boost, sure felt good after those experiences. I believe I have a gift for teaching, and it's a pleasure to share the gift with others. The energy it gives me for my other efforts is reward in itself, and the students have been a prompt for me to get on with those, 'One day I really want to….'

Christin finds himself much in demand at libraries, bookstores, churches, nursing homes, hospitals, and in classrooms from first grade to high school seniors. He has also picked up on interests that go back many years.

"I always liked acting, taking on a role I would never have in real life, enjoying the feeling of living that role, getting a sense of what it must have been like," Christin says. "Since I retired I've acted in films produced by New Dominion Pictures, shown mostly on the Discovery Channel.

What are the roles he's played?

"In a series called *The Prosecutor,* I was a bad guy who brought up a nephew, helped him bury his first wife after he murdered her, and kept quiet about the murder of his second wife. After that, I played a judge. I was a civilian yachtsman with a trophy wife on an island near Hawaii where I met what later turned out to be a couple who murdered another couple to get their yacht. I was a Texas Ranger solving a murder."

"I wouldn't want to be any one of these characters," he says quickly, "but I enjoyed the feeling of 'living' out their lives temporarily."

"When my wife died two years ago I was glad to be as busy as I am. I attended excellent AARP bereavement sessions for widows and widowers for two years. I am so grateful for the help they gave me during one of the worst periods of my life that I plan to take lessons to become a facilitator to help new widows and widowers through this tough period. This group meets one evening a week."

"Now, my days and a lot of evenings are filled with activity. My only regret is the many things I want to do but have no time for: learning Spanish, and doing photography; putting hundreds of photographs in acid-free albums, putting the writings of my wife and myself in acid-free notebooks."

> **"A middle-aged woman claimed the course had helped her adjust back to normal living. I had not known of her illness until then."**

Christin sees each morning as a fresh beginning and is making the most of it.

E-mail: rechris@earthlink.net

# Serving the World at Home and Abroad

For Dennis Jett it was a new but familiar scene—a diplomatic reception. He had been in the Foreign Service for more than 25 years, but had arrived in Lima less than two months earlier as U.S. Ambassador to Peru.

©2003, Greg Undeen

This night's reception was different. It was being held at the Japanese ambassador's residence to mark the annual birthday party for Japanese Emperor Akihito on December 17, 1996. Because the president of Peru, Alberto Fujimori, was of Japanese descent, anyone who counted was present that night. However, Fujimori, himself had not come. He had wanted to attend, but had returned too late from a trip up-country.

Because it was such a power-packed gathering, security was even tighter than normal. Peru had long been a hotbed of terrorist activity. *Fortune* magazine had rated it the riskiest place in the world to do business. On that night, however, nowhere in Lima seemed more secure.

Security is never far from an ambassador's mind. American embassies have taken very strong security precautions and are continually reviewed because American diplomatic establishments are frequently the targets of terrorists. The embassy in Lima and the ambassador's residence had both been bombed twice in recent years. In addition, there were over 10,000 Americans in Peru and the threat of terrorism and common crime was a reality that had to be faced 24 hours a day.

 **In less than three minutes, using surprise, speed, overwhelming force and controlled explosions, all the guerellas were dead.**

Jett intended to stay only briefly. He had gotten back very early that morning from a meeting in Miami and had to go back to the airport that night to meet his mother who was arriving for the holidays. He planned to have a quick dinner at his residence with his wife, Lynda Schuster. A former reporter for the *Wall Street Journal* and the *Christian Science Monitor*, she was pregnant with their first child. After about half an hour, he walked quickly out to the street where his armored car was waiting. Most of the other U.S. diplomats stayed on a bit longer.

About 8:15 P.M, less than half an hour after Jett departed, 14 members of the Tupac Amaru Revolutionary Movement (MRTA), a terrorist group, blew a hole in the 15-foot wall between the ambassador's residence and the house next door. They quickly entered the Ambassador's garden firing their weapons in the air and moved on to the house where the hundreds of guests were taken hostage. Because the security personnel had remained outside on the street, the MRTA was able to carry out the operation without

*It's Never Too Late to Plant a Tree*

exchanging gunfire with the guards. It was an audacious, well-executed, military-style raid.

The hundreds of hostages were gathered together and told to lie facedown on the floor. After a few hours, all the women were released, but about 400 hostages remained.

The MRTA was in decline. Its 1,000 adherents had recently dwindled to a few hundred after most of their leaders had been captured and imprisoned, but it was still formidable. The rebels said the hostages would not be freed unless hundreds of their imprisoned comrades were let out. In addition, they wanted all of them to be allowed to retreat to their war zone in the jungle. If their demands were not met, they vowed they would start killing hostages at noon the next day.

Jett and his embassy team went into a well-rehearsed security posture. It has been long-standing State Department policy not to give in to the demands of hostage-takers. However, an attack on the residence by American military was out of the question. The residence was Japanese sovereign territory and would require Japanese, as well as Peruvian government, approval to launch an assault. The Japanese had in the past preferred to meet the demands of hostage takers rather than use force and risk a blood bath. In addition, the Peruvian government made clear it was in charge and that Fujimori was going to handle the situation his way without foreign assistance.

The negotiations dragged on as the deadline kept being extended. On the evening of December 22, some 250 of the hostages, including the seven remaining Americans, were allowed to leave. They were all in good health and spirits despite being held at gunpoint for five days. The MRTA described the release as a Christmas gesture, but the reality was they still had too many hostages.

From the outset of the crisis, providing for hundreds of those crammed into the Japanese ambassador's residence was a challenge.

While the negotiations continued on and off, the Peruvian government prepared to bring the standoff to an end, if necessary through military means. Ambassador Jett had made clear that the U.S., if called upon, would help in whatever way appropriate. The Peruvian government, nonetheless, insisted on running the operation itself except for limited intelligence support.

When the takeover first occurred, some had predicted that the situation would be resolved in days, a few weeks, at most. Despite their threats, the terrorists had not executed any hostages. But by late April, they were losing patience and sleep. At one point, the police set up sound trucks that blasted music at high volume at the compound 24 hours a day making it impossible for the rebels and the hostages to rest.

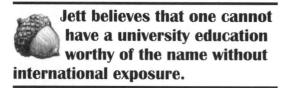 **Jett believes that one cannot have a university education worthy of the name without international exposure.**

The end finally came after 126 days. On April 22, 1997, in a well-coordinated attack, 150 Peruvian army commandos, trained by SWAT consultants from the U.S., Britain and other friendly governments, crashed though the compound walls and emerged from tunnels dug under the lawn. In less than three minutes, using surprise, speed, overwhelming force and controlled explosions, all the guerrillas were dead. A couple of them had the opportunity to kill a large number of the hostages, but in the end only one hostage and two army officers died in the fighting.

The State Department awarded Jett and his staff a group superior honor award for their superb performance. This was not the first time an embassy under Jett's direction had won the award. When he served as Ambassador to Mozambique from 1993 to 1996, it was given in recognition of its efforts to bring that country through its first democratic elections. In 1990, he and the embassy won it for their work during the civil war in Liberia. He was also given the Department's highest recognition, the distinguished honor award, for his exceptional service during that war.

*It's Never Too Late to Plant a Tree*

Jett had faced many difficult moments in other diplomatic posts in Mozambique, Liberia, Malawi, Israel, and Argentina, but the Peru hostage crisis was one of the hardest and longest challenges in his Foreign Service career.

Upon leaving Lima, Jett accepted an assignment at the Carter Center in Atlanta as diplomat-in-residence and senior advisor on Africa. While there, he began writing opinion pieces and appeared on radio and television responding to questions about peacekeeping, democracy, Peru, terrorism and other topics. His over 35 articles have appeared on the Op Ed pages of the *Christian Science Monitor, Miami Herald, Washington Post, New York Times* and other major newspapers.

In the Foreign Service one can retire at age 50 with 20 years of service. Jett knew that if he were to start a second career it would be easier to do then rather than wait until required to leave the Foreign Service in his late 50's. What to do?

Jett decided his second career would be in higher education. While he had a B.A. and an M.A. from the University of New Mexico and had attended the U.S. Naval Academy and the University of Miami, a Ph.D. was important for a career in academia. So while in Mozambique, he enrolled in a doctoral program at the University of the Witwatersrand in South Africa. Based in part on his experiences in Africa, his dissertation was entitled *"Why Peacekeeping Fails,"* and was published as a book by Palgrave/St. Martins.

After a year in Atlanta, in 2000, Jett retired from the Foreign Service to become dean of the International Center of the University of Florida in Gainesville. In Gainesville, Jett and a staff of 30 send 1,200 UF students to study abroad each year. Additionally, they help some 2,800 international students and 1,300 international scholars adjust to academic life in the United States.

By encouraging students, faculty and staff to have a more global perspective, the International Center helps to enhance the academic environment and experience at UF. Jett believes that one cannot have a university education worthy of the name without international exposure. Given the effects of globalization, he says, Americans can no longer ignore the greater world. By studying foreign cultures and languages, students also prepare themselves to be more competitive in today's increasingly globalized economy.

Jett's best retirement resource was the advice obtained by networking with former Foreign Service officers and other contacts. His most important recommendation is to plan ahead five to eight years, set a definite goal, then develop a plan and the contacts necessary to achieve it.

Dennis Jett thinks he's lucky. As a Foreign Service officer he accomplished much for his country and the world. In retirement, he is helping thousands of young students achieve a world of understanding and success. In his case, that may be two different paths toward the same end.

E-mail: djett@ufl.edu

*It's Never Too Late to Plant a Tree*

# Do It Right
# Or Don't Do It At All

It was 1982 and Herb Kamm had a retirement problem. He was an old newspaperman and there was no money in old newspapers. That's an old Henny Youngman joke, but it fit Kamm, a former Scripps managing editor of newspapers in New York and Cleveland. He had reached retirement age but not retirement mentality.

> **He had reached retirement age but not retirement mentality.**

He didn't think he had a lot of options. He could write columns, but there wasn't an opening from syndicates or a big demand from newspapers for off-site columnists. He could move to Florida and play golf. His problem with that was he wasn't that good of a golfer. Then he thought he could join the faculty of a

©2001, California Polytechnic State University

university and teach journalism, but Kamm had never  even graduated from college, let alone earned a PhD.

He turned to Phyllis, his wife of 48 years, and said, "O.K., you decide." "I just don't want to spend any more winters in Cleveland," she said. "Let's try California." So the two of them moved to one of their favorite California locations, San Luis Obispo. No job. No work. Just a pension and 60 years of newspaper memories and contacts. That's all Kamm needed.

Within a few weeks, Kamm was writing editorials for the local daily newspaper *The Tribune.* He bumped into the president of the California Polytechnic State University and offered to help with Cal Poly's public relations and teach journalism courses. The school was skeptical about accepting a free offer from this nationally famous journalist. Universities are often more concerned with process than substance and if there's no previously approved handbook ruling, many great opportunities from outside the ivory tower world of senior executives are lost.

To the surprise of many, Cal Poly's president, Warren Baker, invited Kamm in, first as an adviser to the

**"I wouldn't be a reporter today without Herb's influence on my life."**

university's vice-president, then as a consultant to the president, and finally as a part-time faculty member. In addition to teaching journalism classes, he designed special projects including seven media forums, a celebrity lecture series for the community, and wrote speeches for the university president.

But it was the students that gave him the most satisfaction. He trained them, rather than lectured them. He coached them in how to select news stories, spot the right peg, the tricks of in-depth interviewing, and how to write with honesty and schmaltz, his New York word for finding deep human interest.

"I wouldn't be a reporter today without Herb's influence on my life," said a writer for *The Washington Post.* He quickly became an adviser to the university's student newspaper *The Mustang Daily,* and a former editor credits him with teaching "the nuts and bolts" of journalism and becoming the "biggest role model I've ever met."

Here was a major figure in journalism, an editor and columnist who had interviewed Presidents, befriended celebrities like Marilyn Monroe and sports stars like Joe DiMaggio and now, in shirtsleeves, their classroom teacher. "He is a newspaperman who seems hewn from the very trees that were pulped into the ink-stained sheets he loves to peruse and talk about so passionately," wrote columnist Steve Moss. "He wants us all to be better, and those at the university who follow him with such devotion have become known as 'Herb's tribe.'"

Students eagerly sought his guidance and contacts to help them start their careers. But that was not enough for Kamm. He kept in touch with graduates as they skipped from one job to another. "When I grow up," wrote the higher education reporter for the local newspaper, "I want to be like Herb Kamm. I want to be able to walk into a room full of a hundred strangers and be able to gain their camaraderie by night's end. I want to have the stamina to retire but then keep doggedly working as if I'm fully employed. I want to be 85 and still act like I'm 35. I want to be married to the same woman for 66 years."

One of his proudest days was when he delivered the Commencement Address before 1,700 graduating seniors and their families in 2001.

Kamm's most famous off-campus activity was his "lunchtime bull session," his own take on the famous book, *Tuesdays With Morrie*. Each day he took a few students to lunch, lets them talk about everything from sports writing to girlfriends. From this introduction, it was an easy segue to caution and the necessity to be honest. His advice was spiced with the salty language he brought from the newsrooms of New Jersey, New York and Cleveland. Every student left the lunch believing Kamm was his best friend, a larger than life persona with a down-to-earth personality. "Do it right or don't do it at all," was his mantra.

"If you want to be successful," he told them, "you should observe the traits of successful people." So whenever he /could corral them, Kamm invited his celebrity friends and *New York Times* sportswriters to address his class. When Kamm told his class one day he would have Bob Costas deliver a lecture by a conference call, one of his students doubted him. Sure enough, when the young man entered the classroom the next day, there was Costas on the telephone. Kamm insisted that the skeptical young man be the first to start off the Q & A. Kamm was never doubted about anything he promised from that day on.

Recently Cal Poly announced the creation of a Herb Kamm Lifetime Achievement Award presented annually to an outstanding journalism professional. There is also a Herb Kamm Scholarship for worthy students.

Retirement provided him the opportunity to write two books, but more important he was a perfect example of how good professionals can be productive long past the time of societal pressures to retire.

# Save Your Life
# and Save The World

When your first retirement dream runs aground, it's a good idea to have a lifeboat.

That's what happened to Bill Sams and his wife, Jan, when his first retirement project nearly cost them their lives.

For 17 years, Sams had been VP and general manager of several semiconductor firms in California, the last being LSI Logic in Silicon Valley. It was a time when earnings and stock options were making millionaires of many computer industry executives. An astute Sams decided it was the time to cash in and follow his star.

His dream was sailing the South Pacific. "I wasn't trying to get away from life," he said. "I felt I was going toward something."

©2003, Andrew Eiler

*Education*

And that's just what he and Jan did. They traded in much of their bank account for a 46-foot Liberty 456 cutter rigged sailboat, which they named *Camelot*. And in 1995, after10 years of weekend sailing in the San Francisco Bay area, they set sail under the Golden Bridge for the South Pacific and its countless romantic islands.

**"Wave after wave dash over us and around the flooded dinghy until, with just one lucky break, I land on top of the dinghy."**

For nearly two years, *Camelot* was home, honeymoon cottage and retirement paradise. They toured hundreds of beautiful islands, made scores of new friends and pinched themselves that it was really happening.

Then one calm day it happened. Here is Bill Sams' reconstruction of events:

"First comes the dreaded impact along with the sound and thud of grounding. 'We hit something,' the fearful cry of every sailor. They have run aground on an uncharted coral reef four miles west of the Fijian island of Vanua Levu. With each jolt, Jan and Bill are thrown forward.

"Nothing can shake them loose. Bill frantically tries to power off the reef, shifting the engine forward and reverse with the rudder hard over both ways. The boat doesn't move an inch. Coral heads astern and on the port side have trapped the keel from both directions.

"What is worse is that developing low tide will worsen the entrapment by at least four feet of water over the next four hours.

"Another escape plan of using the anchor to pull the bow around to starboard doesn't work either. Distress calls to the Fijian Coast Guard come to naught when the authorities demand $5,000 up front in cash, just to dispatch a rescue boat. Sams has the cash, but the Coast Guard wants it paid at the dock before they will come to the rescue.

"To make matters worse, if one can call it that, what started out as a lovely, calm day is suddenly turning into a raging storm. Waves start to slop against the low side of the deck, causing the boat to rise and fall. With each fall, the boat smashes harder and harder against the reef. The flooring starts to crack, and *Camelot* begins taking on water.

"'I take to the water to monitor and adjust the boat's fenders, but a wave throws me hard against the hull, and a stanchion whacks me on the head. It's time to get out of the sea.'

"Finally an American boat, the *Silver Cloud*, answers Jan's distress radio calls, but limited visibility, 25-mile-an-hour winds and four-foot seas make a side-to-side rescue impossible. As weather conditions worsen, the friendly rescue boat soon will have problems of its own, if it doesn't immediately head for a safe harbor. Now, as each wave starts to break up the *Camelot*, saving the boat becomes secondary. The main objective is for us to save our lives.

"'Abandon ship!' We put on life jackets, grab our credit cards, passports and boat papers and push them into canvas boat bags.

Everything else, such as personal valuables, wedding rings, and photo albums, is left on board.

"Getting off the sinking boat also proves to be a challenge. An Avon inflatable dinghy is totally flooded, but it still floats. Jumping into the dingy, which is rising and falling 10 feet in the air with each crashing wave, would be a feat for an experienced gymnast. Jumping into the water with coral all around is equally dangerous.

**Experiential involvement in real life is the path Sams and Stinson are researching.**

"'I'm drowning.' 'No, just hold on,' we shout back and forth to each other. I know that time is running out for us and the rescuers on *Silver Cloud*. No choice left. We jump into the turbulent waters. Wave after wave dash over us and around the flooded dinghy until, with just one lucky break, I land on top of the dinghy. Seconds later I'm able to catch Jan and pull her in as well.

"As breaking surf rolls through the flooded dinghy, we're sitting in water up to our waists, I try to get the 3-hp engine to start. Miraculously, it does. We pray with each turn of the prop, as the inflatable chugs forward loaded with a ton of water, narrowly missing razor sharp pieces of coral, jutting up all around the raft.

"As the crew of *Silver Cloud* finally pulls us from the raging seas, our first reaction is to hug each other and say, 'I love you.' Our second is to watch tearfully the last few moments of the rapidly disappearing *Camelot* and say goodbye to our home and dream way of life. Our third is to thank the crew of the *Silver Cloud*, who put themselves at great risk to rescue us amidst dangerous reefs under storm conditions."

A dream has ended as a nightmare, albeit with a final silver lining.

Back in California, Sams has lost his enthusiasm for long ocean passages, the rigors of the open ocean and the worry of difficult anchorages. It is time for his second retirement project, which he denies is really retirement, just doing something else.

Now he is involved with his passion for information. And along with an associate, Professor John Stinson of Ohio University, he is developing a new educational system that he hopes, "will save the world."

There are three major routes to education, he claims: lecturing, reading and experiential involvement in real life. It is the latter path that Sams and Stinson are researching.

They are developing computer animation techniques, popular in video games, to create software, which places the user in stories and case histories where choices have to be made. In this way, students discover knowledge on their screens by making choices that the computer will instantaneously evaluate with real-time feedback.

"There won't be right and wrong decisions," claims Sams, "but the opportunity to deliver experiences in real life in a user friendly environment." Education can be entertaining. "We shouldn't be afraid of making learning fun," says Sams.

It's an exciting educational innovation in unchartered waters. So obviously Sams, whether he admits it or not, is still sailing.

E-mail: samsw@ohio.edu

# Entertainment

Bob Hope lived a full century in a career that stretched from vaudeville to motion pictures to radio and television. But most memorable were his personal tours to the men and women of America's armed services on battlefields around the world. And he wasn't even born in the United States.

None of the men and women profiled in our book came to their callings by a direct route. Carol Shedlin did most of her singing behind closed doors or in the shower, the way many of us do. Jack Mertz didn't set out to be an actor. He'd been head of an agency, specializing in editorial and public relations work in the food field. Jim Layer made his living as a physician. Joan Wood was a top-flight public relations executive. Jack Chilton in "real life" was an engineer with the Naval Air Systems Command Pacific, albeit a serious jazz aficionado.

And as you'll read in the *Helping Kids* section of the book, there are others who use their skills as clowns and magicians to engross, entertain and help children. In the *Humor* section, you'll find more than a joke. Without a trace of pomposity, these entertainers are trying to improve the lives of those who hear and see them. You may not see the names of our entertainers in lights, but they light up the lives of those they touch.

# Retirement Is Only A Beginning

The full name is Harrison R. Chilton, but you can call me "Jack." I was an engineer with the Naval Air Systems Command Pacific, based at the Naval Air Station North Island in San Diego, California, when the place was reorganized. We lived in Coronado, a small paradise. I rode a bicycle to work every morning. The prospect of moving to Patuxent River, Maryland was not attractive. I chose to retire. That was 1977.

**"I applied for and was awarded a grant to produce 'Vision and Flight: San Diego's Aviation Heritage.'"**

Retirement requires adjustment, but less so in my case. I had a number of avocations. The most enjoyable of these were music, photography and writing. There was a monthly jazz jam session that I participated in with some big time musicians (those of you who love swing will know the names): John Best, Bob Haggart, Bobby Gordon, Skeets Herfurt. Bob Crosby occasionally dropped in.

One day I spotted a story in the *San Diego Union* about a group called PACE, short for Public Access Cable-television by and for Elders. Dr. Michael Real, a professor at the University of California in San Diego, had formed it.

Mike had written a book, "Mass-Mediated Culture" in which he pointed out that the media, controlled by fewer and fewer people, had great influence on public attitudes and the danger this offered. He proposed that use of the Public Access channels of cable television by minority groups might mitigate this danger to some degree.

Mike had obtained a grant to train one such group—seniors—on how to access these channels. The training was done by putting seniors into an undergraduate class at UCSD where they were trained to produce, shoot, write and edit television shows and to get them exposed through cable television.

Here was a chance to do all three of my favorite avocations. As a class project, I arranged to film the story of John Best, a trumpet player from North Carolina who had played with many of the top swing bands of the 1930's and 1940's and had been a studio musician in Hollywood for many years.

John was doing a Sunday afternoon monthly gig at The Little Bavaria, a club and restaurant in Del Mar, a short distance up the coast from UCSD. He brought some of the finest jazz musicians of our time down from Hollywood, and we taped them at The Little Bavaria. To meet the class deadline, my sharp undergraduate co-producer, Sharon Lukomski and I decided to limit our 30-minute tape to the session at The Little Bavaria. We titled it "John Best and All That Jazz." It was awarded Best Show of the Year by the San Diego Community Video Center in San Diego. Later, I took the raw footage for "John Best and All That Jazz," filled in with additional shots and made a one-hour show titled "Best of the Big Bands." The cable companies aired it for a number of years.

> **"I ran for office at a slow walk and was beaten in the first primary."**

Next, the Foundation for Community Service Cable Television in San Francisco offered a grant for productions using the cable public access channels. I applied for and was awarded a grant to produce "Vision and Flight: San Diego's Aviation Heritage."

We focused on two experimental aircraft designed, built and tested in San Diego. They were the Sea Dart, manufactured by Convair and the Vertijet, manufactured by Ryan Aviation. Both were highly advanced concepts and had experienced dramatic moments in tests. The Sea Dart, for example, came apart in a high speed, low altitude pass in front of a reviewing stand of 300 people. Neither plane ever went into production.

*From left: Jim Hoag, Bass; Jack Chilton, Guitar; Randy Lobb, Drums; Hans Gunder, Sax.* ©2003 Adrienne Helitzer/Still Productions

But for me, it was a very exciting project. I'd been through World War Two as a Navy carrier-based fighter pilot and had seen combat in the Pacific during the attack on Tarawa in the Gilbert Islands and the Marianas campaign.

During the Korean War, I was assigned to the Navy's Bureau of Aeronautics office at Douglas Aircraft Company in Santa Monica, CA. I was made Engineering and Inspection Officer and was flying acceptance flights on aircraft being produced by Douglas for the Navy and Air Force.

With the support of the San Diego Aeronautical Museum I was able to reach back and interview people involved in the concept, design, prototype development and test flights of the Sea Dart and Vertijet. I also obtained and used film and documents from the archives of the Aerospace Museum. Unusually large audiences for public access channels viewed the 30-minute shows we produced on these two aircraft.

In 1988 I came into a Democratic 75th Assembly District meeting late and found that I had been selected as their candidate for the State Assembly. I ran for office at a slow walk and was beaten in the first primary.

I'm pushing 89 at this point, and all in all, I'm doing fine with no aches or pains. I play tennis four times a week (I need a nimble partner), ride a bike for all transportation (except to parties), have prostate cancer but doing nothing about it except taking periodic PSA blood tests. This is called "Watchful waiting," using the excuse that at this age something will get me before the cancer. What the hell, I've lived past my time!

In my spare time, I play guitar with the Coronado Swing Band and write letters of protest to the San Diego Union-Tribune.

What am I protesting about? It's a pretty long list, and if you're interested you can send me an E-mail.

Still, life is very good. My advice? Live it up! Do those things you've always wanted to do. Keep active and don't look back. A great old pitcher by the name of Satchel Paige said it best a long time ago, "Don't look back. They're gaining on you!"

E-mail: jchiltz@juno.com

# Keep an Eye Open for This Doctor. And an Ear, Too

If your ophthalmologist told you he could perform perfectly well with his eyes closed, you'd be a bit nervous, wouldn't you?

Well, I'm Jim Layer, an ophthalmologist, and I can. Except...I'm performing on stage, and it's not surgery I'm doing. I'm singing, and even then I keep my eyes open

It all started around 1996, during my family's yearly winter getaway to Palm Springs. We were invited to a party at a friend's home. He had rented a karaoke machine, and my family, knowing my love for Frank Sinatra's music, persuaded me to get up and sing. Come to think of it, they didn't have to try that hard.

The last time I'd sung in public was in a church choir when I was in grade school. I don't remember anyone going wild then, and this group didn't either, but neither did anyone run for the door. Best of all, I discovered that I really enjoyed singing in public. So much so, that I bought my own karaoke machine and began to practice regularly. Golfing, sketching, and my other pastimes took a back seat.

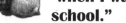

**"The last time I'd sung in public was in a church choir when I was in grade school."**

Not that I quit my daytime job. In fact, I continued to practice ophthalmology with fresh enthusiasm. Unfortunately, singing wasn't a cure for an old neck injury that resulted in cervical arthritis. My motion had become so severely limited that I had to give up microsurgery and limit my professional activities to medical ophthalmology. The upside was that I had more time for singing.

Okay, I was addicted, and in December 2000, six months after turning 62, I retired from ophthalmology. Even before then, I felt that I needed a change of pace. I just didn't know what it might be, until that One Enchanted Evening.

There must be something about Palm Springs. On our next winter vacation there, after I'd retired, my wife, Judy, and I had dinner at a local restaurant that often featured live entertainment. That night, a mother and daughter were singing. That was all Judy needed. She approached Tony, the owner of Pepper Maggies, and asked, "How would you like to have a male singer perform on Wednesday evenings? I know a singing doctor from Minneapolis."

Tony didn't jump for joy, but he didn't laugh either. "Tell him to come in and sing for me. If he's any **"I've appeared in an independent film, Cliché, as a lounge singer."**

good, I'll let him perform here," he said. That Wednesday at 2 PM, I sang for Tony, his wife, and several waiters and busboys. Four hours later, my public singing career had begun.

To be on the safe side, Judy and I invited some of our Palm Springs friends to my first formal gig. Even though I didn't have any musical training, the audience actually enjoyed my singing. With my brand new karaoke machine playing background music, I belted out some of my Sinatra favorites—"Witchcraft," "I've Got You Under My Skin," "Come Fly With Me." For the remainder of our three months in Palm Springs, I performed at Pepper Maggies once a week. Several groups of people came to hear me on a regular basis. I had a following!

When we returned to Minneapolis in the spring, I began singing once a week at my golf club, to the amazement of the members. Soon I was singing twice a week, and the club had added a dance floor, transforming a staid dining room into a swinging nightclub. I tried to emulate the styles of the greats: Sinatra, Tony Bennett, Mel Tormé, and Dean Martin, who I think is really underrated. Or maybe he just didn't do as much with his voice as he might have. My repertoire grew from a few Sinatra classics to more than 200 selections. With relentless practice, my voice also improved and my range increased.

When Judy told my father that I'd taken a part-time job in California, he asked if I'd have to retake the board exams. "No," she said, "the job isn't in medicine." "Is it golf-related?" he asked. Again, she just said, "No," before she broke done and told him I was singing in a restaurant. He just stared at her. "This is the last thing I would have expected of my eldest son," he finally said.

©2003, Richard Tsong-Taatarii

To be honest, it's not the first time I surprised my dad, or myself. When I graduated from high school, I enlisted in the Navy. I'm the eldest of 12 children, and Dad was very upset with me. He said I'd ruin my life and never come back or go to college or make much of myself. As it turned out, once in the Navy, I got sick and had to spend a few weeks in the Navy hospital. That gave me a chance to watch the Navy doctors and I thought, "That's not a bad life. They're in the military, but not strictly under the military as far as their own schedules."

When I was discharged from the Navy, I had some money saved and, much to my father's relief, I went to college and then on to medical school. Surgery appealed to me, and thanks to an older ophthalmologist, I decided that was the specialty for me.

As for my singing career, at this point I'm still an amateur, mostly singing without pay for my own enjoyment. But I have appeared in an independent film, *Cliché*, as a lounge singer. I've recorded three CDs including a Christmas CD, featuring classical holiday songs. You can hear me on my website, www.TheSingingDoctor.com.

All things considered, I'm pretty content with how things are going. I sing twice a week at my country club and fairly frequently at private events and parties. I don't see going to Las Vegas. My kids come to hear me when they can, and I've done some duets with my younger daughter. Of course, Judy my wife/manager, is a fixture in all my audiences. I'm not sure where this new career is headed, but Judy, who can take the credit or blame for what I've been up to, has been talking about my getting an agent. By the time you read this, I hope to have sung with live background music. And the thought of retiring again hasn't crossed my mind.

Do I have a favorite song? Hard to say. Maybe it's "I've Got You Under My Skin," because somehow my songs have gotten under the skin of my audiences. And that's without the benefit of ophthalmic microsurgery.

Wed site: JLayer2539@aol.com
Web site: www.TheSingingDoctor.com.

# They'll Always Need Older Men

In this scene a man in his 70's is posing nude for a pregnant young woman. No, it's not a kinky dream. It's from the film, *Life Drawings,* which was made by a young Croatian director, Arsen Anton Ostojic. It's been shown at film festivals in Morocco, Croatia and at the New York International Independent Film & Video Festival.

Jack Mertz's performance in *Life Drawings* won him a nomination for best actor at The Moroccan Film Festival. "I didn't win," he says with a shrug, "but at least I was noticed. I did receive a Best Actor Award in a short drama from the New York International Independent Film and Video Festival and also from the Sulzbach-Rosenberg Short Film Festival in Germany."

©2003. Thomas Hart Shelby

"In *Life Drawings,* I play an old man, a widower, living alone with a cat. Through a series of events I re-discover my easel and say, 'Maybe if I start painting, it'll get me out of the rut I've fallen into.' So I hire a model, who in real life was eight months and three weeks pregnant, and start sketching her in my house. Well, it goes from bad to worse. Finally, she puts her clothes on and says, 'What the hell do you do you think you are? You're no artist. You're just an old pervert.' And as she gets ready to leave, she turns and says, 'Take your clothes off, all of them. I'll show you what nude painting should be like.' So I do. She does the drawing and as she's about to go, she picks up a large paintbrush, defaces her drawing and storms out.

"Well, three months later, I'm coming back to my brownstone in Brooklyn, and there she is at the top of the steps. I figure she's come back to finish what she's started.

"'Remember me?' she says.

"'Yes.'

"'Well, I behaved rather badly when I was here the last time, and I wanted to apologize and also show you my baby.' Which she does. 'Now, if you'd like, you can have two models, instead of one.'

"In the last scene I'm at my easel again," Mertz says, "painting the two of them together. It's like a Renaissance Madonna and Child. Just a beautiful piece of work.

"I consider myself to be a director's actor. I like being directed by someone who's really good. That was the beauty part about *Life Drawings.* This guy was such a brilliant director. You find what he wants and then you try your damnedest to create it. It's very rewarding."

Mertz's first serious push to act came as he was winding towards retirement. "Retirement can be deadly," he says. "Most men are defined by their careers and income. When that's no longer there, they don't have anything but an easy chair."

Unlike his film character in *Life Drawings,* who returned to his easel, Mertz did not have old scripts tucked away waiting for him to pick up. The closest he'd come was conducting an electronic puppet show that *The Pittsburgh Press* sponsored in the early 1950's. He had gone to work for *The Press*, after teaching English literature at Duquesne University, following graduation from Syracuse University.

**"I re-discover my easel and say, 'Maybe if I start painting, it'll get me out of the rut I've fallen into.'"**

"I was Donny Dingbat," he says, "and I went to a lot of school auditoriums in the Pittsburgh metropolitan area, working with the appropriate police groups, showing the kids the importance of safety. So that was performing, and I've always been a theatergoer. But, I'm not going to say that I nursed this long-held dream. I'm not good at starving, and I don't look well in a garret."

Instead he went on to a successful career in editorial and public relations work in the food field. In time, he formed his own agency, which he continued until he turned 60 before returning to teach at a middle school on Long Island. At that time, he also started doing Little Theater and Community Theater locally.

When Mertz retired at 65 in 1990, his wife gifted him with a set of headshots, the publicity photos that are a must for actresses and actors. Mertz wasted no time sending his photos and resume off to listings in the trade paper *Back Stage.* Love Creek Productions, an off-off-Broadway company, accepted him, and he worked with them for several years before going on its Inactive List. ("My memory just isn't what it used to be, when it comes to retaining my lines.") As a result, he has emphasized films rather than stage performances in the past few years. But he hasn't given up live performances entirely. He still plays Santa Claus at Christmas.

"And I do have one endearing story," he says. "It was at a brokerage firm's party for the children of employees. A thin, little girl about 11 or 12 came through. I asked her what she wanted

Santa to bring her this year, and she said, 'A million dollars.' 'Well, that's a pretty big order,' I said, 'and I can't promise anything, but I'll work on it and do the best I can.' 'Do you know why I want it?' she asked. 'No.' 'So I can buy a house for my parents, and the rest will go to help the poor.' What a story."

To this day, Mertz continues to send out his resumes.

"A lot of the time, you don't get a response, or if you do, you don't get a call back You just keep doing it. I have an audition this Friday. What I find most gratifying

> "Most men are defined by their careers and income. When that's no longer there, they don't have anything but an easy chair."

in my work is being involved with creative young people. I do a lot of student films. I don't make any money at it," he says with a laugh, "but fortunately I'm at that point of my life where that is not the primary reason. In my second or third year, I made about $1,800 and I spent $2,900. It's called a deduction from my taxes."

He has no regrets that he didn't start his acting career earlier. "I would have missed all the things I did do," he says. Nor does he have any second-career retirement plans on the horizon. "They'll always need older men," he says, and he chuckles.

# She Sings
# At Your Supper

It was midnight when Carol Shedlin's rotary phone rang.

"Hello, Grandma." She didn't recognize the caller's voice immediately.

"Who is this?" she asked. "It certainly wasn't any grandchild of mine."

"This is Bob," he said. "I want to know when you're going to stop using that rotary phone of yours and climb into the 21$^{st}$ century and get e-mail."

Having her phone ring at midnight wasn't unusual for Carol, but Bob? And "Hello, Grandma?"

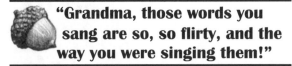 **"Grandma, those words you sang are so, so flirty, and the way you were singing them!"**

"Oh, of course. *That* Bob," she says. "Okay, the rotary phone. I like old things, and Bob's a friend, a successful composer, and I was pleased he'd called. The only surprise was that he was still working at midnight. Speaking of old things—don't tell him I said this— Bob is 94. Come to think of it, his calling at that hour wasn't that much of a surprise. 'Early to bed, early to rise' isn't a known concept in the world of music and entertainment."

As for being called "Grandma," Carol laughs, "It's really a big extended family. I've been singing professionally for 12 years now, and being accepted by my peers is tremendously rewarding. I feel truly blessed, and I love being in the spotlight."

The songs Carol sings in cabarets, or "supper clubs" as she prefers to call them—"to some, cabarets sound a little seedy"—are from composers who are anything but seedy: Gershwin, Rodgers and Hart, Cole Porter, Ellington. They are revered figures in Music's

Flyer "Fresh as a Daisy" Judy's Chelsea 2002

*It's Never Too Late to Plant a Tree*

Mount Rushmore, yet to a much younger generation, their lyrics of 70 or 80 years ago, can come across as risqué. Go figure.

"My granddaughter, yes my real granddaughter," Carol says, "and her fiancé came to one of my shows a couple of

**"That first moment in the spotlight changed my life. Today, I'm a glamorous blonde. I'm never too shy to sing."**

years ago. After the show, she said, 'Grandma, those words you sang are so, so flirty, and the way you were singing them!' I think she blushed a little, but she managed to survive and is married now."

Growing up in suburban Harrison, New York, Carol never projected herself as a flirtatious woman center stage. Becoming a professional singer was something of a fluke. She explains:

"I was painfully shy growing up, an only child with a vicious dog. But I wasn't lonely, thanks to my passion for reading all the time, a lively imagination, and a glamorous, older cousin who befriended me and actually took me along on some of her dates. So there I'd be on one of her dates, in the rumble seat of some jalopy, hearing romantic stories of evenings of dancing at the Pennsylvania Ballroom while inhaling the music from the car radio. When my cousin married and moved away, she gave me her huge collection of 78-RPM records, big band, boogie woogie, my heritage.

"After college, I married and, in the style of the times, raised children in suburbia. Spending so much time driving, I listened to the car radio a lot, and at home to my record collection. I loved it, but all my singing was done in private. When my 18-year marriage ended, being a life-long bookworm, I quickly went to work in the nearest bookstore. It was the beginning of a very rewarding career as a book buyer and bookstore manager.

"As a manager, I opened a huge bookstore at the concourse level of the World Trade Center for a Canadian chain and then moved to their flagship store in Rockefeller Center. Eighteen years passed, and I was living happily in Manhattan. Then, I found myself 'suddenly' retired and with a problem. The problem was a bad throat, maybe from the air down in the World Trade Center or all the screaming I did—'The business section is over there!'

"The physician I consulted was brilliant. He removed a huge mass and warned that unless I took voice therapy and brought my speaking pitch down —'I was high and squeaky'—I'd get polyps and he'd have to do more surgery. I went assiduously for the therapy, but it didn't kick in, and I did get the polyps and had surgery again."

"Now, here's the fluke," says Carol. "The doctor said, 'Your life must be very stressful. Surely, there's something you've always wanted to do that can relieve the stress, and I answered, 'Well, I've never told this to anyone, but I've always wanted to sing.' Bingo! He said he had just the person and referred me to a patient, who was also a voice therapist and an opera coach. One day, she asked me to sing something, and when I did, she said, 'You have a rather respectable voice.' That did it. I took my first singing workshop. In secret without telling friends or family. As a child, had anyone asked what I wanted to be—No one ever did—I would have amazed them by saying, 'I want to sing in a nightclub.'

"Since that first workshop, I've taken at least twenty more, which led to my first break. The director of the workshops took me to a club owner she knew. The owner heard me, hired me for a performance and has kind of fostered me over the past decade.

"What can I tell you? That first moment in the spotlight changed my life. Today, I'm a glamorous blonde. I'm never too shy to sing. Just show me an open mike. I ignore the bulges, the wrinkles and the creaks, because it's so easy when you get a chance to be just you. After a dozen years, I can look forward to longer engagements and solo acts. I've developed an enormously supportive extended family, and I'm a respected professional in the cabaret community.

"It's never too late to follow a dream to fruition. Sure, it's hard to get there, but if you can open the door to your dream world and bravely walk through you'll find acknowledgement and joy and fulfillment. I do volunteer work, singing at hospices and senior citizen homes, and I'm a published poet.

"For much of my life, I was on the outside with my nose pressed to the glass, looking in. Now, I sing these old songs to audiences of all ages. I belong somewhere, and it's just heaven. Yes, I'm finally on the inside."

# Fancy Feat

Joan "Joanne" Wood went into a tailspin when her husband, David, died in 1988 at the age of 68.

For nearly 32 years, he had been a successful lawyer, and Joan was a top-flight public relations executive handling such blue chip accounts as Quaker Oats.

Suddenly, at age 58, she closed her business and found herself alone and retired.

> **While competing in Los Angeles, she says, "I arrived late. In order to catch-up, I had to dance 466 heats in over three days."**

It wasn't that she was inactive. She was on the boards of several arts centers and opera associations in her retirement home in Sarasota, Florida. She established a faculty chair in business journalism and four scholarships at her favorite university. She served as a board member of the university foundation, was named alumna of the year and was an honorary chair of her college's bicentennial campaign.

"But when you've voluntarily retired, you need another challenge," she said. So for exercise, she went to several Sarasota dance studios and studied ballroom dancing. "It got me out and permitted me to be with fun people," she claimed. Suddenly, her tailspin life found new wings. She turned out to be an excellent ballroom dancer. She found a teacher, who encouraged her to turn her exercise hobby into a serious amateur endeavor.

Now, at the age of 72, she travels to dance competitions in different places in the country and in 2002.became the top female ballroom dance student in the country. She won top honors in the United States DanceSports Competition in the 2001 Ohio Star Ball, the largest pro-am dancesport competition in the world

©2002, Albert T. Parker/Park West Photography

*Entertainment* 129

Don't think that dancesport, sometimes erroneously called ballroom dancing, is easy. Her repertoire must include 23 different dance styles, exhibiting precise international requirements that demonstrate the waltz, the foxtrot, the tango, the Viennese waltz and the quickstep. While competing in Los Angeles, "I arrived late. In order to play catch-up," she reported. "I had to dance 466 heats in over three days." Each heat lasts for approximately one and a half minutes.

 **"Find a dance instructor who is encouraging. We all start off with shaking knees."**

She must practice two hours a day, five days per week. In those 10 hours, she exercises, studies videotapes and finally works on step choreography with her partner, John Moldthan, whom she calls "the #1 dance teacher in the country." There is also a great need for the ability to improvise. "You never know what will happen on the dance floor," she said. Wood claims she lost a championship competition one evening when one of her shoe soles came off in the middle of her routine and she and her partner fell ignominiously to the floor.

Competitive ballroom dancing is not inexpensive. Each year, she enters eight to ten of the eighty sanctioned competitions all over the country. She must have a wardrobe of at least three custom outfits, with couturier gowns and dresses appropriate to the Latin, standard and American swing music she must dance. Each outfit can cost from $1,800 to $5,000. And dancing pumps must be of superb quality. In addition, her extensive travel accommodations range from first class to luxury.

She frequently travels with several others of her studio's outstanding students. Each is assigned an age classification and within that, a gold, silver or bronze ranking. Wood has silver ranking, and in each world-class event, she is often pitted against eight to ten nationally ranked competitors. . Her partner is her dance instructor, so the exhibition is classified as a pro/am competition.

Her fame has changed her social life. Often, she is asked to give dance demonstrations at small parties. As for her friends, their most frequent reaction to her exhibition is "I don't know how she does that? How old did she say she is?" Her answer is, "The only way you'll find out is if you'll all get out on the floor and start learning how to dance."

Her advice to those who are thinking of learning ballroom dancing is that one should start off going to the "party nights" that reputable dance studios use to organize classes. "Go to several," she advises, "and find the facility and people with whom you feel comfortable. Most important of all, find a dance instructor who is encouraging. We all start off with shaking knees."

"Kids, today, don't know what they're missing by not learning ballroom dancing," she claims. "It's graceful, it's challenging, and it's romantic. And you can't beat a combination like that."

E-mail: jhwsrq@aol.com

*Joan Slattery Wall of Ohio Today contributed to this profile.*

# Health

Good health is something many of us take for granted. As long as we have it.

You know the "should's" and "ought-to's" about exercise, diet and regular checkups. Certainly, having good genes helps. Still, there are silent stalkers that doing everything "right" can neither thwart nor allay. As John Jay Daly says of his wife's irreversible descent into quietude with the progression of Alzheimer's disease:

"Remember, Alzheimer's doesn't discriminate on whom it hits, not on the basis of sex, color, ethnicity, religion, political affiliation, geographic location, or economic status."

Daly is a veteran public speaker, an activist, as the title of his piece indicates, *A Cure for Alzheimer's Is More Than A Personal Cause: It's a Passion.* He's fund raising, lobbying for a U.S. postage stamp for Alzheimer's, all the time pursuing a highly active professional life. "When people ask what I do now that I'm 'semi-retired,'" Daly says, "I tell them the 'semi' part keeps me busy/busy/busy."

In a different vein, Dr. Doris Howell, who spent more than a half century as a pediatric hematologist and oncologist, heads a foundation that focuses on issues relevant to women's health, with heavy emphasis on awarding scholarships for study in that area. "Research on women and children just wasn't done," she says, and seeing the need she stepped in to do something.

Ironically, advances in medical science have bumped into cost problems that, at the very least, are hampering if not disabling. Typical of these situations is an aggressive and expensive lung operation that might save the lives of tens of thousands of elderly patients, according to an article in *The New York Times*. For Medicare the problem is what the cost burden would add to an already heavily stressed budget.

None of which will stop people like Daly and Howell.

# A Cure for Alzheimer's is More Than A Personal Cause: It's a Passion

After working since I was a teenager, my major role, as I approach the three-quarter century mark, is to ensure that Lu Corbett Daly, my wife of 50-plus years, is well taken care of as she sleeps through her final days in a nearby home for eight Alzheimer's patients. The caregivers are true angels.

I want to be clear that we didn't put Lu in a home without much thought and planning. And tears. We cared for her at home, followed by a daycare system for 15 to 18 months; after that, at home with one daughter, Maura, taking a leave of absence from work for six months to supplement a nurse. I did nights and weekends. Key characteristic of Alzheimer's is that as disease progresses the patient regresses. The end often comes when patient forgets how to breathe or swallow! Imagine that!

©2003, Allison Shelley

Four million Americans now suffer from Alzheimer's. To try to ensure that millions in the future don't suffer the fate Lu has endured for the past decade, I'm seeking at least 50,000 signatures on a petition to have the U.S. Postal Service issue a fundraising stamp, similar to the one for Breast Cancer. I pass out petitions at every opportunity—at meetings which I attend or where I speak, such as National Speakers Association, the Direct Marketing Association or a local Kiwanis club.

I'll even make my pitch to those of you reading this book: Go to my website, www.johnjaydaly.com, click on Alzheimer's Fund Raising stamp, download the petition, get signatures and send the petition to Mrs. Gene Siggins, who initiated this effort in memory of her husband. Her address is on the petition. Or telephone, toll-free to 1-866-259-0042 for a free supply. Ask friends to do the same. Remember, Alzheimer's doesn't discriminate on whom it hits, not on the basis of sex, color, ethnicity, religion, political affiliation, geographic location, or economic status.

**"I'm seeking at least 50,000 signatures on a petition to have the U.S. Postal Service issue a fundraising stamp."**

Lu was a prize-winning copywriter before and after I married her, a bright, vibrant, life-loving woman, but that didn't provide immunity. Tragically, she can't now enjoy the happy fruits from the incredible efforts she daily put into raising eight children, and, sadly, doesn't recognize them (or me) or our 10 grandchildren.

For the fourth year I'll be working with the local Alzheimer's Association on its fundraising184-mile bike ride along the C&O Canal in September. It's a two-day ride and while I'm not a biker, I use my talents as an organizer and publicist to generate new riders and to ensure that the complicated logistics run smoothly. I'm also a volunteer spokesman and appear on TV and radio and give newspaper and magazine interviews about ways to cope with the disease. The overall objective is to increase public awareness in the hopes that Congress and the public will provide more research monies to find a cure.

When people ask what I do now that I'm "semi-retired," I tell them the "semi" part keeps me busy/busy/busy. Which is all to the good, because without balance, especially as an Alzheimer's caregiver, you're not going to last long. It's a transcendent disease that can be all consuming.

The average patient suffers eight to 12 years, but I know several who've had it for almost 20 years. What's more, I try to live by what I preach in the many platform presentations I still make. One of my half-dozen topics is *Humorize Your Life*, for I firmly believe humor is a language, and, with serious application, anyone who so desires can become fluent in that language. I'll share four points from *Humorize* and urge you that Right Now, promise yourself that most every day for the rest of your life *(take your birthday off)*, you will work diligently to *memorize and record* the following 4 key elements:

- A clean, *appropriate, brief* joke (complete with punchline)
- An *illustrative* anecdote (from your life or from history)
- An *apt* quotation (preferably a witty, pithy or humorous one)
- *At least* one new word (or a word you need to *re*-learn)

One of many advantages of "speaking humorously" is that when it's done well, you can communicate memorably. Another is that you are likely to be happier in your personal and professional life—and lots more fun to be around. After all, no one gets out of this life alive, so it's best to have as much fun as possible while going through it.

While I try to follow my 4 points of advice about "humorizing one's life," I'll admit doing it each 'n every day is quite a goal. But it's worth the effort. I've been at it for decades, and it helps keep me upbeat. I'm a 5th generation Washingtonian, and in DC you need a sense of humor to survive. For 30-plus years I've been presenting a live audio-visual tour, *The Wacky Wondrous Worlds of Washington,* and it remains popular regardless of who's in the White House. Harry Truman said, "Anyone who had my job and didn't have a sense of humor wouldn't still be here," and Will

Rogers said, "I don't make jokes. I just watch the government and report the facts."

I remain active in professional organizations including the Public Relations Society of America, the Direct Marketing Association of Washington and the National Speakers Association, especially its 200-member DC chapter, which I founded in 1980. My presentations are based on a half-century of varied communications experience and as head of Daly Communications, since Gerald Ford was in the White House.

There are organizations I belong to just for the fun of it, such as *The Lincoln Group,* which meets monthly for dinner to discuss aspects of our 16th President's life. I also go to monthly meetings of The Association of Oldest Inhabitants of D.C., a division of the Historic Society of Washington. That's a double-header since it dovetails with one of my speech topics.

Yes, balance is the key. So I serve on an advisory board for the Salvation Army, as well as one for the Alzheimer's Association. I'm a lector/Eucharistic Minister/usher and an Arimathean for the Shrine

**"In my platform presentations I try to live by what I preach. One of my topics is, 'Humorize Your Life.'"**

of the Blessed Sacrament the Roman Catholic parish in Chevy Chase where I've spent my life.

Of course I keep in regular touch with my eight children ("all girls except for the four boys") and ten grandchildren, read several newspapers daily plus a dozen magazines, lots of books and always have two hardcover books "working." I also love movies, new and old.

A question that I'm often asked is, "What are some of the activities that help to brighten and lighten your wife's current life. Until a year ago, my answer was:

"Nothing fancy, but *while patient can enjoy doing them*, take walks, go to movies, concerts, visit museums, have friends over or go there to dine together. Look at family pix. Do whatever either or both of you enjoy. Sing or read aloud. Don't worry if patient doesn't recall activity a minute later, it's important to keep the mind active and "in the present." Yes, it may be frustrating, consider what it must be like for the patient not to have the intellectual faculties we blessedly possess. The brain is the most powerful gift from God and its loss is so tragic in so many ways. In fact, I've found the loss of intellectual companionship to be the most profound. No longer can we discuss anything of substance. I show slides and pix of our family since conversations are largely prosaic. Sadly, in the final stages that's not possible so I urge caregivers do what they can while they can."

E-mail: speaker@johnjaydaly.com

# At Last, Research on Illnesses of Women

Dr. Doris Howell spent 52 years as a pediatric hematologist and oncologist, but now instead of cultivating the physical well-being of young people, she's focusing on their minds.

As the honorary chair of the Doris A. Howell Foundation for Women's Health Research, she's been instrumental in awarding 56 scholarships to college students studying issues relevant to women's health.

The Howell Foundation became a reality after she joined Soroptimists International of La Jolla, a women's club similar to Rotary.

"There I found myself caught up with a group of women between the ages of 30 and 50 and all relatively successful," she says. "What they didn't know very much about was their own

©2003 Adrienne Helitzer/Still Productions

health. I found that disturbing. I wasn't an obstetrician, gynecologist or even an internist, but as a woman, I had experienced enough to enable me to use my training as a physician to alleviate their fears by lecturing them on women's health. In the meantime, I did my homework and kept current with research."

In 1993, Soroptimists held a symposium on menopause that brought many well-known speakers to the San Diego area and

*It's Never Too Late to Plant a Tree*

helped Howell see a serious problem in women's health. "The conclusion from [the symposium] is there's not enough research done about menopause, and other illnesses of women. Research on women and children just wasn't done, because it was considered wrong to do on anybody of reproductive age; therefore, all the work was very limited."

> **Research on women and children just wasn't done, because it was considered wrong.**

After the symposium, the Soroptimists wanted to use their profits from the event to fund research "but $4,000 to a research lab hardly buys enough pipettes to get through the day, because research is so expensive," Howell explains.

Forced to find another use for the money, Howell suggested the Soroptimists "invest the money in scholarships for university students who would write up a research proposal about something related to the health and welfare of women and find a faculty member to mentor their work." A competitive contest was held and the Soroptimists awarded $2,000 to each winner to use towards the research project.

This continued until 1996, when six of the Soroptimists created the Doris A. Howell Foundation for Women's Health Research, which would be independent and responsible for the further fundraising and granting of scholarships.

"And since that time we have continued to raise money by giving educational lunches at which we always have a well-known speaker talk about a topic that is very pertinent to women's health," she says.

Howell and the 23 foundation board members sift through numerous proposals sent to them by California universities.

"[The proposals] are so unbelievable," Howell says. "I have trouble reading them myself. They're so profound. I can't believe how bright kids are today."

*It's Never Too Late to Plant a Tree*

But why focus only on women's health?

"We don't limit the grants to women," she says. "We just want the research to focus on improving the research done on women until it becomes par on what's been done on men. As a pediatrician, I also have a hidden agenda. I feel strongly that women are the backbone for the family and that what happens in a household is what the woman makes happen. She buys the food, she does the cooking, she makes people eat what they should eat. If she exercises, they exercise. What she does, they tend to do by habit, just following her."

"I'm hoping that as I educate women in the importance of taking care of their own health that

**"I feel so strongly that women are the backbone for the family."**

they in turn will be able to raise healthier children," Howell says. "So I feel I'm meeting my role as a pediatrician after all."

In addition to her duties as the honorary chair of the Howell Foundation, she is also the Director Emerita of the San Diego Hospice which she founded in 1977.

"[People] remind me I'm no chicken and ask why I don't relax and enjoy my retirement," she says. "But if I didn't have a problem or job to do, I'd probably cause trouble."

And at 79, Howell is not done.

"I still feel I want to do a lot of living," she says. "If you go to bed every night knowing you're doing something worthwhile, you never have to apologize for the way you've spent your time."

# Helping Kids

Count the ways in which you can help kids. And when you're finished, there are bound to be still more.

We offer a sampling.

Mary and Robert Longacre's youngest son, Steve, is hard-of-hearing. "Steve was never embarrassed by having to wear hearing aids when he was small," says his mother without crediting herself or her husband for playing a role in their son's positive attitude. Steve became principal of an elementary school for deaf and hard-of-hearing children in Santa Ana, California. The senior Longacres formed a foundation, DEAFinitely 4 Kids, to provide opportunities for the hard-of-hearing that school budgets do not.

Luther Haseley and his wife, Jeanne, are *guardians ad litem* in Athens, Ohio. *Guardians ad Litem?* Is that some kind of fraternal organization? No, it's Latin for adults who represent foster children in court. Haseley is a retired university professor. Being a *guardian ad litem* is not limited to Ohio. Maybe you'd like to give it a try.

Al Stetz was a Navy pilot in Vietnam, who flew more than 8,000 mission hours. Today, he teaches kids to fly on the computer, but not satisfied with that, he's arranged to have them experience actual "stick time" in a real plane, with takeoffs and landings.

Burrell Ross is a former high school principal and university professor who looks like Santa Claus. He cuddles babies whose mothers can't or won't. Ross's gift giving is not limited to Christmas-time.

Search the Yellow Pages nationwide and you won't find a listing for Dr. A. Ken Foote, a bona fide retired podiatrist, who formed a clown troupe called *The Happy Heartbeats*. They entertain seriously ill children several times a week at a hospital in New Jersey. Now, sound out his clown name—Dr. A. Ken Foote.

Three days after Joe Zacherman retired as a special education high school principal, he was back on the job. This time as Executive Director of Lifeline Center for Child Development, a day treatment center and special school in New York for seriously disturbed children.

Count the ways.

# To Those Who Abuse Kids: "We'll See You In Court!"

For a retired professor, Luther Haseley spends a lot of time in court these days. He's not an attorney, and he's not a spectator. He and his wife, Jeanne, are *guardians ad litem* in Athens, Ohio.

Their job, and it is a job, is to represent the interests of children who have been neglected, abused or abandoned.

"We knew a couple who were serving as Guardians, and they said there was a real need for help in our area," Haseley said. While he does not practice as a psychologist, he does have training in psychology. Mrs. Haseley agreed and they volunteered their services, working with the courts, children's services, foster parents and parents.

*Guardians ad litem* are important in court cases, because they do not represent the parents or Children's Services or the State. Their clients are the children.

©2003, Terry E. Eiler

*Helping Kids*

The Haseleys are each assigned children with whom they work. Whenever the children appear in court, they go to the hearings with them. When the children have visitations with their parents, the *guardian ad litem* sits in during the visits to make sure everything goes smoothly and to see how the children and parents interact.

"Many of the kids have been neglected or abused," Haseley says. "Some have been abused physically, some verbally and some sexually. Sometimes it is the parents doing the abusing and on rare occasions it is the foster parents"

The *guardian ad litem* spends a lot of time talking to the children, talking to school counselors, meeting with the parents and foster parents, discussing the children with social workers, appearing at court hearings and working with Children's Services to put together overall assessments of each child. The Haseleys agree that serving as *guardians ad litem* is a tough and unusual job.

"When you see kids like this, it's difficult. It's emotionally draining. It's hard to see the children going through trauma and abuse, but it's rewarding to know that we're helping them and watching their lives improve."

**"It's hard to see the children going through trauma and abuse, but it's rewarding to know that we're helping them."**

He and his wife continue to do it, though, for one main reason. "We think there's a real need for it, and the kids we deal with make it all worthwhile. It's easy to get attached to the kids we're assigned to work with, some as young as a year old. You see some of these kids really grow and progress....they do some really nice things."

The situation for the children can't change much, unless the parents want to change and show love to their children, the Haseleys point out.

"It's really a great feeling to see the change that can take place. Most of the children come from dysfunctional families, but despite all the problems most of them want to remain in their families. Helping the children through the tough times and helping the families improve is a wonderful thing."

Their work as *guardian ad litems* varies from week to week depending on when hearings are held, when the

**"It's really a great feeling to see the change that can take place."**

children have visitations and the other things the Haseleys have going on. They figure that all in all, they each average about five hours a week doing their jobs.

They also spend time seeing members of their own family; working on community boards; attending reunions of friends from their days working in Botswana; spending time at elder hostels; and continuing to work in education. Haseley is currently involved with a doctoral program for a university in Mexico. He travels there one or two times a year to work with students and teach seminars. The Haseleys have a farm and plenty of friends and they enjoy being retired. They love the freedom of being able to travel and continue working in the ways that they choose.

The feeling Haseley and his wife get from helping these kids, and the fact that they know the children need their help keeps them going and going and going. If they ever did a TV show called "The Guardians," Haseley says," they'd never run out of material."

E-mail: haseley@ohio.edu

# Oh, My A. Ken Foote!

At Hackensack University Medical Center in New Jersey, a lot of patients ask for Dr. A. Ken Foote. His name isn't on the directory of physicians, but if you come on Monday, Tuesday, Wednesday or Thursday, you may see him working at Tomorrow's Children's Institute with children who have serious cancer or blood diseases or in the Pediatric Unit of the hospital. He's a big man, 6 feet, 2 inches, easy to spot. Look for someone in a white coat with a stethoscope around his neck, a clown's outfit, a red hat, a red nose, and a clown face.

Dr. A. Ken Foote (sound out his name—AKenFoote; Got it? Aching Foot) is a real doctor, William H. Kelley of Ramsey, New Jersey, a retired podiatrist with 40 years of practice behind him. And he's still a professional. For the past five years, he's been a member of "The Happy Heartbeats," a hospital based clown care unit.

"I knew I could go into clowning. For me, it was something waiting to happen. I've been involved with The Rotary Club for 46 years,

©2003 Mia Song

*It's Never Too Late to Plant a Tree*

and about 10 years ago, when I was getting ready to retire, a friend, Ben, brought a clown to one of our meetings. All that the clown would say was, 'Hello. My name's Dolly.' Later, I found out she was a working professional. At the end of the meeting, the president of the club asked Ben what was with the clown.

**Smile Kids, The Elephants Are Coming!**

"Ben stood up. 'I have a dream,' he said, 'to start a troupe of clowns to work in the community at hospitals and make someone happy, and I need volunteers.' I raised my hand so high, I thought I'd touch the ceiling. Our first gig was at a nursing home where I had worked for years. It just kept going from there. But you can't be a clown by putting paint on your face and a big red nose. You need training. Five years ago, I went to Mooseberger Clown Camp in Minnesota, where I learned a lot. Six of us were at the camp and when we finished, five of us organized 'The Happy Heartbeats.' Today, there are eight of us."

How did he get started with his second vocation?

"I began playing Santa Claus, when I was 16, that's more than 60 years ago. I found out that once you get behind that façade, you're not yourself anymore. You become the person you're portraying. I'm not Dr. Kelley. I'm Dr. A. Ken Foote. Different clowns have different specialties. I latched on to hand magic. Sleight of hand, and I've become adept at it. It mystifies people, and kids, especially, love it. It's been terrific also in working with kids who are very frightened.

"I came into a ward once, and a little boy was fighting to keep them from getting an IV into his arm. I said, 'Hello,' but he just kept struggling. So, I went up to him, put my hand behind his ear and a little red ball came trickling down along his jaw up to his nose. I took the ball, but when I opened my hand, it was gone. Well, his eyes were getting bigger and bigger. 'Where is it? Where is it?' he wanted to know. I pulled the ball out of my pocket. By the time I was finished, the IV was in his arm and he didn't know what had happened."

The clowns work in teams of two for five-hour stretches.

"It gives the clowns emotional support playing off each other. Sometimes it can be heavy going. There are days we laugh. Days when we cry. Having been in medical practice, I'm able to have a little more detachment. Some of the others break up. When something isn't working, we have a code word to take a breather, "Elephant.""

"The Elephants Are Coming!"

"Do I hear an elephant in the hall?"

"When doctors come by with their retinues, they expect 'civilians' to leave. When they see us, more often than not they'll say, 'What you're doing is important. We'll come back later.' Of course, you're bound to get involved with the kids. Sometimes, they're in and out of the hospital, then they're gone, and we hope they get better. Other times they may be in and out for a couple of years.

The toughest part is watching a child get sicker and sicker.

"There was one little boy, we really got attached to. He didn't make it, went to The Clown Camp in the Sky. When it came time for the funeral, the family asked 'The Happy Heartbeats' to come, dressed in our clown costumes.

"'The Happy Heartbeats' is a not-for-profit corporation. It exists solely on donations from the public and private corporations. The money is used to cover expenses for give away gifts for the children and for projects with them. Our reward is the love and laughter of the kids and their parents. 'The Happy Heartbeats' will make you happy in a heartbeat."

Clearly, Kelley relates well to kids. He and his wife, Isabella ("the Clown Mother"), whom he married in 1948, have four children, Sandra, Gayle, Bill

**"There are days we laugh. Days when we cry."**

and Patricia (in chronological order) and 10 grandchildren, several in college. They're still waiting for their first great-grandchild.

Kelley was born in Paterson, New Jersey, went to school there and trained in Ohio. In 1953, the Kelleys moved to Ramsey where they've been ever since.

Does he miss his old life?

"No, after 40 years of practice, I still hadn't gotten it right, so I decided it was time to quit. Practice, practice, practice," he says with a small laugh, then goes on, " Like other retirees I know, I'm so busy now, I don't know how I had time to work all those years."

As for podiatry, his son, Dr. William S. Kelley, is carrying on the practice. Dr. Kelley, Sr. lives on the second floor of the building with offices on the first floor, so he's apt to pop in to see how things are going or to shmooze with old patients/friends. "I eased off, did some of the bookkeeping, not any more. Now, in the office, I'm just Dr. Kelley's dad."

Born on December 10, 1923, his advice to others is predictable: "Do something. Don't just sit and read the newspapers. It's tantamount to putting yourself in a chair to die. You've got to become involved in something. Offer to drive people to the store or to the doctor. Get involved with the church or some community project. Do something."

The elephants may be coming, but old clowns always manage to cope.

# DEAFinitely 4 Kids
# Is Definitely Working

"I didn't raise my boy to be a magician," is something you'll never hear Mary or Robert Longacre say.

To the contrary, the Longacres are proud of how their youngest son, Steve, who is principal at Taft Elementary School for deaf and hard of hearing children in Santa Ana, California uses his magic skills to capture students' attention and encourage them to learn.

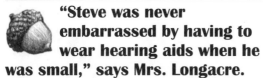

**"Steve was never embarrassed by having to wear hearing aids when he was small," says Mrs. Longacre.**

The success of their two sons, Richard and Steve, both hearing impaired, inspired the Longacres to form DEAFinitely 4 Kids, Inc., a non-profit organization in 1998, after Mary had retired as a registered nurse and Robert as a civil engineer,

"Steve was never embarrassed by having to wear hearing aids when he was small," says his mother. "The three older boys by my husband's first marriage treated Richard and Steve as normal. Both of the younger boys grew up not feeling handicapped. Steve didn't care who knew he had a hearing problem. That kind of positive attitude obviously made a difference."

As for the value of DEAFinitely 4 Kids Mrs. Longacre explains, "The school districts supply some things for the children, but not nearly enough for what they need, so we wanted to thank society for the help our boys got when they were young, by starting this public benefit corporation. The funds we get, mostly by donations, allow the students to do things the regular school budget doesn't provide for, like giving teachers spending money for class projects and for little trips away from the school. A lot of the children are underprivileged and don't have a chance to do these things with their own families.

"Even though we don't spend a lot of time fund-raising, we manage. Besides, some regular contributors, for which we're grateful, the children at Taft sell T-shirts with the school's logo and others with the manual alphabet proclaiming, 'Let's Communicate.' Those are moneymakers. Then we have a silent auction once a year, and some other small fund-raising activities.

"There's also a secondary program in Irvine, that's connected with Taft. It's a regular 6th to 12th grade middle and high school with a deaf and hard of hearing program. At graduation, we give several small scholarships to high school seniors who went through Taft's program and are continuing on to junior college, the way Steve did, initially."

DEAFinitely 4 Kids also runs sign language classes for the parents at the Taft School, so they can learn to converse with their child, as well as for siblings. And we provide baby-sitting so parents can attend those classes.

"Parents are very taken with Steve, because they understand he has a good understanding of hearing loss," says Mrs. Longacre. "And the teachers are so dedicated. California has a new law where all newborns are tested for hearing, so it doesn't go undiagnosed the way it did with Steve and with Richard, who's a year older than Steve. What's great is that Taft has a program where a teacher goes into the home with the little ones until they are three years old. They, of course, like to get the children at as early an age as possible. I just 'melt' when I see the little pre-schoolers using sign language! They're absolute angels in my book!"

For the last 13 years of her career as a registered nurse, Mrs. Longacre, now 71, was employed at one of the

**"I just 'melt' when I see the little pre-schoolers using sign language!"**

state's special schools for neurologically handicapped children— children who were not retarded but had learning problems. She worked with doctors, putting the youngsters through the special state schools, testing them, then returning them to their home schools.

Robert, who is 82, spent 32 years as a civil engineer for the city of Alhambra, then a final 12 years as a Street Superintendent for the city. "I retired early, when I was 60," he says with a chuckle. "People said I'd be bored, but I haven't been bored for one day. We're in a senior community at The Fountains, with our own condo and loads of activities. The best part is that we don't feel like we're in an old people's home, and we have plenty of time for something like DEAFinitely 4 Kids, and, of course, for our grandchildren. By the way, both Richard and Steve have children, and none of them has a hearing problem."

And what about that magic business? Mrs. Longacre chimes in, "Steve just loves magic, has ever since he was a little kid, and he works real hard at it. Of course, the kids love it, too. They'll go to principal's office to see him do his tricks. Steve has a best friend from college. The two of them go around and do little shows. This past year they participated in the 9th World Deaf Magicians Festival in Moscow, Russia, capturing 1st place in Comedy Magic. In two years they hope to attend the 10th Festival in Leipzig, Germany."

Yes, the magic is great, but what makes DEAFinitely 4 Kids work isn't magic. It's Hard Work.

E-mail: mrlongacre1@cox.net

# Rockabye Baby

If Burrell Ross lived in Los Angeles and were so inclined, he could have a full time job auditioning for Santa Claus roles.

Not only does he look and sound like Santa, Ross tops Santa when it comes to gift gifting. What Santa does once a year, Ross does twice a week.

Ross is a baby cuddler.

A baby cuddler?

That's right. Twice a week for two hours a day, Ross shares his warm touch, robust body and ample cheeks with premature babies

©2001, Michael J. Gallegos/The Albuquerque Tribune

who need security and personal closeness as much as they need food and medicine at the Newborn Intensive Care Unit of Albuquerque's New Mexico University Hospital.

"They need someone to hold them," he says. "That's what I do." The need originates from the fact that these babies were born with problems, most prematurely; others from mothers too sick to care for their children, let alone nurse them. Many have heart, blood or lung problems.

**"Being a cuddler gives me the joy of having a baby in my hands, and I love that. They so desperately need someone to hold them."**

"Mama can't always be there, and the nurses can't do it all," he explains. Some children were born from mothers who cannot be with them; some mothers need help because they cannot tolerate the sight of their newborn infants with i.v. units attached to their head, arms or legs, or with breathing tubes in their noses to provide them with desperately needed oxygen.

No so for Ross, who has a strong stomach as well as a jolly one. "Babies need love," he said. "Love is beneficial to their growth and development."

"He's a wonderful man, very warm, soft-spoken and gentle," says Jan Wade, director of volunteers for the hospital. "He has a special bond with babies."

The Albuquerque cuddler program was pioneered in 1980 by Genny Munsing, an occupational therapist, and Dr. Herb Koffler, director of children's neonatal unit services at University Hospital. Since 1999, Ross has been one of 40 volunteers who work with needy infants.

"Being a cuddler gives me the joy of having a baby in my hands, and I love that," says Ross. "They so desperately need someone to hold them. How can you leave them isolated and never touched? It helps me to know that I am providing the security and love that are part of their growth from the start. I get more out of it than the babies do."

According to Ruth Florman, one of the first cuddlers, Ross was accepted into the program after a one-day orientation, which included a TB test, a background check and being finger printed. That was followed by three hours of specialized training on how to feed babies and how to hold their heads to keep them from flopping over. Volunteers continue to receive in-service training twice a year. They must know how to check vital signs when babies are hooked up to monitors or when they suddenly stop breathing and maintain their skills.

Ross is busy from the moment he walks into the intensive care unit and greets the nurses who supervise his work. First he puts on his ID tag, scrubs up, dons sterile gloves and puts on a fresh hospital gown, then makes his way to the first infant. He may spend one to two hours with one baby or divide his time between two or three infants.

Ross sits alone, permitting nurses and staff to perform their duties. He calms fussy babies by snuggling and rocking them. Everything that makes a person **"I hate retirement. I didn't want to retire from something. I retired to something."** bond with another human is present in cuddling–eye-to-eye, skin-to-skin, facial expressions, even the smell between him and the baby. He always speaks and sings softly. "They are very obedient when I start singing," he jokes. "In fact, they'll do anything to get me to stop singing."

"There's something about touch," he claims. "You can live without every other sense, but you can't live without touch." Ross uses a soothing but not tickling touch around the abdomen that keeps the internal machinery working. Research indicates that premature babies who are cuddled leave hospital care about six days earlier than those who are not massaged.

He sometimes helps with the feeding, an act that sparks a lot of jokes from friends who wonder if he ever tries to breastfeed. Ross laughs with every punch line, as if he's heard it for the first time. That's an Academy Award performance right there.

Each baby stays in the intensive care unit being cuddled until they are brought to term. There are all kinds of benefits, such as easing indigestion and supplementing cognitive development that was not completed in the womb. Many are born weighing less than a pound. "Volunteer work is not only heartwarming, it can be heart wrenching, especially when we lose one I've worked with," admits Ross.

"Yet, with very few exceptions, I feel good about what I've done each hospital day, " he says. "I feel sad when I have to leave because I feel for the kids who are in a tough situation. You hate to see a kid who hurts. There's no glory in it, and I'm not asking for a thank-you. I do it because it needs to be done." But the thank-you's do come. Often mothers will come to the unit to see their babies and marvel at the care their children are receiving. Ross is easy to spot because he's one of four men, and his distinctive Santa persona is so memorable that Ross is often approached years later in the supermarket by a grateful mother and her child.

A former high school principal and university professor who left education in 1994, Ross, now in his 70's, also teaches children about the zoo's inhabitants at the Albuquerque Zoo and is a co-director of religious training for his synagogue, Congregation B'nai Israel, in addition to his baby cuddling.

Ross thinks of his retirement as a gift. "People sitting at home and doing nothing are missing so much of their lives. I want to encourage seniors. There are so many things they can do."

He recommends thinking seriously of a retirement project several years before the professional curtain comes down. You need to read, study and even try each possibility before just suddenly being thrust into a dramatically new era of your life. "I hate retirement," he said. "I didn't want to retire from something. I retired to something."

You've read that before, and it's not surprising. No one ever thinks Santa will retire, either.

E-mail: buross@aol.com

# Come Fly Away.....
# With A Difference

A decorated Vietnam War pilot, who'd flown all over the world, been to the North Pole and mapped the South Pole, Commander Elias "Al" Stetz decided, at age 45, to retire from the U.S. Navy. His reason: It was time to quit.

Which, as it turned out, was not quite the case.

"When I retired," Stetz says, "people asked, 'Why don't you be an airline pilot? The money is good and so forth.' That just didn't appeal to me. There's a great novel by Ernest Gann, *Fate Is The Hunter*. Gann had been an airline pilot, and he was flying out of what was then Idlewild Airport. One day he picked up his navigation bag and walked away and never went back to an airplane. It was just after a near miss and he said, 'That's it. No more. The next one's going to get me.' And I had that feeling. Some 8,000 mission hours, and I'd had a lot of close calls. These

©2003, Thomas Hart Shelby

days I fly on airlines and in small planes, but not the hairy missions I was flying in the Navy.

"So, looking for other things to do, I went to work for National Westminster Bank in computer operations, which was a new technology in 1980. Not the most exciting thing in the world, but I had a master's degree in computer science, and because I have an analytical mind, I liked it. Kept doing it for 16, 17 years. Finally, I left and did some high school teaching, not far from my home in Locust Valley in New York. Frankly, I just didn't have the patience for it."

In fact, Stetz can be a patient man. He's just selective about what he's patient about, such as self-publishing a book, *In Search of Eagles*. It's about golf courses on military bases. Stetz, a ranked player, and at 70, the super-senior champion at his club, wrote and composed the book on his computer and marketed it, himself, to the tune of 7,000 copies in two editions.

All of which seems miles distant from getting back to flying.

"Well, yes and no," says Stetz. "Here in Locust Valley, we have the Grenville **"I can teach kids to fly on a computer.' Holy smoke. She almost came out of her seat."**
Baker Boys and Girls Club. It's a place where kids, most of them from blue-collar families, can have activities like baseball, basketball, soccer or just a place where they can do homework or get tutoring, because there's nobody at home. And I've been active in the community.

"Initially when I went to the club, I talked to the program director and said I could teach life skills, spreadsheets, database searches and word processing. She's sitting there kind of 'ho hum.' As we were talking, I said, almost as an aside, 'I was a flight instructor in Pensacola for two years, and I can teach kids to fly on a computer.' Holy smoke! She almost came out of her seat. I told her I could get these kids to solo on the computer after eight sessions. They'd be able to make virtual takeoffs and landings. But it would only have

*It's Never Too Late to Plant a Tree*

meaning, if we could get them out to Republic Airport and put them in a real airplane.

"Later, talking to the club director, I said, 'We can get a certified instructor and an airplane for $120 an hour. We get four or five kids up there for two hours, and they'll get 30 minutes stick time each, and it'll be a fantastic experience.' And the director said, 'We're going to get you three hours.' That's how enthusiastic they were.

 **"I want to give these kids a heads-up and stimulate their interest."**

"The club has a nice computer lab. Lot of desktops. Maximum of six in a class. Three computers. Three operating. Three watching. We meet twice a week, but kids will be there other times, on their own. They can turn on the computer and do their own practicing with Microsoft's Flight Simulator 2002. Microsoft even kicked in with a donation of 10 Flight Simulator CD's. But the first time the kids think it's a video game and start zooming around the place, I'm going to ground them.

"We have both girls and boys in the class. And while I have zero interest in being an airline pilot, this gives me a chance to close the loop, to come back to flying in a different way, using my computer skills. I want to give these kids a heads-up and stimulate their interest. I'm even building my own model airplane for them. I'm not sure that these kids ever get a chance to talk to professionals.

"Our first class graduated in June 2003. It was a great class and a great experience for me, and we'll be doing more classes. Out of the seven who started, five finished. Only one guy was asked to leave, and the other had a schedule conflict. The five who finished are really outstanding students. I told them that they all have the intelligence and aptitude to fly.

"The final 'safe for solo' check was comprehensive and required all of their newly attained skills. They had to make a virtual takeoff from LaGuardia, climb out straight ahead to 500 feet and make a climbing turn to the downwind leg and level off at 1,000 feet on the reciprocal heading. They then had to maintain a wing-tip distance from the field and start their cross-wind leg 30 seconds past the landing point. In a descending turn to the field, they had to lower flaps, reduce power and airspeed and rollout on the runway heading.

"On the final approach, they adjusted power and airspeed to touch down on the first one-third of the runway. On the runway, rolling straight ahead, they then had to raise the flaps, cut power and apply breaks to stop on the runway. The five kids did this unassisted. Not bad for a bunch of 12-year olds."

As Stetz explains, the club works on donations from the community, cake sales, used clothes, a big black-tie ball once a year. Fund raising at Locust Valley has enabled them to build a new gym with expanded facilities.

©2002, Al Stetz at First Flight, Kitty Hawk, with grandson

For his two children and five grandchildren, Stetz has done an extended narrative on his military career. His high point: Operation DeepFreeze to the South Pole and the Antarctic in 1959-1961,

*It's Never Too Late to Plant a Tree*

where his team photographed about 75 percent of the Antarctic, photographs that a geological team will use in 2003 when they trek up the mountains and climb onto the Polar Plateau. The low point: his year in Vietnam. "Every time you're shot at, it's like the first time," he says, "but it wasn't being shot at that discouraged me. It was the way the politicians were managing and running the war."

"What happens though is cumulative. In my case, I was doing proficiency flying out of Oceania in Virginia Beach in a Grumman Intruder. Bang! We had an emergency on board. It turned out to be an electrical wiring problem, but there we were calling, 'Mayday! Mayday!' Because of my rank at the time, proficiency flying was optional, not required. When we landed, I said to myself, 'That's it. Enough is enough.' I did a final tour and retired."

Obviously, Stetz's flying days are not over. Having seen the first of his Boys and Girls Club kids soar into the air, he's waiting to see how far their dreams will take them, perhaps remembering himself as a boy in World War Two, watching planes overhead and saying, "One day I'm going to do that."

E-mail: alstetz@aol.com

# They Call It "Lifeline" For A Reason

Mention "G" Building to anyone who knows New York's Kings County Hospital, and you need say no more. Some 25 years ago, a widely publicized serial killer, calling himself "Son of Sam," was taken there before being imprisoned for life.

About the same time, Joseph Zacherman found himself in "G" Building—not as a patient, but as a volunteer. How did it happen?

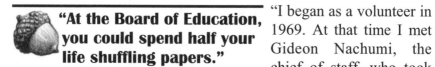

**"At the Board of Education, you could spend half your life shuffling papers."**

"I began as a volunteer in 1969. At that time I met Gideon Nachumi, the chief of staff, who took me under his wing, and we kind of bonded. I continued to volunteer, but at the same time got a job with the Board of Education and taught at the in-patient unit of 'G' Building for about a year. Actually, Nachumi encouraged me to go to medical school, but I was never that interested in doing the science part of it.

"After awhile, the Board of Ed transferred me to Livingston High School, an all-girls school for emotionally disturbed students with behavioral problems. It focused my interest on working with a population for emotionally and behaviorally challenged kids."

In combination with his experience in "G" Building, Zacherman was launched on a 32-year career in the New York City school system in special education as a teacher, supervisor, and high school principal, mentoring kids with a variety of learning disabilities. Along the way, he picked up two master's degrees and a PhD before retiring in 2002.

He stayed retired for three days.

"I'd been recruited to be Executive Director of Lifeline Center for Child Development," Zacherman explains, "and they wanted me to

*It's Never Too Late to Plant a Tree*

start right away. That gave me three days off over Labor Day weekend."

Lifeline Center is a day treatment center and special school for seriously disturbed children and their families from the New York City metropolitan area. It is licensed and supported by both the state and the city with a large professional staff of psychologists, psychiatrists, social workers, speech and language therapists, music therapists, art therapists, physical and occupational therapists, a full-time nurse and special education teachers. The Center has been around since 1959, now housed in two modern buildings on a three-acre campus that includes a swimming pool. There is no charge for its services.

©2003, Thomas Hart Shelby

*Helping Kids*

"These kids couldn't function in a regular school environment. They present a lot of emotional problems, a lot of behavioral problems and emotional problems. We have two programs, Pre-School for children ages 2 to 5 years, and the Upper School Program for children ages 5 to 18. They're grouped in small classes of six to nine per class. Lifeline is also a training institution for Master's level students in social work and art therapy, and a training site for child psychiatry fellows."

Has it been a major transition for Zacherman to move from the public school system into the nonprofit sector?

"Yes and no. Personally, I knew a lot of the clinical staff here, and they knew me. In that way it was a smooth

**His proudest achievement is seeing kids from Special Ed come back years later. Many of them made it to college.**

transition. I felt coming here, I would grow professionally, as well as bring new leadership to the agency. The big difference is that I'm free of a lot of red tape and bureaucracy. At the Board of Education—Department of Education, as it's called now—you could spend half your life shuffling papers, being accountable for a lot of stuff that didn't have much to do with education, justifying what you were doing.

"Here, I answer to the state and city regulatory agencies, but I don't have to do it on a daily basis. As a principal I had a superintendent whom I had to answer to, and be accountable every step of the way. Here the demands are very different, since we are a not-for-profit organization with fiduciary responsibilities, as well as compliance requirements with the Office of Mental Health and State Education. Many times their regulations compete with each other. The only other people I answer to are members of the Board of Trustees that hired me. I'm in touch with the president of the Board on a regular basis, but he's not asking me, 'So what did you do today?'"

Not that Zacherman automatically followed the rules when he was in the public schools.

"Something like 20 years ago, I was working as a special education supervisor in Manhattan in the high schools. Going back to the 1950's, early 1960's, the Board of Ed had bureaus for special disabilities, a bureau for socially and emotionally disturbed, a bureau for mental retardation, one for neurological problems and so on. You could walk into a school where they had special education classes, and whatever the category of handicapped condition, the bureau had a supervisor. Four conditions, four supervisors in a single school. One day, I decided this didn't make sense. Why not one person to supervise the programs, with one caveat: you couldn't mix the kids. So I get this assignment at Seward High School in lower Manhattan, and find that there are still separate classrooms for each condition. After awhile, I said, 'Why are these kids being kept separate, three kids with one disability in one class, nine kids with a different disability in another class? I don't see any difference between their cognitive levels—their ability to learn. Why don't we just combine them and even up the class sizes?' I called it cross-categorization, and I did it.

"Let me tell you, you'd have thought I'd set the system upside down. I get hauled to downtown Brooklyn, the main headquarters for the Board of Ed, 'How dare I do this?' I thought I was going to get fired, but I survived. And you know what? Today, cross-categorization is standard in the system, even if they call it by a different name. It's called 'Unified Service Delivery System.'"

Looking back, Zacherman says his proudest achievement is seeing kids from Special Ed come back years later. "Many of them made it to college and are succeeding professionally." And looking forward he points to Lifeline's record of returning more than 95 percent of its children to public schools in their communities, a mark he intends to continue. "It really is a lifeline," he says.

As for burnout, which Zacherman admits is a common problem, his answer is, "Give it 100 percent on the job, but when you close the door, leave it at the door, and get on with your life."

E-mail: drzat23@aol.com

# Humor

"Make 'em laugh! Make 'em laugh! Make 'em laugh!"

That's Donald O'Connor singing and shouting, as he takes pratfalls and crashes into scenery in his classic performance in *Singin' In The Rain.*

Not bad advice. Decades later, Dr. Dale Anderson, a highly reputable, board-certified physician in Minneapolis, offers that prescription to audiences in Asia, Australia, Africa, Europe and North America.

A smile, a giggle or a chuckle won't do, Dr. Anderson says. It's real, up from the gut, belly laughing, the kind that makes you shake and gasp for breath. Take it to the bank. It's good for you and for your health.

Best of all, you don't have to be a patient to get the prescription. Dr. Anderson tells you how to do it in *Laughter Is A Health Prescription.*

Enter Art Gliner, a 68-year-old professional humorist, who retired in 1999, but hasn't stopped thinking funny. His message is addressed to kids, and it's simple. "Don't smoke." It's not cool. It's hot. And it's dangerous. Kids who smoke are no laughing matter," he says. But using humor to get them to stop or, better yet, not to start in the first place is something else.

And John Cantu turned a deadly colon cancer into a 20-minute comedy routine, as he marched through the gloom with a smile on his face.

*Laugh, and the world laughs with you* still has a strong resonance.

# Laughter Is A Health Prescription

Here's an offer you can't resist: Whatever your age, you can laugh your way to the bank every day and come backricher than when you left. All this without leaving your home, because the bank is not a savings bank. It's your "Good Health Bank."

The offer comes from Dale L. Anderson, M.D. together with a prescription that you can fill by yourself. Free of charge. It's the Laughter $R$ that Dr. Anderson has prescribed to audiences in Asia, Australia, Africa, Europe and North America. Here it is:

> $R_X$  *In front of mirror*
> *Belly Laugh*
> *15 seconds, 2x/Day*

A smile, a giggle or a chuckle won't do, he says. It's real, up from the gut, belly laughing, the kind that makes you shake and gasp for breath.

For those who are skeptical of the credentials of this funny man-physician, Dr.Anderson has a wall full of diplomas and certificate.

"I am a traditionally trained medical doctor, who has 'practiced' for more than 40 years as a board-certified surgeon and board-certified emergency physician," he says. "And since 2001, when I was 68, I was board-certified as a Holistic Medicine physician. I still practice as a Medicare-card-carrying doctor by treating patients in the Urgent Care clinics of a large health care group in the Twin Cities Metro area of Minnesota."

He has written four books; his most recent, "Never Act Your Age: Play the Happy Childlike Role at Every Age." As a seminar keynote speaker, he prescribes "Method Acting" techniques to more than 100 major audiences around the world each year. It's all part of Anderson's ACT Approach (Action<->Chemistry <->Thought).

Typically, Anderson starts before a roomful of people who arrive with a blend of hope and "show me." He begins with his "Minnesota cold car start." First, a gurgle in the diaphragm. "A-haa hah," Anderson sputters, and everyone joins in. When the doctor's laughing engine revs up to "A-ha,ha, ha, HA-HA-HA-HA-HA!" the laughter shifts into high gear, and Anderson is off and running.

 **"Fake it till you make it."** Does the engine ever fail to turn over, like in real life? "Not very often," says Anderson, "and if it does, there are other tricks. There's a great book that Irvin S. Cobb wrote about 70 years ago. It's called 'Exit Laughing,' and that's how I want to leave my audiences at the end of the seminar."

For those who demand scientific evidence that laugh therapy is more than hocus-pocus, Anderson explains, "There is scientific, measurable evidence of the physiological links of emotional states and overall health. Feelings are chemically measurable. Happiness releases PNI's, the acronym for the jaw-braking 'psychoneuroimmunology chemicals that lay people refer to a 'endorphins.' People with a happier chemistry are happier people."

Tell Anderson that you just don't feel happy, can't act happy, and his advice is the familiar, "Fake it till you make it. INNERtain yourself." He offers the following "success stories."

"In a store, place a mirror in front of the salesperson, and he or she will sell 17 percent more. Waitresses and waiters who put on a happy act make 27 percent more in tips. In 'method acting,' actors and actresses prepare themselves for a role in the 'green room' before a performance by smiling into a mirror, if the role is a happy one, by surrounding themselves with colors, music and aromas of happiness. When they are fully in the role of 'happy,' they have actually altered the chemicals in the body and released the PNIs

*It's Never Too Late to Plant a Tree*

©2003, Richard Tsong-Taatarii

that change their bodies into happier bodies, emotionally and physically.

"There are great, personal side effects of happiness. Better posture, less wrinkles, healthier aging, greater attractiveness. We bolster the immune system and promote well being. A solid minute of laughter is worth 40 minutes of deep relaxation. And 100 laughs burn as many calories as a 10-minute jog."

Anderson does not claim to be able to cure diseases or take years off people's lives. But he cites the case of Norman Cousins, former editor of the *Saturday Review*, who suffered from ankylosing spondylitis, a painful, degenerative disease that is often fatal. Cousins took charge of his medical treatment by moving his hospital bed to a nearby hotel room. He created a home-like environment and paid attention to his mental and emotional states. He watched classic comedy films such as Laurel and Hardy. His health improved dramatically and he wrote two books about it, "Anatomy of an Illness" and "Head First: the Biology of Hope."

Anderson's work as an urgent care physician attests to his belief that traditional medicine has a necessary role alongside of holistic practice. Furthermore, he knows first hand the power of humor.

When he was 18 months old, he suffered severe burns on his face, neck and hand when he pulled a saucepan of boiling cake frosting off **"Growing up, doctors were my heroes."**  the stove. Sixteen surgeries, the most recent three years ago, have helped repair the most serious scars. His accident also influenced him to choose medicine as a career. "Doctors were my heroes—and still are." And growing up in Austin, Minnesota, Anderson became known for his humor rather than his scars.

When Anderson asks a patient, "How are you feeling?" he refuses to accept as an answer, "It only hurts when I laugh, doctor."

Web Site: www.acthappy.com.

# He Walked Through The Gloom With A Smile On His Face

John Cantu knew he was sick. He was losing five pounds a week and soon his six-foot frame was carrying only 140 pounds. Still the doctor's diagnosis was a blockbuster. "You've got colon cancer," he was told. "If we don't operate immediately, it could be fatal in three to six months."

For most, these words would be life shattering. Cantu made two major decisions. The first was easy. "Doc," he said, "Let's schedule the operation as quickly as possible."

"Don't you want a second opinion?" the doctor asked.

"O.K.," joked Cantu, "if you insist, I'll come back tomorrow."

> **What is grisly to some he turned into a 20-minute comedy routine.**

The second was a wake-up call. For Cantu, humor in the face of death was not an act. He had died several times–but on stage at the Holy City Zoo, a comedy club he ran in San Francisco. For years, from sunset to sunrise, he went to work when most people were going out to play. Now the nightclub manager, who had worked with such comics as Robin Williams, Jerry Seinfeld, Steven Wright, Paula Poundstone and Margaret Cho, decided to face one of life's most dreaded challenges by entering a new retirement arena. He would devote his energy and his talent, not by entertaining people, but by helping people become happier, more skilled and more popular through humor.

Concerned that his sudden inspiration might seem trivial, he consulted with close friends, Patricia Fripp and David Garfinkel, two of the country's most famous professional speakers. He regaled them with stories about his operation that removed a sizeable tumor from his colon but left one on his brain. He humorously detailed his radiation and chemotherapy procedures, his loss of hair, and his

©2002, Susan Cerce

thoughts during long periods of isolation. What is grisly to some he turned into a 20-minute comedy routine as he mimicked the medical staff and ridiculed his rehabilitation procedure.

Teary-eyed from laughter, both Fripp and Garfinkel strongly urged him to go public. "Share your experience," they told him, " and by adding humor you may take the fear out of it for others."

They were right. Cantu's new retirement project soon became a fulltime business. Within a month he organized three-hour workshops for small groups of adult humor neophytes and installed an Internet humor website. He became a popular convention keynote and after-dinner speaker.

Can anyone be funny? Of course, claimed Cantu. There are many widely accepted formulas and structures. For seniors, he advocated three main styles of comedy: storytelling, exaggeration and self-deprecating humor.

His favorite for seniors was storytelling, a sharing of witty observations. "Talk about common experiences," he preached, "you're not doing a documentary." He urged them not to give up on an amusing anecdote they were struggling with. Keep writing different approaches and try it at least three times.

He recommended exaggeration, which is permissible in humor. Sometimes it's funnier to call the car a Mercedes, rather than a Chevy, and often one name is funnier than another. "It's okay," he claimed. "No one ever challenged a comedian for veracity." As an example, he started many of his professional speeches by introducing himself, "My name is John Cantu. I'm not excited about that name but it was a birthday gift from my parents. When I was ten I learned you could exchange birthday gifts but, by then, it was too late."

Self-deprecating humor is the most common comedy technique. It actually helps bring re- **"It's a humor workshop. Encourage each other," he urged. "It's not therapy."**  spect into your life because we appreciate someone with a modest sense of humor. "Don't pity yourself when things go wrong and complain to your friends," warned Cantu. "Fifty percent don't care and the other fifty percent are glad you're getting what you deserve." He told the infirm, "For peace of mind, find humor in your life. You'll discover a positive attitude that will help alleviate your pain and speed your recovery. He pointed to the therapeutic healing power of humor made famous by Norman Cousins in his book *Anatomy of an Illness.*

"While young people have a one-dimensional point of view ("Am I going to get drunk tonight and have sex?"), the varied experiences of seniors increase their appreciation of life, and the best humor is often based upon shared tribulations," he claimed.

Because humor can be inspirational in normal conversation, he urged his senior students to participate in their surroundings. "And don't be afraid of bombing," he said. "There isn't a professional comedian alive who hasn't bombed many times. Since laughter is the only payoff for a joke, if a punch line doesn't work, don't accuse someone of not having a good sense of humor. Just keep on talking. People will just think you're talking normally. Oddly, but normally."

Cantu's creative principles are so universal they can often be applied in other areas. That's why the man with cancer on his mind, talked enthusiastically about the future. "Every once in a while someone goes from rags to riches and," he adds with a smile, "that's no joke!"

# Smoke Gets In Your Eyes...
# And It Doesn't Stop There

Kids who smoke are no laughing matter. But using humor to get them to stop, or, better yet, not to start in the first place is something else. Enter Art Gliner, a 68-year-old professional humorist, who retired in 1999, but hasn't stopped thinking funny.

©2003, Allison Shelley

"The fact is I never really retired. I just stopped working full-time. I've used humor for 43 years in radio, theater, professional speaking and in teaching," Gliner says. "I can probably do it forever. Well, forever is a long time, but it seemed to me that humor might be a way to reach young children and that it could be put to work in a good cause. What prompted me to do the kind of programs I have in mind began 30 years ago when I was doing talk-radio and public service interviews."

> **"It seemed to me that humor might be a way to reach young children and that it could be put to work in a good cause."**

Gliner goes on to describe how a recent anti-smoking program featured a humor contest for young children. The contest is effective in different ways. First of all, it teaches children about humor and how to use it to teach a lesson. In addition, the contest gets kids thinking about anti-smoking messages and helps them understand why smoking is bad for their health. Another key element is to get kids thinking about the problems associated with smoking, so that they internalize that message. The contest was for children 7 to 11 years old, before they have to face peer pressure to perhaps light up. Here are a couple of winning entries:

Smoking is bad for you.
Second-hand smoke is bad for me.
If you can stop smoking,
Think how happy and healthy we will be!
—Emily Rose Peikin, 2nd grade

*(To the tune of She'll be Comin' round the Mountain)*
She'll be Smokin' like a Choo-Choo
She'll be smokin' like a choo-choo when she comes.
She'll be smokin' like a choo-choo when she comes!
She'll be huffin' and a puffin', her lungs, they will be snuffin'!
She'll be smokin' like a choo-choo when she comes!
She'll be chokin' cause she's smokin' when she comes.
She'll be chokin' cause she's smokin' when she comes!
Her fingers will be yellow, her lungs will be like Jell-O,

She'll be chokin' cause she's smokin' when she comes!
She'll be drivin' her own casket when she comes.
She'll be drivin' her own casket when she comes!
She'll be drivin' her own casket, her smokes in a basket!
She'll be drivin' her own casket when she's done!
    —Emily Sobel, 5th grade

Awards were given in two age groups: Grades 1-4 and 5-7. There were two categories, graphic arts (cartoons, comic strips, posters) and written humor (poems, songs, slogans, bumper-stickers etc.) First prize was $150, second, $100, third, $50.

Before Gliner could launch such a program, however, he needed a vehicle. He found his inspiration in his favorite humorist, Benjamin

**"She'll be chokin' cause she's smokin' when she comes!"**

Franklin. He quotes a passage Franklin wrote, "Life, like a dramatic piece should not only be conducted with regularity, but methinks it should finish handsomely. Being now in the last act, I began to cast about for something fit to end with."

The quote made a lot of sense to Gliner, who decided to "do something fit to end with." He started by speaking with officials at the University of Maryland about setting up a scholarship. Endowed scholarships are always attractive, but the provost at the university suggested, instead, that Gliner sponsor a center.

Before long, The Art Gliner Center for Humor Studies was born, dedicated to teaching humor and developing programs to use humor to help senior citizens, teach children and present health information to the general public. One program is taking humor into hospitals and senior citizen centers.

"The idea is to try to bring some laughter into those venues," Gliner said. "They really appreciate it." Studies show that humor can be beneficial to the health and happiness of senior citizens, so Gliner is doing what he can to make humor programs more available.

Gliner has videos of Johnny Carson on the Tonight Show, and he has put together 40 minutes of spontaneous items from the shows.

He wants to test different programs to see what works best for people in need of good cheer.

"This is something I've been testing in senior citizen residences," he says. Gliner is also working at the Center on a program to use humor in teaching, putting together information on this topic in hopes of creating a course for teachers. He also is working on a book on how people can effectively use humor in their jobs and everyday lives.

Besides his programs and classes, Gliner is honoring renowned humorists. The first two persons honored were political cartoonist Herblock, and nationally known humorist Art Buchwald. A third was presented in March, 2003 to Jim Boren (www.jimboren.com) whose 40 plus years of poking fun at the bureaucracy has been a great contribution. Gliner said it is important to honor people like these for their creativity and the work they did.

He has also established a humor collection at the Center. Gliner hopes eventually to have the largest humor collection on the east coast. "We've had close to 1,000 books donated to the Center with many more promised," Gliner says. "In addition, we've received teaching materials and recordings that will help people gain a better understanding of what humor is all about. They are prominently displayed as a special collection in the Hornbake Library of the University of Maryland."

Gliner continues to teach humor, write about humor and uses his knowledge and expertise on the subject at the Art Gliner Center for Humor Studies in order to help people in all walks of life. He also still works part-time as a radio personality at a classical music station where he uses humor to bring a lighter touch to music seen as highbrow by many people. The Center is his first love, though, and he is dedicated to making it grow and prosper.

Art Gliner is a man who would make Benjamin Franklin proud.

E-mail: gliner@erols.com
Web site: www.humorcenter.umd.edu.

# A World Without Boundaries

If the title of this section caught your eye, and you're looking for a travel cruise website, this is the wrong place. Nothing about boundless space travel, either, although John Glenn, who became the first American to orbit the earth, then served for 24 years in the U.S. Senate, went back into space at age 67. A tree planter extraordinary, Glenn is another startling reminder of what seniors—some anyhow—can do.

A World Without Boundaries has its own share of drama.

Ed Artis, a modern knight, brings food and medicine into war-torn areas throughout the world in old trucks, armed with a white flag and boundless determination. Don and Judy Asman, working with Aloha Medical Mission, provide free health care and health education in developing countries and Hawaii. E.J. McClendon fights on in his mission to eradicate polio from the planet.

Paul J. Meyer, a multimillionaire, has a long-term financial plan that you won't find in the business section of your newspaper or in the bookstore. Having grown up in poverty, Meyer is giving his wealth away by establishing family trusts and foundations that will continue to distribute his largess in perpetuity. The beneficiaries include educational and religious organizations, community beautification programs and civic centers, Boy Scouts and Boys and Girls Clubs, and more than 100 miscellaneous charities with spiritual and humanitarian goals.

And Burns Weston, through The University of Iowa Center for Human Rights, battles a host of worldwide ills, in particular sweatshops and child labor violations.

All in all, a heady combination.

# Food for Thought

As a kid, Ed Artis was a car thief, truant, and juvenile delinquent. Given a choice of going to a youth detention camp or enlisting in the U.S. Army, Ed enlisted in the Army.

Soon he was a medic with the 82$^{nd}$ Airborne Division, where he first saw combat in the Dominican Republic and then as a medic in Vietnam. Although he had been wounded in action, he learned how to survive under fire. And for the first time in his life he experienced the horrors and destruction of war.

After his honorable discharge in 1973, Artis spent nearly 20 years working in mortgage banking, real estate, television and film production. But something was constantly gnawing at his conscience. How could he enjoy a comparatively luxurious American lifestyle without trying to help the world's most helpless and often the world's most hopeless?

©2001, Walt Ratterman, Knightsbridge International

*A World Without Boundaries*

So in 1993, at age 48 he retired from his various commercial endeavors, and soon thereafter helped form Knightsbridge International, a private non-profit relief organization. Together, with his partner, Dr. James Laws, an osteopathic cardiologist from Dayton, Ohio, Artis began waging peace in 11 war-ravaged parts of the world including Cambodia, Thailand, Rwanda, Nicaragua, Albania, Kosovo and most recently Afghanistan and the Southern Philippines.

The two partners met when Artis was invested as a member of a "self-styled" Order of the Knights of Malta in Moscow in August 1993. Now titled Sir Edward Artis and Dr. Sir James Laws, they were inspired to practice a brand of chivalry rarely seen in modern times.

These modern knights ride trucks and airplanes. Their sword is a cell phone. Their ammunition is food and life saving medicines. Their banner has one word on it, "HOPE." Their battle cry is, "We're going to get food and medicines to these people." Yet, they realize their relief missions are not much more than band-aids on a hemorrhage. Their objective is a basic sustainable program that can save lives. But no matter how difficult the terrain, fighting for financial support is also part of their battle.

"Simply put, we're DHL, UPS, FEDEX with an attitude," jokes Artis.

**"Simply put, we're DHL, UPS and FEDEX with an attitude," jokes Artis.**  They raise the funds and supplies that they need from other relief organizations, such as The Buddhist Tzu Chi Foundation, The REMEDY Program at Yale University and numerous others. Much of their medical needs are supplied by Dr. Laws. Neither of them accepts a salary for their efforts, and both scrape and scrounge for whatever supplies they can find.

Artis's small teams often include fellow retirees with basic skills in education, communication, history, sciences, biotech medical

*It's Never Too Late to Plant a Tree*

equipment, alternative energy and construction. All are volunteers, and since their living conditions are often primitive the team excludes "disaster tourists" who go to war zones simply to say they've been there or to have their photos taken.

They provide sustenance such as food, clothing, blankets, basic medical supplies, tents, **He has a simple rule: those with guns will not be served. Amazingly, his rule works.**  cooking oil, and simple farming tools in trucks that can carry 15 to 45 tons of wheat. On one of their recent operations in Northern Afghanistan distributed more than 300 tons of food, enough to feed nearly 15,000 refugees for up to four months.

Their borrowed or hired trucks, often with broken parts, travel at night, get stuck in sand and mud. Winter's snows frequently make the mountain passes treacherous and travel painfully slow. In addition, visas into some countries don't get approved in a timely manner; relief offices get ransacked by bandits, and caches of supplies get bombed mistakenly.

Teams sometimes must drive close to the front lines to reach small, desolate villages and crowded refugee camps that need help immediately. That's where the humanitarian program is most limited, because of the danger caused by war still pounding in their ears. Other charitable organizations, steeped in bureaucracy, take months longer to reach disaster areas and lose as much as 80% of their supplies to inefficiencies, blatant larceny and bribes.

On many missions the members put their lives at risk on a daily basis, unable to wait for security to be in place. As soon as Artis's trucks arrive in a camp, hungry, shouting refugees start fighting and shoving to get preferred treatment. Artis immediately jumps into action. He has a simple rule: those with guns will not be served. Amazingly, his rule works. Soldiers begin handing their weapons to others waiting on the sidelines. A bloodbath over food has been avoided. Once or twice, members of the teams have been shot at or come close to being beaten up, so Artis often travels with a bulletproof vest. And, even though many war-ravaged natives assume American bombing caused their suffering, Artis always displays a U.S. flag patch on his shoulder.

"We're not heroes," he claims. "We're simply doing what's right. There has never been a better time than right now for chivalry—for good guys and gals to step forward. We'll go where others don't or won't. We'd rather do something, instead of sitting on our hands and complaining about what we see going on."

His admonition to all present and future retirees: You don't have to travel to war zones to have a positive impact on the quality of life for those in need. You have a chance to do something meaningful in your own community every day. Spot a local problem and do something about it. There are homeless people even in affluent communities; there is also poverty, health problems, deficient educational resources, and growing numbers of infirm. He challenges fellow retirees not to become emotionally bankrupt. "If you call yourself a good person, and you're not doing something to help somebody else, you're a fraud."

Just before he falls asleep these nights, Ed Artis can truthfully say, "Today, I did a good thing."

E-mail: knightsbrg@aol.com
or visit the Knightsbridge International website at: www.kbi.org

*It's Never Too Late to Plant a Tree*

# It All Starts
# With A Seed...

Judy and Don Asman are veteran tree planters. Their stories are best begun with their own verse.

> We had the call when we were small.
> To be joyful, caring and compassionate to all.
> Especially were we to consider those with needs.
> Through parents and mentors, God planted the seeds.
>
> The seeds sprouted dreams outrageous and daring.
> Dreams keep us working and moving and caring.
> The journey has been challenging, bumpy and wild.
> The journey continues as we help each child.
>
> Judy's dreams involved medical missions in faraway places.
> She dreamed of small orphans with joyful faces.
> Don dreamed of bringing light and hope, maybe with magic,
> Of building bridges where separation was tragic.
>
> We pray, listen, learn and hope to discern
> What we should be doing to help in our turn.
> When new doors are opened, we trust we'll decide
> To walk through in faith with God as our guide.

**After the beginning:**

Following 34 years as a registered nurse, her staff was downsized, and Judy retired in 1996. That suited her fine. She still felt the call to serve the frail, lonely and disenfranchised, but did not want a full-time job.

As it turned out, the Pacific Health Ministry, the local chaplaincy agency, was looking for precisely someone with her skills and knowledge. "Can you develop a program with a spiritual component," she was asked, "that might improve the quality of life of the frail, who do not meet criteria for other services in the home?"

*Judy and Don Asman with sponsored child and her mother.* ©2003, Judy & Don Asman

Being a "can do" woman, Judy wrote grant proposals, received funding, developed and implemented the Interfaith Health Ministry Program. It exists to this day, providing free in-home nursing assessment, information, referral and mentoring of volunteers. Local churches and temples help provide volunteers to serve the clients and financial support for the program.

**Don, a pastor for more than 40 years, has had magic as a hobby since his teens.**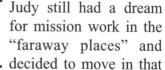

Judy still had a dream for mission work in the "faraway places" and decided to move in that direction by developing her own travel and group missions business. In 1999 she was invited on her first truly "medical mission" through Aloha Medical Mission (AMM), a Hawaii based non-profit, volunteer organization. Begun in 1983 by a small group of doctors from the Philippine Medical Association of Hawaii, AMM provides free health care and health education in developing countries and in Hawaii. Because of her experience and openness

*It's Never Too Late to Plant a Tree*

for new adventures, Judy was asked to help with AMM's first mission to Luang Prabang, Laos.

"What a thrill to help organize supplies, packing and transport a team of 32 doctors, nurses and staff to a small dirt-road town in Northern Laos," she says. "In just five days, we provided medical and surgical care for over 500 people. And then to assist in the operating room. Talk about a dream come true!"

**In the middle:**

During this same period, Don, who has had magic as a hobby since his teen years, began honing his skills in preparation for retirement in 2000. After 40 years of providing full-time pastoral care in church settings, he became chaplain at the Veteran's Administration Center for Aging in Honolulu between May 2001 and June 2002. His model for working with physical and occupational therapists in helping patients improve coordination, attention span and other motor skills was Project Magic, begun by David Copperfield, a well-known stage magician.

*Don Asman entertaining patients in Laos.* ©2003, Judy & Don Asman

*A World Without Boundaries*

As for Judy and Don, they were finally ready to move ahead jointly. "Since all six of our children are independent adults, we could now spend more time on the journey together," Judy says.

To begin, they helped three different church youth groups to plan, train and then provide vacation bible school in poverty areas in Mexico. The groups helped build church halls, made new friends and learned that they could go a week without TV, radio, a bath and flushing toilets. Don and Judy were also able to help four different Christian groups to travel and learn together in Europe and Israel.

On the next mission to Laos, they were both part of the team. While Judy again assisted in the surgery suite, Don helped spread joy and entertain the crowd with magic as well as assist in procuring supplies, daily meals for the team members who could not leave the hospital area, etc.

"Since we knew that we would be focusing our mission's work in the Asia area, we began sponsoring children via Compassion International with hopes that we would someday be able to meet the

*Judy Asman with a friend at an orphanage.* ©2003, Judy & Don Asman

*It's Never Too Late to Plant a Tree*

children. Compassion International is a Christian child development ministry formed in 1952 to help bring children out of poverty and to promote lasting change and development.

 **"In just five days, we provided medical and surgical care for over 500 people," Judy says.**

"Since the Laos government was in turmoil in 2001, we could not do a return mission there, so we took that opportunity to visit our sponsored children in India on a Compassion International Tour. We now sponsor six children, one in Thailand and five in South India. We've met all but two in India, and we hope to do that as soon as we have arranged a short-term mission there in 2004. These short term missions help keep us humble and thankful. If nothing else, we can be bridge builders by sharing love, compassion and a bit of our skills."

**Still on the journey:**

"We are blessed with good genes, good health and much support from family and friends. We recently returned from our third trip to Laos with Aloha Medical Mission. We visited missionary friends in Thailand, took gifts from our home church to a Christian Orphanage and visited with our sponsored Compassion child, Narubed, his family and church in Chiang Mai Province of Thailand. Shortly after our return home, Don was asked to fill a position as interim chaplain with the VA Center for Aging as the resident chaplain is on medical leave.

'As our journey continues, we make time to exercise our bodies and souls and maintain relationships with our children and grandchildren here on Oahu as well as the many relatives on the mainland. What next? We are open."

E-mail: asmand001@hawaii.rr.com

# For This Choctaw Indian, All Things Are Possible

Dr. E.J. McClendon fights no small wars. Years after he was out of the Navy, he went into a different kind of battle in Africa. This time he carried a World Health Organization flag, a United Nations flag and a white flag. All that was lacking was a pennant bearing his motto, "Eradicate Polio from the Planet."

With a PhD. in public health and the rank of professor emeritus at the University of Michigan in Ann Arbor, McClendon makes no prediction as to when he will be victorious. Born on the Choctaw Indian reservation in Southeast Oklahoma in 1921, he has been engaged in a lifetime mission, but can point to substantial progress. "I've been to eleven major countries and six smaller ones, inoculating their populations," he says. "The Western Hemisphere

©2003, Lon Horwedel

is free of polio. So is Europe and most of Asia. In Africa, it's probably two-thirds."

McClendon's mission reaches back a half-century, when his sister's only child died of polio in 1952 and his two children had played all afternoon with their cousin four days before she died. He was an observer of the first use of the polio vaccine when it was tested at the University of Michigan, and his children were the first to be vaccinated in the Midwest.

Since then McClendon says, "Three great events have occured in the war to eradicate polio. The first was the discovery and/or refining of the Salk of 'killed virus' vaccine. Few of us up to then thought we had any serious chance to ever get rid of polio. Second was the Sabin of 'live virus' vaccine which provided a superior means for achieving immunity. Third and last, the elimination of the 'Shoot,' as labeled by kids in many countries, meaning a needle injection, which children often feared. The use instead of sweet drops on the tongue made most kids double happy. No polio, no iron lung, no needle and a candy taste as a reward."

At age 76, McClendon traveled to Zaire on behalf of both Rotary International and the World Health Organization (WHO) to conduct vaccinations. The members of his team met with great resistance, initially. Not only did they prevail, they stopped a war temporarily between African countries, in order to get their people vaccinated.

By now, running against odds is force of habit for McClendon, having developed a sense of independence from his grandparents who raised him on the Choctaw Reservation.

"I've been involved with Native Americans all my life," he says. "I still like to be called 'Indian,' because that's what I was taught when I was five years old. I was Indian and that was a good thing to be. Growing up on the reservation, we didn't have any schools. My grandfather got very involved in helping to create schools. He and some of the other elders got the Presbyterian and Methodist churches to help, too.

"My parents lived off the reservation, and the reason I was raised there was my parents agreed to leave me there for what they thought would be a short term after my sister was born. I already had three brothers. But my grandfather got so attached to me that whenever my parents tried to take me home with them, he'd say, 'You can't take my boy away from me.' So I stayed on until I went off to the University of Oklahoma, where Indian kids got free tuition and books. But I still needed money for food and other things. Working in a restaurant just took up too much time. I wanted to go to medical school, and I knew that if I was going to make it, I'd have to study a lot harder. Anyhow, when I learned that by joining the NROTC, they would pay me $55 a month, I signed right up.

"That also got me a full first and middle name. 'E.J.' was all I'd been, named after the doctor who came to deliver me on the reservation; except by the time he arrived I was already born. Eight weeks later when my uncle went to find out what the E.J. stood for, the doctor had left the territory, so that's what I was left with. When there was no more avoiding it in college, my mother decided it was Edwin James, but everybody still knows me as E.J."

McClendon was called to duty exactly one month after Pearl Harbor and was sent to Northwestern University to

**By now, running against odds is force of habit for McClendon.**

finish up for an engineering degree. Aboard ship, thanks to a gruff surgeon to whom he was assigned, McClendon was ordered to read a medical or science book each week and write a report. Unbeknownst to McClendon, those reports earned him college credits in public health, a big step towards his becoming Deputy Chief of TB Control for Wayne County in 1954. In 1960 he received his PhD. in public health. Subsequently, he was elected National President of the American School Health Association, and in 1976 received the William Howe Award, the Association's highest honor.

Ten years after retirement in 1986 he was inspired by Rotary International's worldwide effort to wipe out polio worldwide. He discovered that, although the U.S. was basically free of the disease, there were ten countries that had not rid themselves of this killer. What keeps him going is a feeling of fulfillment from the work.

McClendon relates an episode on a trip to New Guinea.

 **"In Zaire, I said to a boy on crutches, 'You get the kids all to take the vaccine, and nobody will die.'"**

"I was walking up the road to a school where the kids had not been immunized, when I saw this kid with a homemade crutch walking on the other side of a gully. I shouted ''Polio,' and he shouted back, 'Polio.' He got to a log bridge made with grass rope, but I couldn't see how he'd get across that gully. He laid his crutch down, and sure enough he got across the bridge. On the other side, where we were, he picked up a second crutch that he had waiting. We started talking, and he wanted to know what we were doing. I told him about the vaccine, and he said he had two sisters who had both died of the polio, so I said, 'We'll never have that again. You get the kids all to take the vaccine, and nobody will die.' And he asked, 'Nobody will die?' I repeated, 'Nobody will die.' Then he said, 'That's a miracle!'"

To this day, he acknowledges the contribution to his work by the medical staff of the University of Michigan, as both guides and practitioners. "I've been able to convince people that by getting involved they really can eradicate this terrible disease," he says, "and that as retired people we really have the time and understanding about tackling large problems."

As for how to get involved, "The best way," he says, "is by working with the thousands of Rotary International Clubs, almost worldwide and in nearly every city in America. You can also help make others aware of the disease by just talking about it. You can challenge people by raising their sense of responsibility about how blessed we are in this country and how destitute other people are around the world."

By chance, during the war McClendon met Eleanor Roosevelt on several occasions. Each time she recognized him, calling him by her version of his name, "McLeeendon." When she asked what she could do to help him, he hesitated, feeling it would be too much of an imposition. The first time they met was at graduation from Northwestern, and he had already been assigned to a ship. She insisted, and he said he would like to see his grandfather who was old and frail, but that it couldn't be done. Her reply, he says, with a chuckle, was "All things are possible."

"Great woman that Mrs. Roosevelt was," McClendon says thoughtfully, "the most important person to me was my wife, Ruby Scott McClendon, a Cherokee from Tahlequah. She did more to enhance and guide everything I did than any other person. She died in April, 2001, but her even temper is with me to this day."

# The Family That Prays Together, Pays Together

Texas multimillionaire Paul J. Meyer plans to die broke. This hard driving entrepreneur from Waco not only believes Andrew Carnegie's admonition, "A man who dies rich, dies in disgrace," he plans to go out in style.

In his retirement, Meyer is giving his wealth away by establishing family trusts and foundations that will continue to distribute his largess in perpetuity. In so doing, he has become a happy man. "Death will snatch it away anyway," he claims, "so why not have the pleasure of giving it away before you go?"

Meyer grew up in poverty. His father treated him harshly. He decided against spending time in college, devised his own curriculum and read voluminously. 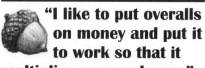 **"I like to put overalls on money and put it to work so that it multiplies over and over."** Meyer made his first million selling life insurance. In 1960, he founded Success Motivation Institute for the purpose of helping people develop their leadership skills and personal potential. Within a few years, he had become the pre-eminent leader in the self-improvement industry and made millions more.

"The question isn't whether I can afford to give, but whether I can afford not to give," he says. He encourages his executives to take off 10 to 20 percent of their work time to do something for their community or religious affiliation.

"I have always believed that what you do is more important than what you say. So I constantly ask myself, 'Where would Christ be today if He were in town? Who would He help?'" Meyer believes missionary work is one of the best routes to reach the world's population with the gospel of Christ. So he is a major benefactor to The Haggai Institute that specializes in evangelism and leadership training of individuals from third world countries. "I'll get paid back by laying up treasures for myself in heaven," Meyer believes.

©2001, Joe Gonzalez Photography

His multimillion-dollar foundation, called The Paul J. Meyer Family Foundation, has given away tens of millions for charitable purposes, including educational and religious organizations, community beautification programs and civic centers, Boy Scouts and Boys and Girls Clubs, and more than 100 miscellaneous charities with spiritual and humanity goals. It has helped more than 1,000 Waco teens to attend college. "Let others donate to the arts," he says, "I like to put overalls on money and put it to work so that it multiplies over and over."

Meyer has five children and a classroom full of grandchildren, so he had the typical philanthropists' dilemma that by giving millions to public causes he would be alienating his children and shortchanging his grandchildren.

His solution was advanced planning. "I started brainwashing my children 20 years ago," he admits. During family gatherings he would talk about the legacy he wished to leave them. "Here's where

I'm coming from and here's where I'm going," he would tell them. "I want you to buy into the belief that the least important thing in this world is money." Before they could challenge him, he would tell them, "When people make their top priority the acquisition of material possessions, they become progressively more selfish, self-centered, egotistical and proud."

He continued to pound away with this message for two decades. When they were old enough, Meyer set up an endowment fund of $500,000 for each child, enough to give them incentives and bank credits but not enough to retire on. "I made them aware that inherited wealth rarely breeds strong leaders. The immense wealth that came from one individual's shirtsleeves dissipates so quickly that by the third generation, the progeny are not only back in shirtsleeves but often lacking the skills to contribute to a renewed upward cycle."

His prediction: "The charitable foundation is here to stay and almost anyone can found one—and probably many should." He envisions the day when business people in every town in America will be doing the same thing.

Meyer invests his time and money in what he calls "high payoff" activities and ventures. Whenever one of his **"Meyer's foundation, The Paul J. Meyer Family Foundation, has given away tens of millions and provided more than 1,000 Waco teens the tuition to attend college."** foundations helps set up a business by guaranteeing loans, Meyer demands that 50 percent of the profits be turned back to the issuing foundation. Each unit must first make money. He believes in the philosophy of leverage and multiplication. Family foundations must have a business formula and a trustee group manages many. He sells properties and companies and then places that money in a foundation to perpetuate selected charities.

His formula works. By now all of the Meyer children have their own businesses and professions and are totally independent. They are also deeply involved in their church. His message to his children is still "I want to be known by my children and grandchildren, even 100 years from now, as a man who walked with God and lived for Christ."

At age 67, Meyer retired. "I was the principal owner of 30 corporations and supported 25 charities through my nonprofit family foundations. I didn't want to be a CEO any more. I wanted to be a servant of the Lord, to pass on values such as honesty, integrity, discipline and, most importantly, faith in God. I wanted the freedom to write, to speak and to start more foundations."

Meyer has written several books that include chapters on charitable giving. His most recent book, *Unlocking Your Legacy,* focuses on using what God has given and maximizing it for the benefit of others. This includes money—and helping people use their God-given potential. For example, a highway construction worker Meyer met in South Dakota when driving in the Great American Race was standing at the side of the road as she was waiting for traffic to clear. Meyer asked her what she dreamed of doing with her life; she answered, "Be a nurse." Meyer's scholarship program, Passport to Success, enabled her to attend college, and now she is fulfilling her dream—she is a nurse. Not only that, but she is helping her younger brother and sister attend college.

One of his biographers, John Edmund Haggai wrote, "Meyer is a creative life enhancer. He makes life easier and more meaningful for thousands on all continents."

Meyer doesn't spend a lot of time in meetings or interviews. "I have more words to write, more people to impact and a whole lot more giving to do. I want to be able to say I amounted to something. That I made a difference in the world."

E-mail: www.paul@pjm1313.com
Web Site: pauljmeyer.com

# Just Weighing In
# Is What
# It Must Come Down To

> Two sides to every question, yes, yes, yes...
> But every now and then, just weighing in
> Is what it must come down to...
>     —Seamus Heaney

If it's worth doing, it's worth fighting for.

That's the motto of Burns Weston, the Bessie Dutton Murray Distinguished Professor of Law Emeritus at The University of Iowa, and it's more than a figure of speech.

Flash back to 1985. The scene is Seoul International Airport, and an American delegation, Weston among them, has come with Kim Dae Jung (then dissident and recently President of the Republic of South Korea) and Mrs. Kim to protect the Kims.

KaPow! Half-way down the ramp, as they disembark, they encounter (in Weston's words), "a phalanx of Korean CIA (KCIA) goons with no necks. They all looked alike. All were dressed in blue-black suits; all had a little red KCIA boutonnière. And we couldn't get past them. They grabbed Mr. and Mrs. Kim, whisked them out a side exit, and proceeded to pummel the rest of us to prevent us from coming to the Kims' rescue. I had a few bruises, but that was it. I was lucky."

Burns was more than lucky. He'd been foresighted enough to borrow the flack jacket of the Iowa City's Chief of Police, with whom he had considerable political differences, but who was so proud of the episode, he went around boasting afterwards, "Weston wore my flack jacket."

Weston is not a street fighter. To the contrary, he regards force as a final, if sometimes necessary resort in international action. But he certainly takes a rolled-up sleeves, hands-on approach to the "non-retirement" project he was instrumental in founding in 1999, The University of Iowa Center for Human Rights (UICHR).

The UICHR (*www.uichr.org)* is dedicated to battling a host of worldwide ills, in particular sweatshops and child labor abuses. At the top of its agenda are the gathering and evaluating of information on child and sweatshop labor and the improvement of workers' rights and conditions at work sites worldwide, especially those that produce for the U.S. market.

**The UICHR is dedicated to battling a host of worldwide ills, in particular sweatshops and child labor violations.**

The direct impetus for the UICHR's formation was a yearlong university commemoration of the 50th anniversary of the Universal Declaration of Human Rights of 10 December 1948.

In Burns Weston, the university has a major asset. Since launching the UICHR, he has raised more than $1 million from the U.S. Department of Labor and other granting agencies to underwrite the Center's efforts. It was a matter of being connected with a broader world beyond the university walls.

What does Weston expect will come of the project?

"Well, some of the information is being housed in an electronic database and will be available to people all over the world," he says. "Some of it is going to be in a collection of essays on which I personally am working. Some of it is going to be in courses that we're developing for college-level instruction and modules for high schools. We also are working with a university labor center on public education programs about child labor for union members of the American workforce."

Weston's passion for human rights goes back a long way.

"Human rights is something I've been passionate about since I was a young boy in high school, maybe before that," he says. "French

*It's Never Too Late to Plant a Tree*

©2003, Brian Ray

*A World Without Boundaries*                                    *209*

was my first language (his mother was French). I played the piano. I was once embarked on a concert piano career, and at an early age I was seen by some of my peers as a 'sissy' who from time to time would get beat up by the 'tougher' kids. Probably I've been committed to fighting for the underdog ever since."

**"We see barefoot and undernourished children as young as 2 or 3 years old picking at refuse on municipal garbage and trash heaps."**

While databases, essays, and curriculum development may seem a bit abstract, one of his Center's task forces is working to provide safe-haven sanctuary for scholars and activists at risk from war and other human rights abuse.

In addition, Weston points out that on his missions abroad his group always visits factories and other sites.

"The human side of the equation can be appalling. We see barefoot and undernourished children as young as 2 or 3 years old picking at refuse on municipal garbage and trash heaps to find something to sell in order to earn a mere dollar per day."

The UICHR is also planning annual awards for human rights scholarship and activism to deserving students, faculty, and off-campus persons and groups. And it makes every effort to respond to informational inquiries and requests from near and far.

Weston points out that while other universities have established human rights centers and programs, Iowa's Center is innovative in several ways. Though naturally influenced by the disciplines of law and politics, it does not limit itself to a traditional legal/political approach and counts in its organization faculty from throughout the University.

The result is an integration of anthropological, educational, environmental, geographic, historical, medical, journalistic, literary, philosophical, psychological, sociological, even artistic, as well as legal and political perspectives into its diverse agenda.

Second, the Center makes a self-conscious effort to involve students in its activities and to reach out to local citizens and citizen groups not officially associated with The University of Iowa to facilitate its ultimate mission, the promotion and protection of human rights at home and abroad.

Finally, believing that the broad dissemination of information about human rights is central to the advancement of such rights, the Center seeks regularly to inform both human rights specialists and the general public about its activities and about human rights issues and developments generally.

Not all of Weston's travel is work-related. He and his wife, Marta, spend two months a year in Sweden, his wife's homeland, and three months in the Adirondack Mountains in New York, where Burns grew up during summers. As a visiting professor, he will teach in the Hopkins-Nanjing Center in Fall 2003 and at the Vermont Law School in Fall 2004. They also visit a son who is a professor of Chinese History at the University of Colorado, their daughter-in-law and granddaughter, and a daughter, who is a clinical social worker in San Francisco, their son-in-law, and a new grandson.

Burns sees no end to his career and, already a prolific scholar, looks forward to further research and writing in the international law and human rights fields. Looking back, he says, "Teaching was the best part. I think the thing I have found the most thrilling, though it doesn't happen often, is when, five to 10 years down the road, some former student will cross my path, in a letter, a phone call, or a chance encounter somewhere and say, 'You know that day you did such and such?' or that course I took from you?' Well, it changed my life."

Says Burns, "I always have told my students: 'Be ashamed to die until you have given of yourself to humanity.' So if that is how I have influenced them, then that is to me the highest possible compliment."

Web site: www.burnsweston.com

# Never Too Old

None of the men and women whom we've profiled had a long-term plan that led them to what they're doing today. Nor will you find any of them creeping to the grave, as represented in *The Seven Stages of Man*. Yes, there's a decline in physical powers, but there's no landmark age at which one becomes "old." Their positive attitudes make an enormous difference.

At the time of the American Revolution, when life expectancy was in the 40's, John Adams lived to be 90; Thomas Jefferson until he was 83. Both died on the same Fourth of July in 1826; both in the mainstream in their final years.

Three of our seven nominees are in their 90's; three others in their 80's. Roland Sharer at 93 is, with his partner the 90-and over national doubles champion for 2001, 2002 on clay, hard and grass courts. Allan "Bud" Reid, age 94, is still skydiving, and Tyler Davis is a familiar figure on the ski slopes of Pennsylvania, a leading member of the ski rescue squad.

Louisa Groce is the oldest person to be ordained in The Evangelical Lutheran Church in America. A brisk 81-year-old, she is older than the biblical Abraham was when he set out for the Promised Land. It took Tom Farley a half-century between the times that he entered a Catholic seminary, fresh out of high school and celebrated his first Mass. Not that he was a slow learner, just that he followed diverse paths before responding to a call that he found impossible to ignore.

Rubin Weser has nurtured a boyhood dream of becoming a lawyer, but it was not until he retired from the commercial insurance business that he turned his attention seriously to into getting into law school. He's been rejected time and again, but in his '80's, he marches forward, representing himself in court, refusing to say "Never."

The youngster of the group, Jeannette Graves, is a hospital chaplain and director of a New York City councilman's office in Co-Op City in the Bronx. In her '60's, she'll tell you, "There's much work to be done out there, and as long as God gives me the strength, I'm going to try my best to do it."

# He Just Saved Your Life, But Don't Check His Birth Certificate

All the injured skier remembered clearly was the examining doctor looking down and saying, "You've got a serious boot-top fracture. It's a good thing the ski patrol found you, or you'd have frozen to death."

"I'd like to thank the person who brought me in," the injured main groaned.

**He has rescued skiers hanging by their skis upside down in trees.**  "Look behind you," said the doctor. "He's just coming in now." The injured man looked back and saw a 91 year-old skier with sunglasses, knit cap and a red-and-black parka, standing by the snowmobile.

"Do you mean that elderly man," the patient growled," he's only five feet tall. I mean the tough guy who skied the mountain and rescued me."

"Same guy," said the doctor. "Shake hands with Tyler Davis, the most outstanding member of the National Ski Patrol in the country."

The injured man wasn't the first to doubt that a five-foot, 125-pound, 91 year-old could be an active hero on the bitter cold, dangerous ski slopes. Nevertheless, some 20,000 skiers a day on the 31 slopes of Pennsylvania's Seven Springs Mountain Resorts owe their safety and some of their pleasure to Tyler Davis and the 140 person ski patrol.

Davis didn't start skiing until he was 24. His father was a maintenance supervisor at a cinema in Uniontown, Pennsylvania. Tyler liked to go to the movies and watch the newsreels, especially skiing segments from Switzerland or the Olympics. Intrigued by the sport, he went to the local hardware store, bought a pair of wooden

©2003, Guy Lombardo

skis that were two feet taller than he was, went to a backyard hill and, without even reading the instruction book, put on the skis and pushed off. It was a big mistake. His arms flailing, his legs trying to correct his skis from a cross over to a snowplow position, he raced down the 100-foot hill and ended up in a small stream known as Coal Lick Run.

Instead of giving up the sport on the spot, Tyler decided he'd stay with it but finally read the instruction book. His day job was with the Fayette Count Board of Assistance, an agency of the state welfare department, and he retired as executive director after 41 years of service. But skiing became his dream sport and it has been for 65 years.

In its early stages, skiers used a rope tow if available. If not, they skied down a mountain, took off their skis and walked back up. Accidents were frequent. Bear trap bindings kept the ski boots locked in no matter where the ski went. Either the ski broke or the leg broke, so getting the injured off the mountain was a constant challenge. There were only primitive first aid patrols to find them. To transport them, there was often just a toboggan with 2-by-6 inch boards as side-rails to prevent the patient from falling out. An injured skier was lucky to survive the fall first and the lightly guided toboggan ride next. The ski lodge's first aid box, complete with a few bandages and splints for fractures, was kept in front of the fireplace. First aid teams, often out on the slopes, had to leave signs warning strangers that the splints weren't to be used for kindling.

**In World War II Davis came home with a Bronze Star, a Legion of Merit and the Italian Military Cross, thanks to his skiing skills.**

Once retired, Tyler helped to organize his local National Ski Patrol teams on a more professional basis. Today, an ambulance is as much a part of the ski scene as a chairlift. Highly trained personnel are equipped with state of the art radio communication, use snowmobile powered rescue sleds and have the facilities to airlift victims to neighboring hospitals within minutes of an accident.

Tyler has trained thousands of people in first aid, CPR and rescue mission techniques. Younger members are in awe of his sheer energy and his enthusiasm for volunteer service. He is an expert in lift evacuations and mountaineering rescues. He has rescued skiers with every conceivable off-slope injury, including some found hanging by their skis upside down in trees and other buried in deep snow from avalanches.

Dick Barron, director of operations at Seven Springs Resort, claims, "Without a doubt, Tyler is the most respected, highly regarded person among the 6,000 members of the National Ski Patrol's Eastern Division."

His associate, Guy Lombardo, director of the Western Appalachian Region, has to keep pushing the modest bachelor to accept all the awards being offered. Recently, he was elected into the Pennsylvania Ski and Winter Sports Museum Hall of Fame. In fact, since Tyler has received every award the National Ski Patrol offers, so in 1995, they created a new one "The Tyler Davis Eastern Division Outstanding Instructor Award."

Tyler has skied in every continent except Antarctica, and while an infantryman in World War II used his skiing skills so successfully in combat that he came home with a Bronze Star, a Legion of Merit and the Italian Military Cross.

Tyler claims that his selection to the Hall of Fame is a little overwhelming. "Actually," wrote Larry Walsh, a newspaper columnist, "it is Davis's accomplishments that are overwhelming."

*Larry Walsh of the Pittsburgh Post Gazette and Tom Lavis of the Johnstown Tribune-Democrat contributed to this profile.*

E-mail: guylom@juno.com

# Reaching His Promised Land

In May 2002, Thomas Farley completed a journey begun 50 years earlier. At age 68 he celebrated his first Mass in Ellsworth, Maine, a newly ordained priest in the Catholic Church.

"I felt completely at ease," he says. "I wasn't nervous or uncertain."

When 25-year-old Tom Farley dropped out of the seminary in 1959, he was just a few years from ordination. He had gone from high school into Boston's St. John's Seminary. Maybe it had all been too quick, he says in retrospect. After he left St. John's, he traveled abroad, became a teacher, returned to school and took a graduate degree, worked in a variety of jobs in a bank and business. Then, in middle age, when many of his friends were retiring, he became a parish business manager in Ellsworth, Maine.

©2003, John Ewing

Becoming a church administrator was not a conscious step to resume where he'd left off, says Father Tom, as he prefers to be called. Neither was it accidental. For some time, he had been researching records on Father John Bapst, a 19th century cleric. He turned to the Boston Archdiocesan Archives on the grounds of St. John's Seminary, which he had left some 40 years ago. In the archives, Farley discovered that Father Bapst had gained a singular distinction in Church history in the United States.

> **"Was it serendipity, or Father Bapst's intervention with God that spurred me on once again? I don't know."**

In the 1850's, the "Know-Nothing" Party was organized to oppose the great wave of immigrants who entered the United States after 1846. Know-Nothings claimed that the immigrants—who were principally Irish and Roman Catholic—threatened to destroy the American experiment. The Roman Catholic Church, they charged, was subservient to a foreign prince (the pope), was growing in power, and potentially could exert political control over a large group of people.

The Know-Nothing's anti-Catholic, anti-foreign church activities were particularly rampant in the Northern States. Prompted by their agitation, hostile mobs burned churches in Bath and Ellsworth, Maine. Bapst was pastor of one of the churches in Ellsworth. There, he was tarred, feathered and run out of town on a rail. Father Bapst survived the ordeal and went on to become the first president of Boston College.

By coincidence, or otherwise, Farley lives in Ellsworth today.

"Was it serendipity, or Bapst's intervention with God that spurred me on once again? I don't know. I had been resisting the call quite a while to come to the ministry. I realized that it was not so much my choice that made me accept. I really feel that it was coming from God, Himself. I had pushed it aside for so long Now, I felt that I should resist no longer.

"A few days later I applied to Blessed John the XXIII in Weston, Massachusetts, which is strictly for men embarking on second careers. They'd been doctors, lawyers, teachers, businessmen before, and of course, are much older. Some were widowers. I wasn't even the senior member of my class. That went to a man who was 70 on graduation."

The seminary has changed in many ways since Father Tom was at St. John's in the 1950's.

"The way the theology is taught is different. Back then, it was a six-year program, after college. Today it's four. The atmosphere in the 50's was much more monastic. You needed permission to leave the grounds. Now you don't. I can't say that those restrictions were a burden at the time. We just didn't know any differently. The entire seminary enrollment was 500 students, and maybe half made it. At Blessed John the XXIII, from which I graduated, seminary enrollment is about 75. It was a much more comfortable experience.

"My going to the seminary right out of high school wasn't unusual. I **"Personally I feel at ease being a priest. I'm pretty much the same person I've always been."**  can't say that it was because of my parents' urging. They were happy that I had made the choice and disappointed when I dropped out, but they didn't put pressure on me, one way or the other. I was completely satisfied with walking away, when I did. It wasn't really right for me at that moment. Now it is. I think the experiences of every day life with its ups and down have given me a much better appreciation of my parishioners and of myself than I would have had when I was younger. I'm able to bend and change, not just be rigid."

As for his transition from a church administrator to a priest, Father Tom says:

"Most people treat me with a little more deference as a priest than as a layperson. Personally I feel at ease being a priest. I am open with people and feel comfortable with myself. That's especially important in Confession. It's such an intimate setting, and I don't feel thrown by the confidences that are given to me. I feel that I have greater understanding and compassion for the human condition."

Nor does he have concerns about age differences with his parishioners, or his own age.

"I just don't let my age bother me. I believe I can relate to both younger and older parishioners. As far as worrying that my time is running out. I have no fear of dying. I've come to my vocation, and I'll work as long as God gives me the time and strength to do what's been awhile in coming."

*It's Never Too Late to Plant a Tree*

# The Chaplain
# Is A Grandmother

"You don't have to call me 'Chaplain,'" Jeannette Graves tells you straight away. "But I really am one." Her formal designation, which appears on her recently minted diploma, is "Healthcare Chaplain."

A high-energy 64-year-old grandmother, Graves has the distinction of being the first African-American woman to achieve that position and is officially registered as a Protestant chaplain.

"I'm proud to be able to contribute to a field that is largely dominated by males," she says. "We need more African Americans in this field, particularly women with a caring attitude and true concerns for others."

Achieving and moving upwards is what Graves has done all her life, as she moves seamlessly between the secular and religious worlds. She served as a manager with Empire Blue Cross/Blue Shield until her retirement in 1994, all the time remaining active in the Community Protestant Church of Co-op City in the Bronx.

**"I was reared by my God-fearing, loving grandmother and mother."** Earlier in the late 1960's, while working for Empire Blue Cross/Blue Shield she learned that a supermarket was for sale in the East Bronx. Residents of the area had been working voluntarily, but without much luck, to gain ownership of the supermarket so that they could control the means of food distribution. Then Graves stepped in to become chairperson of the Publicity Committee. Through newspaper ads, leaflets, bumper stickers, banners and buttons, she organized a membership drive to buy shares at five dollars each in a cooperative venture. The drive was so successful that with the help of the United Methodist Fund, where Graves was also active, and the Coalition

©2003, Thomas Hart Shelby

Venture, the Coop bought the supermarket. In July 1970, with Graves on hand in the company of national and local officials, the "Bronx River Food Co-op" opened.

Even so, how did this lead to her becoming a Healthcare Chaplain?

"After I retired from Empire after 36 years," she says, "I traveled to Africa, visiting various cities, distributing educational supplies and clothing. On my return, I received a call from the Assistant Executive Director of the Co-op City Senior Services, whom I knew only casually. She said she'd had a dream about me and invited me to become Director of Interfaith Volunteer Caregivers, a program of Robert Wood Johnson Foundation. I accepted.

"In that job, so many times when I would accompany a volunteer, the patients would need a faith-based prayer, or something of that kind. Coming from Empire BlueCross/Blue Shield, I had a lot of healthcare background. So I applied at the Healthcare Chaplaincy and received a scholarship. I was sent to Beth Israel Medical Center for my Internship. To gain certification involved cramming a year's worth of training into five months of intensive study. It was hard but rewarding."

The group of seven 2001-2002 Chaplain Interns, besides Graves, included two rabbis and a cantor. Rabbi Jeffrey Silberman, Graves' supervisor at Beth Israel in Manhattan, says of her:

"Jeannette was a truly unique presence here. The fact that she is an African-American woman and was working in this position had a significant impact on the staff here. It is clear that she brings a special level of commitment to a position where few minorities are assigned. She is a deeply religious woman and a very serious student who brings both determination and compassion to the position."

> **"The fact that Jeannette is an African-American woman and was working in this position had a significant impact on the staff at Beth Israel Medical Center."**

Today, you can find Graves at Montefiore Hospital in the Bronx, involved in the Palliative Care Grand Rounds. Palliative Care provides information and education to the community and to caregivers about choices people with serious and complex illnesses can make. She is also in regular attendance as Healthcare Chaplain for Christian counseling at Full Circle Health in the Bronx, part of a team of psychiatrists, psychologists, social workers and educators, working to promote personal and spiritual well-being. And she recently became Director of New York City Councilman Larry Seabrook's office in Co-op City.

If such is possible, it appears that Graves has not reached her full stride yet. Between 1997, when she became Director of Interfaith Volunteer Caregivers until 2001, when she left to study for the chaplaincy she offers an abbreviated list of accomplishments:

- Organized and recruited over 100 volunteers within the community
- Developed and organized a program for Income Tax counseling for Senior Citizens.

- Founded the Grandparent Connection in 1998 (a support group for grandparents raising their grandchildren).
- Founded the Read Aloud Program in 1998 (a program designed for volunteers reading to children in elementary and preschools in Co-Op City).
- Coordinated with DOROT a Senior Telephone Partyline— 'University Without Walls'—primarily for the homebound, to bring the world into the home by taking classes over the telephone.
- Revived a successful Senior Trip Program.

While she is reluctant to single out an award of which she is most proud, she does mention the "Point of Light Award." It is the nation's highest award for a volunteer program, which she received from the first President Bush at The White House. But she is quick to acknowledge her pride in having been awarded the "2001 City Council Citation" as an outstanding citizen and being named "Principal for A Day," at P.S. 160 in the Bronx.

Where does the drive come from? In what Graves calls her "Spiritual Biography," she writes:

"Born into a faith-filled family, I was reared by my God-fearing, loving grandmother and mother. Our Christian home, located on a farm in Maryland, served as a meeting place for relatives and friends. Sunday School was an important part of my Christian foundation. We were in church all day long on Sundays. A member of the Junior Gospel choir, we were regularly in fellowship with other churches spreading God's Word through song and radio broadcasting. Some of the most memorable experiences of my youth include school intersession spent on the campus at Maryland State College."

Following high school, Graves moved to New York, graduated from Grace Institute Business College and completed several certificate programs at NYU. In New York she met and married her husband and later moved with him and their daughter to Co-op City in the Bronx, her home base for 32 years.

In Co-op City, Graves serves as a trustee, member of the Missionary Board and Steering Committee of the Community Protestant Church, a very visible member for the past 24 years, as well as President of the Gloria Wise Boys and Girls Club. Her husband, James Graves, died in 1990, but her daughter, Cherie, son-in-law, William and granddaughter, Monei continue to live in Co-op City.

As for conventional retirement, it's as distant as ever for Graves. Her next step is to complete the next stage of the chaplaincy and get a second certificate.

"That way," she says, "I'll be able to perform marriages and provide other services. There's much work to be done out there, and as long as God gives me the strength, I'm going to try my best to do it. My true passion is helping others."

E-mail: jgraves@chesma.com

# Older than Abraham

Louisa Davis Groce has yet to meet a challenge she won't tackle.

The prospect of becoming pastor of a century-old church in New Jersey might have daunted someone half her age. Not Louisa Groce, the oldest person to be ordained in The Evangelical Lutheran Church in America.

Well, that's not 100 percent true, and being truthful is a cornerstone of Pastor Groce's life. Looking back at that day in 1999 just before graduation from The Lutheran Theological Seminary at Philadelphia, she says, "I'll admit that I was a little afraid about whether I'd be good enough to handle the call."

The parishioners at The Redeemer Lutheran Church in Jersey City, New Jersey, didn't share her doubts, and since that September day, when she was ordained at the age of 81, they've been proven right.

**"I'm really not special, exceptional or unusually talented. My only claim to 'fame' is my trust in my God."**

Groce decided to come to The Lutheran Seminary "because I'd never really had any formal education on the Bible, and I wanted to know more." She says her call to the ordained ministry "wasn't a lightning bolt kind of thing. Being involved in the church was something I always wanted to do."

She credits a Missouri Synod Lutheran pastor, Paul Trumpoldt, with influencing her in her younger years, but it was Bishop Roy Riley of the New Jersey Synod, she says, who surprised her in the Spring of 1996, when he heard she was attending the Seminary.

"Would you consider ordination?" he asked.

"Bishop Riley," she responded, "Do you know how old I am?" He told her that age didn't matter.

Indifference to her age was borne out in a Lenten sermon at the Seminary by Dean Philip Krey, who noted that Groce was "older than Abraham when he left for the Promised Land."

"To be perfectly honest with you, I don't feel old at all," she says. "I'm ready to go wherever I'm assigned and do whatever work the Lord gives me to do. I believe in looking ahead and not behind. I hope to become a great preacher someday."

Most striking is Groce's modesty. "I'm really not special, exceptional or unusually talented. My only claim to 'fame' is my trust in my God. I trust in this quote from Jeremiah 2:11: 'For I know the thoughts that I think toward you, saith the Lord, thoughts of peace and not of evil, to give you a future and a hope.'"

Groce's faith found expression outside a church setting for 30 years, as she worked in the Philadelphia public schools. Her pupils were often hard-to-teach children in special education. A teaching colleague was Lolita Bluford, mother of America's first African-American astronaut.

Later, she instructed high schoolers who'd gotten in trouble with the law and couldn't be placed in regular schools. She'd give the children her home telephone number in case they needed someone to talk to. She saw that they took class trips to New York and Washington—even China. For the latter adventure, she did the fund-raising herself in a matter of months. She was successful, if at times a bit crazy, in her approaches, she says.

"I found these children needed someone who would be loyal to them," Groce says. "I would tell them that even though they might think of themselves at the bottom of the ladder they are worth something. I respected them and let them know they were loved. I told them that they needed to strive for excellence and respect themselves."

On more than one occasion, she took them into her home on an emergency basis. After two young women fought each other and a blouse was torn, she took them both to a department store to shop

*It's Never Too Late to Plant a Tree*

together for a new one. A male student once began to attack her after she tried to coax him away from riding a cart in a school hallway. He stopped after she offered to find help if he wanted it. Her last 10 pre-retirement years were spent at Antioch College, focusing on "teaching others to teach" in special education.

Louisa Groce has built her life on looking ahead, but she can take satisfaction in looking back, as well. Although married for many years, she virtually raised five daughters as a single parent. Today, the daughters hold jobs like Deputy Director of the Social Security Administration, CEO of a New Jersey hospital and Student Services Coordinator of the International School of Abidjan in the Ivory Coast of Africa.

After "retiring," Groce continued her involvement in the Church, teaching Sunday school and serving on the church council. She also served as a lay associate

> **"I'll admit that I was a little afraid about whether I'd be good enough to handle the call."**

with the Camden (NJ) Lutheran Parish, then as an Associate in Ministry at Emanuel Lutheran Church in South Philadelphia. She played a role in invigorating church attendance and ran a campaign to pay for new building downspouts at the church. "I always worked alongside people at Emanuel," she says. "I always told them I would do anything at all, including scrub toilets, but I wouldn't do it by myself."

How is she getting on in her role as pastor?

"I get tired," she admits, "but I'm feeling real excitement. My work in the congregation is a brand-new adventure."

Helen Oriole, who has been secretary of the church for almost a half century, says, "Louisa Groce has done a wonderful job. She's our fourth pastor, since the church was founded in 1898. The first, Dr. John Heindel was here for 43 years. Dr. Edwin J. Grubb for 25 years and Rev. John W. Johnson, Jr. for 29. It's a warm, family congregation, 85 percent African-American at this point, and Pastor Groce has fit right in."

Louisa Groce may not match the tenure of her predecessors, but there's no question that she'll leave her mark.

Mark A. Staples of The Lutheran Theological Seminary at Philadelphia contributed to this profile.

# Some Jump For Health On A Trampoline, Others....

Look! Up there! It's that's 94-year-old guy jumping out of an airplane! Extraordinary? Mind-boggling? Unbelievable?

Right on counts one and two. Wrong on Count Three. As of May 2003, Allan "Bud" Reid has sky jumped two times. And he says he's not finished.

Reid made his first skydive June 22, 2002, in Germansville, Pennsylvania, near his hometown of Eddystone; the second time was four months later at Sky Dive City in Zephyr Hills, Florida, near The Fountains, the retirement village where he now lives.

Looking back on that first jump, Reid laughs, "I was praying for rain, or that the parachute club would turn me down because of my

©2003, Dirk Shadd

age. No such luck. I had to do it to save face, especially after passing my physical on the ground before being cleared to jump." Ironically, a considerably younger friend, whom Reid was visiting, took the test also and failed due to his weight.

Reid claims he had no previous interest in flying until a friend got him interested in skydiving. "You'll love it," the friend told him. "There's nothing like that sensation of free falling."

"There are a lot of people to thank for getting me to the point where I could do this including my niece, who's a flight attendant near Knoxville, TN," Reid says. "She was the one who arranged for the flight. And believe it or not, one of my doctors says that skydiving was the best medicine I ever had."

**"There's nothing like that sensation of free falling."** 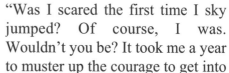 "Was I scared the first time I sky jumped? Of course, I was. Wouldn't you be? It took me a year to muster up the courage to get into that airplane, but I did it. And the first time I free fell, then saw the parachute pop, the fear dissolved and I felt the most unimaginable thrill. There I was floating high over the Pennsylvania countryside with my family and friends on the ground below, all cheering and shouting and waving. I waved back. I made a nice soft landing and they almost smothered me with hugs and kisses."

Making that first jump took more than Reid waking up one summer morning and deciding to astonish his family, friends and fellow residents at The Fountains, a retirement community in St. Petersburg, Florida. What's truly astonishing is that seven years before when Reid moved to The Fountains, he was bed-ridden with Guillain-Barré syndrome (GBS).

GBS typically begins with weakness and/or abnormal sensations of the legs and arms. It can also affect muscles of the chest, face and eyes. Although many cases are mild, some patients are virtually paralyzed. Breathing muscles may be so weakened that a machine is required to keep the patient alive. Many patients require an intensive care unit during the early course of their illness, especially

if support of breathing with a machine is required. Although most people recover, the length of the illness is unpredictable and often months of hospital care are required. The majority of patients eventually return to a normal or near normal lifestyle, but many endure a protracted recovery and some remain wheelchair-bound indefinitely. In Reid's case, he was told he might never walk again. Although the cause of GBS is not known, nor is there is a known cure, Reid, with the help of nurses and physical therapists at the Fountains, responded aggressively with special exercises. Now, Reid walks with the slight assistance of a cane, a far cry from succumbing to a doctor-prescribed electric wheelchair. "Two years ago," he says, I was taking four different kinds of medicine. Today, the only medicine I take is regular exercising."

Reid was born on February 23, 1909 in Eddystone, PA. Right out of high school, he went to work at Baldwin's Locomotive Works in Eddystone, designing locomotives, then tanks during the war. At night he attended Drexel Institute, an engineering college for three years.

*Never Too Old*                                                                 *235*

He retired on May 1, 1974 from Babcox and Wilcox where he'd worked for 18 years, designing buildings including one for Florida Power. Previously, he had done electrical work on buildings and houses in Philadelphia area for 20 years.

After retiring, Reid enjoyed playing golf, traveling with his niece, and just "taking it easy." He traveled to places like the Grand Canyon, Knoxville, TN, and his

> **"Two years ago I was taking four different kinds of medicine. Today, the only medicine I take is regular exercising."**

hometown of Eddystone. On one visit to Eddystone, he visited the house where he grew up as a boy.

"The people living there now couldn't have been nicer," Reid said. "They invited me in and had me look around. It was quite an experience."

Reid loves children and often visits Pennsylvania to visit his great-great nieces and nephews and his flight attendant niece who arranges his flying adventures.

"My goal is to jump once a year until I'm 100 years old," Reid says. "Each year I'll go up an extra 1,000 feet, so I can break all the records. I can't wait."

*It's Never Too Late to Plant a Tree*

# 93-Year-Old Champ
# On and Off the Court

When Roland Sharer left Lincoln Electric Company at 73, he went to a court, where he could represent himself. And he won.

Before line judges and a stadium of critical jurors wishing, "I hope I can do that when I'm his age," he became the men's 90-and over national doubles champion with his partner, Emil Johnson, in 2001 and again in 2002 on clay, hard and grass courts. In fact, Sharer and Johnson have yet to lose a set in tournament play.

Early in his career, he was employed by Lincoln Electric. Within a few years, he became a district sales manger and, during his 46

©2003 Bruce Strong/Light Chasers

years of service helped Lincoln become the world's largest manufacturer of arc welding equipment. Sharer lectures on developing employee compensation systems that produces quality products built on teamwork and is a favorite case history at business schools, like Harvard.

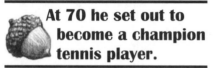

**At 70 he set out to become a champion tennis player.**

Father of six children and a division of grandchildren and great-grandchildren, when Sharer left Lincoln, he immediately founded Roland Sharer and Associates. Long-time colleagues were hardly surprised that he would become a management consultant to clients, who could benefit from his Lincoln Electric profit-sharing concept.

What startled family and friends was Sharer's decision three years earlier to set off at 70 to become a champion tennis player. "Why not?" he said. "I've been competitive all my life. In high school, I was a student council president, a member of the debate team and an honor student. At Lincoln Electric, I always had great fun on the firing line. And I don't like losing."

It helped that he had been an athlete all his life. Born in Nashville in 1910 (his former home is now the site of the Grand Ole' Opry), in high school he ran the mile, pitched for the baseball team and played tennis. During the summers he played semi-pro baseball and was disappointed that he never reached the major leagues. The only serious sports injury he ever suffered was a broken nose while swimming.

Now a day he beats opponents who were professional tennis coaches or had played on their country's Davis Cup team. "We're more mobile than our opponents. I can get to the drop shots." In tennis, he's a smash with a string of gold trophy balls he's won.

"Competitive tennis fame and business contacts are a great one-two combination," he claims. The tennis tournaments Sharer enters all over the country give him the opportunity to visit present and potential clients.

"I want to wear out, not rust out," he says. "I'm blessed. My mother nursed me, so I had the best of health from the crib." He avoids smoking or drinking alcohol or coffee. Dairy food and bread is a mainstay of his diet, plus meat, potatoes and green vegetables. He never uses supplements and is a strong believer in exercise including yard work.

Today, he grows apple trees, harvests raspberries and grows dinner plate dahlias. He sleeps six to seven hours a night. Up at 5:30 a.m. he plays tennis three times a week. When he's not playing tennis, he exercises for 10 to 30 minutes per day and prefers to walk up stairs rather than take the elevator on short trips.

His retirement advice is don't retire, maintain a positive attitude and stay active–physically and socially in your community. Sharer directed Cub Scout baseball for 25 years and also maintains social contact with friends all over the country. His goal is not only to beat other players but also outlive them. He often quotes George Burns' famous quip, "I don't get any joy out of it, but each year I notice I have less and less peer pressure."

How does he stay young? "Love your fellow man. See the good in people," is his answer. His lady-friend is 20 years younger, and when we have dinner, he says, it starts out with a blessing before and a kiss afterward.

Asked why he dates younger women, he answers, "What choice do I have?"

# Never Say "Never" Even When Time's Not on Your Side

Rubin George Weser is past 80 years old and since 1991 he's been trying to get into law school. Only to be turned down time and time again. If you ask him what's going on, he'll tell you, "Their strategy is to stall it, so I will go away, fly away or expire."

**"It was time to follow my dream. So in 1991, I applied to law school. I was**

Weser is not likely to go away or fly away, and he has no plans to expire. What he's doing is suing the law school to be admitted. At first, he hired lawyers to represent him. As the bills mounted, he decided to do the legal work himself and now represents himself (*pro se* in legalese) in appealing his case to a higher court. You might call it on-the-job training for a law career to which he's always aspired.

The story goes back to after World War Two, when Weser started a commercial insurance business. Why commercial insurance? "It was the closest I could get to the law, and there's a lot I learned that'll be of help if I finally become a lawyer."

He had done well financially in commercial insurance, first supporting his three sisters, then his wife, Lillian, whom he married in 1954 and their two sons, Lloyd and Matthew. Getting an education beyond his high school diploma was something he squeezed in on the side at Empire State College, a division of the State University of New York that offers adults a flexible way of obtaining degrees. In the late 1980's, he decided to sell his business. Four decades was enough. ("It seems longer," he says.) Now, it was time to move on. The question was what to do next.

"All my life I wanted to be a lawyer. But growing up as a Jewish kid during the Depression, being a lawyer wasn't the greatest idea in the world for making a living. Still, when I was a young man, I'd offer to carry lawyers' briefcases, just so I could hear their arguments." He leans back in his armchair against a pillow, embroidered with the words, "If I had known grandchildren were so much fun, I would have had them first."

"Going to the gym and to the library, reading, playing with my grandchildren was fine. Adam is 12. Erica is 9. What a pair. Adam's a chess whiz, and he says to me, 'Just wait, Grandpa, when I become a lawyer, we'll take care of them.' And Erica draws beautifully, and is she smart!"

If you press him, Weser will admit he has to be busy, and those kinds of activities weren't enough for him. Neither were busy-busy tasks, like doing chores. He leans forward, confidentially, "I try to get out of the house before my wife opens her eyes because she finds things for me to do. Like grocery shopping, which I hate, especially with those coupons she always collects." He smiles, "But I'm very good with the coupons. When the store owners see me coming they want to send me to their competitors." He pauses before going on.

"It was time to follow my dream. So in 1991, I applied to law school, and I was rejected." That didn't faze him. He just kept coming back, six times in all until 1997, when he decided he was being discriminated against because of his age, sex, race, and religion.

The school's lawyers claim that's not true. Weser, they argue, was rejected because his low scores on the LSAT's and the nature of his undergraduate education raised concerns about his ability to complete law school successfully.

Weser shakes his head in disbelief that the federal circuit judge accepted those arguments. "As far as I know, the law school has no minimum or formal cut-off score for the LSAT's. Any judge with good common sense would have said, 'The guy wants to go to law school, put him in law school.' Then if I don't cut the mustard, so be it."

©2003, Thomas Hart Shelby

*It's Never Too Late to Plant a Tree*

Weser's case has now moved to the federal court of appeals, one step below the U.S. Supreme Court, and Weser is acting as his own attorney. "If I can get the 2$^{nd}$ Circuit to reverse the lower court's ruling against me, I'll be in a small group of *pro se*'s who've won such a ruling."

The challenges keep mounting. The 2$^{nd}$ Circuit affirmed the lower court's decision to dismiss the appeal. Weser responded by submitting a petition for a re-hearing *en-banc* (the full court, rather than the 3 judges who regularly hear appeals from the lower courts.)

What makes him keep moving like an irresistible force? His son, Matthew, a lawyer, says he never doubted his father's persistence. "He doesn't give up," he says. "It's just not in his nature. When I was a boy and he was running his insurance business, I'd hear him on the phone arguing about one insurance point or another until whoever was on the other end of the line gave in."

"Wait a minute," says Weser. "Sure, I like to argue, and I'm pretty good at winning, but there were

**Weser says he's stubborn about his case. "Right is right," he argues.**

plenty of times when I compromised. Compromise, negotiation—that's what it's all about. I'll tell you something else. In all my years in business, I never sued anybody."

As for being stubborn, Weser says he has plenty of reasons to be stubborn about his case. "Right is right," he argues. "I'm not making this stuff up. In my neighborhood, we have a bagel store with a bunch of my old cronies, guys in their '70's and '80's. I'd treat them like a jury, and you know what they ended up with? 'What's the matter with them? Why don't they just let you in?'"

"The pit bull" is not ready to give up. *The New York Times* and *Newsday* ran long interview features on him. The networks are interested in bringing him onto their talk shows.

As we go to press, we don't know how this story will end. Weser is considering an appeal to the U.S. Supreme Court. And if some nationally known attorney were to come forward and represent him on a *pro bono* basis, he'd be delighted. What we do know is that Rubin George Weser could teach a law school class on "Never say, 'Never.'"

# New Business

Our new business ventures stretch from "A" to "Z".

It's literally true: from "Alpacas" to "Z Right Bank." If you're not acquainted with either, read on. You'll be enlightened and delighted. Among the 60+ nominees we've profiled, a solid 20% are engaged in entrepreneurial activities. We have growers of exotic flowers to women in their 70's who are vigorous outdoor adventurers.

Previous occupations give little hint of the roads they've taken or the new horizons for which they reach. We don't have any former "butchers, bakers, candle-stick makers," but how about: a long-time printing press operator; a college president; a foreign correspondent, held hostage for seven years; an NFL referee; a physician; a husband-and-wife team from the educational system.

And what is the source of their inspiration? In one case, proud of adventuresome daughters who were having a great time, Mom decided it was her turn. A one-time farm boy, whose grandmother was a first-class cook, picked up her old recipes and sold his culinary treats to supermarkets. A dentist, plagued by silverfish in his bathroom, came up with a solution and turned into a business. A love of horses transformed a vascular surgeon into a trainer.

Wondering about the next offbeat business venture? It could be yours.

# A Hostage for Seven Years, He Has A Right To Sing the Blues

He had stopped to drop off his tennis partner, when suddenly a green Mercedes drifted to a halt in front of Terry Anderson's car. As an AP foreign correspondent in Beirut, Lebanon, he was used to seeing bearded men jump into and out of cars. It was so common, the cars were called "hamster-mobiles." But this one was no joke. Those three men were armed with pistols, and before Anderson could take evasive action, they had surrounded his car. There was no escape. One reached in and yanked off his eyeglasses. Then they pulled him out of his car and shoved him into their Mercedes.

 **They pulled him out of his car and shoved him into their Mercedes.**

"It's political," shouted one of the men. Anderson immediately knew what that meant. He was being kidnapped, just like William Buckley, a U.S. diplomat, and Rev. Benjamin Weir and Father Lawrence Martin Jenco, American missionaries. He had written about these hostages taken by the Iranian-financed Hezbollah. Now he was one of them.

Although the Associated Press and his family reminded the world unceasingly that Anderson was a captive, he remained a hostage in the bowels of Beirut for nearly seven years.

Before his capture on March 16, 1985, Anderson had made his mark for taking on the toughest and riskiest assignments as chief Middle East correspondent for AP. Then for 2,545 days he was living, when often he wanted to die, under the most precarious conditions imaginable.

"Imagine it," wrote Scott McLeod of *Time Magazine*. "You are chained to a radiator in a bare, dank room. You never see the sun.

When your captors fear that a noise in the night is an impending rescue attempt, you are slammed

**"You can't appreciate blues music unless you've suffered," he claims.**

up against the wall, the barrel of a gun pressed against your temple. Each day you have 15 minutes to shower, brush your teeth and wash your underwear in the bathroom sink. Your bed is a mat on the floor. One of your fellow hostages tries to escape, and the guards beat him senseless. Another tries to commit suicide. One day you reach the edge of your sanity. You begin furiously pounding your head against a wall. Before you pass out, all you remember is the blood."

Anderson's story, captured in his best selling autobiography, *Den of Lions,* demonstrated to the world the remarkable potential of the human spirit to triumph over adversity.

Ask Anderson what got him through, and he will name three elements: faith, determination and music. As a former Roman Catholic, who had dropped out of the church as a teenager, he was

©2003, Terry E. Eiler

*It's Never Too Late to Plant a Tree*

searching for his own God. As a former Marine, he was a model of resourcefulness and daring. He was determined that he would stay alive. And it was music, part humor, part lyrics and poetry that kept his mind stimulated when his body often begged him to let it go.

When you're starving, you dream about food, and so often Anderson's hope was that when he was released, he would manage a restaurant that played his favorite music, the blues. That's how humor helped. His cellmate, the Rev. Terry Waite, and he would sit on their mats and plan the details of a New York restaurant. At first they decided to call it "The Hostage." All the customers would be blindfolded, would be served terrible food, and there would be a lot of screaming and yelling. "But it would never be a success," joked Anderson, "In New York, who would notice?"

After he was released, Anderson answered a reporter's question about his attitude toward his Islamic abductors, "I am a Christian. I am required to forgive. There is no other choice."

He decided to retire from being a foreign correspondent but not from journalism. For a few years he taught at Columbia University's School of Journalism; then, when he and his wife, Madeleine, had had enough of New York's "hecktivity," they moved to a farm in Ohio.

"I wanted to make life positive," he said. "I didn't want to work at a profession where you are cataloguing the world's follies one after another. It's no pleasure to watch people die."

He taught at Ohio University, raised horses and cattle, won a multi-million dollar lawsuit against the government of Iran and decided to open his dream restaurant and blues bar.

It took him two years to put all the pieces together. First, he found a partner, Joel Schechtman; then, he found a location in a college town that had 17 bars and restaurants, but not one that catered to adults and blues music.

The partners agreed that the restaurant must have music. "Maybe it's because I needed to sing," said Anderson. "But it had to be the blues.

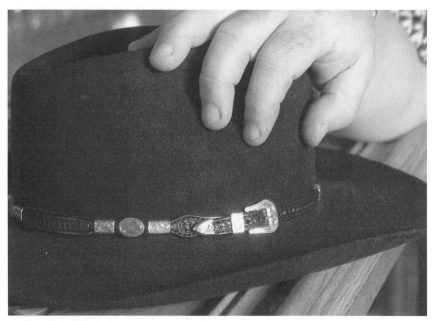

I have a lousy voice. Even though I took voice lessons, I was still the only one whom a parish priest once asked to avoid singing during a service. But anyone can sing the blues."

"You can't appreciate blues music unless you've suffered," he claims. "It's the only music and lyrics that reflect the lives of real people, not sentimental daze, about how many miles you've gone. Artist and vocalists need to be bashed. It's also sexy music," claims Anderson, "and my beautiful wife and I like to dance."

His "Blue Gator" bar brings in national acts from New Orleans and California to his small college town. He works the tables like a Toots Shor, but in his black cattleman's Stetson, cowboy boots and blue jeans, Anderson encourages his growing clientele to "be involved with the music." His menu includes epicurean gourmet food and quality wine, which he personally selects. A year after he started he was making money. Not bad for a retirement hobby.

Now able to invest in almost any kind of business, Anderson still dreams of food, "Good food. Good food," he repeats, "Almost any kind of food." He owns two restaurants, a delicatessen and an international foods business, which produces pasta and imports specialties from scores of countries. He'll never go hungry again.

But he is also a philanthropist, supporting a farm for troubled children in Colorado, a Vietnam children's fund that built 25 new schools, and a committee, that he co-chairs with Walter Cronkite, to protect journalists from physical, financial and legal intimidation.

Anderson's retirement life may be best summed by his own poetry:

*"No man can ever start anew completely*
*He's everything he's ever done or said or failed to do.*
*Each bit is added on, altering the whole,*
*But covering, not replacing what has gone before.*
*A piece of unfired clay, he bears the marks and scars of all his years.*
*Not just clay, though –sculpture, too;*
*Object, artist audience, sometimes, though, larger hands –*
*Destiny, fate, karma, God –take firmly hold and,*
*Wielding fierce events, risk fracture to hack and carve away*
*Some awkward, ugly bits.*
*The final work cannot be seen until it's fired and all fires cooled.*
*Paul knew: suffering and pain are the truest ways, and only ways for some of us,*
*To draw out that within which answers to the purpose of it all."*


E-mail: taa51@hotmail.com

# The Huggable Investment

When Josiah Blackmore retired as president of Capital University, he knew he needed something more than part-time teaching. "I don't play golf and I wanted something that would keep my blood circulating, and that my wife and I could do together," he said.

*So like ol' McDonald, he bought a farm. Ee-i, ee-i - o.*

"We found a historic home built in 1841 in Blacklick, Ohio. We call our farm Blackmore Vale, the English setting of Thomas Hardy's novel *Tess of the d'Urbervilles*," he said. "It was a place where life proceeded more delicately and slowly than the rest of the world. That's just our style and that's exactly what we found."

*And on his farm he had an alpaca. Ee-i ee-i – o.*

Reading an airline magazine article titled *Alpacas: The Huggable Investment* introduced Blackmore to breeding and raising alpacas for fleece, which the industry calls fiber. Perhaps alpacas' biggest

©2003, Bruce Strong/Light Chasers

commercial asset is the value of their fiber. While sheep's wool is valued at ten cents a pound, alpaca fiber is valued at over $30-$50 a pound. Not only is it rare, but also the non-allergic fiber is lighter, softer, and more durable than wool. Suri fiber, from a rare alpaca breed, sometimes is worth $16 per ounce.

After reviewing basic materials, the Blackmores visited some of the state's 140 alpaca farms operating at that time (there are now more than 400) to learn the business.

> **Sheep's wool is ten cents a pound; Suri fiber sometimes is worth $16 per ounce.**

"We both love animals and didn't want to raise animals that we'd have to send to market. You only shear alpacas, and our five-acre farm at Blackmore Vale looked like a perfect place where we could keep them."

They started their farm in 1999 with two alpacas. Soon hordes of people kept coming to see the animals, asking a hundred questions. What started as a way merely to show a few alpaca products has become a busy enterprise. So much so that the Blackmores can't even produce all the alpaca fiber they need. So they keep adding stock until they now have 26 alpacas plus two llamas that guard the alpacas against dogs and coyotes. Customers can see the alpacas in the field, then walk into the barn and browse in the alpaca store.

"We had no intention of creating a growing retail business, but that's exactly what we have now," he claims.

*With an alpaca here, an alpaca there, here an alpaca, there an alpaca, everywhere an alpaca.*

While Blackmore relied on his legal skills (he'd been a law professor) to open the store, he says the real achievement was being creative enough to market a product that isn't abundant anywhere in the area. The Blackmores send their sheared fiber to Peru to process into yarn and manufacture into alpaca clothing, blankets and stuffed animals. The demand is so huge that the Blackmores can profitably sell them in a retail store on their farm.

"Before," said the professor, "I was metaphorically shoveling a lot of stuff, and now I'm doing it for real."

In addition to welcoming visitors to the farm, they participate in a fiber cooperative program and even take a few of the animals to local schools, nursing homes and libraries for show-and-tell exhibits.

Besides being beautiful, alpacas are unusually affectionate and kind. They learn quickly, like to be rubbed on their necks and backs when they trust their handlers, and are unusually obedient.

Breeding alpacas in the U.S. is a baby industry that is growing almost geometrically each year. There are no more than 40,000 alpacas in the U.S. and they are the country's fastest growing livestock. Ohio farms have about ten percent of that census.

A gelded male can be sold for as little as $1,000. A pregnant female can fetch up to $21,000 and has a gestation period of 11½ months. Alpacas live an average of 20 years. Each baby, called a "cria," can be sold for several thousand dollars. Not too many equity investments pay off so quickly.

The maintenance for alpacas is comparatively light. They need to be fed only once or twice a day; eight can graze contentedly on an acre of grass (while horses require an individual acre of pasture). Since their normal habitat is the Andes Mountains of central Peru, they are comfortable outdoors in the winter. During hot summer periods, they require a fan in the barn, and they love to splash in children's plastic pools.

Blackmore's advice to all other retirees: "Let go of the stresses of your former life and enjoy the benefits of your new one."

"I'm living with a value system where harmony and peace are my objectives. The simplicity of this new life permits me to think about other things and not get bogged down in the trivia of the day. And my blood pressure has dropped dramatically.

"After you've served for decades in education and law, you realize you don't have to prove yourself anymore. When you let go of that, you discover you can have an influence on other things. You realize that if you can help one person, then your reason for existence keeps going on, and you find satisfaction in it. I had one of the most fortunate careers that a person could ask for. Now in retirement I'm fortunate to be doing something rewarding and pleasurable. You can't ask for a better sequence than that."

**"No one else will listen to me sing."**

"My wife and I have fallen in love again, not only with each other but with a magnificent animal. Each has a character personality, which is why we gave them names like Jenny Lind, Jamaica, Alex the Great, Amadeus, and Topa Aqui."

They are the only animals that can shed tears, claims Blackmore. "I'll never forget the night I was trying to extract a cria that was attempting to be born but locked in a position in the mother's womb that could strangle her. As I worked feverishly to help, a group of alpacas came to the stable door and just stood and watched. When the female started to cry out in pain, tears came down her cheeks and some of the other alpacas started to tear up as well. It was an amazing sight, crying alpacas. When I was finally successful and the cria emerged, the tears stopped rolling, the group of alpacas "hummed" and they walked away with pleasure."

"Sometimes I think I'm Dr. Doolittle and I can talk to the animals. No one else will listen to me sing. That's when I know my alpacas are not only huggable, they're also grateful for everything I do. Go beat that!"

*With a clip- clop here an' a clip-clop there, here a clop, there a clop, everywhere a clip-clop, Professor Blackmore has a farm, ee-i, ee-i-o.*

E-mail: jblack7629@aol.com

*Betsy Butler, for* Business First Magazine, *contributed to this profile.*

# Don't Call Me a Horse Whisperer

For more than 35 years, Dr. William Evans, a renowned vascular surgeon, improved the lives of countless very sick, often fragile patients.

He was rarely aware, however, that the time expenditure and the high-pressure work environment were endangering his own life. Even the onset of high blood pressure, the discovery of diabetes, the need for a coronary stent and treatment for cancer of the prostate failed to penetrate the sense of immortality so characteristic of surgical personalities.

His doctor insisted he quit, but Evans response was a quote he had heard often from his father, "Hell, doc, the only way to kill one of us hill jacks is to cut off his head and hide it somewhere he can't find it." Evans went back to work.

©2003, Bruce Strong/Light Chasers

*It's Never Too Late to Plant a Tree*

It was only after sudden hospitalization, required for the worsening of his condition, that he admitted that more than minor readjustments in his work habits were required. Retirement, the oxymoron of any surgeon's vocabulary, was not only proposed, it was ordered.

"Maybe you don't know the meaning of the word 'out,'" his doctor told him bluntly. "Get out or you're going to die."

Evans reluctantly accepted the logical solution.

> **Retirement, the oxymoron of any surgeon's vocabulary, was not only proposed, it was ordered.**

He returned to the farm where he and his children had ridden horses for more than twenty-five years. He continued a horse-breeding program, begun a few years before, and he added cattle to the mix. The horse and cattle ventures helped, but didn't fill the void.

He thought writing might be the challenge he needed. Although he had published more than 100 scientific articles and textbook chapters, he rarely read, let alone tried writing a novel. So he studied the writing craft and read all the classics. While he worked part time on a psychiatric service at the local VA, he completed two books and began writing a third. The writing was satisfying, but it was not very rewarding. Editors, he discovered, only wanted books submitted through agents, and agents only wanted to represent authors who were already published. The catch-22 was all too obvious.

Yet, the answer to his conundrum was only two hundred feet from his front door, in his own barn. Evans heard of Buck Brannaman, the famous horse trainer. Buck had just directed the horse work for Robert Redford's film *"The Horse Whisperer,"* so Evans went to one of Buck's training clinics. He was instantly hooked. Through Buck's books and tapes, as well as one-on-one work with Buck's protégé, Bob King, Evans' next few years were spent learning the techniques of horse training that Buck and the others had mastered.

He learned that the initial training of a horse takes place in the confines of a 60-foot round pen. He had that on his farm. The small space provides adequate control of the horse, and most of the training is done from the ground, because almost everything the horse needs to know can be mastered without mounting.

The method centers on the continuous application of light pressure by the trainer until the young horse gives to the pressure, followed by

> **"The owners have tears in their eyes, when they see the progress their horse has made," claims Evans.**

instant release of the pressure. For example, light pressure applied to the halter through a lead rope is maintained until the horse gives in to the pressure, which is then instantly released. With repetition, the horse quickly learns that giving in to the pressure always results in the reward of the release. Pressure is applied to the legs, the neck and the body and in each instance the response is the same. Saddling, bridling, mounting and riding all follow the same pattern creating a gentle, responsive, safe and tractable mount.

Evans' medical intellect was shifted to the challenge of learning how a horse's mind processes information, how that process can be accessed, as well as the development of the physical skills required to put it all together. All this more than met the measure of his previous profession.

Evans decided to start a training farm for pleasure horses and thoroughbreds. And as Buck once told him, "The only bad things that can happen to you once you begin training horses are to run out of daylight or run out of horses that need work."

Today, Evans trains and boards horses. "Just don't call me a horse whisperer. It's not a professional term," he says.

He and an assistant normally work four horses a day over a 30 to 60 day period. The benefits are dramatic when colts quickly respond to proper training. "The owners have tears in their eyes, when they see the progress their horse has made," claims Evans. "After all, the horse has a very important place in their hearts."

More importantly, Evans blood pressure and diabetes soon were controlled, the coronary disease has stabilized and the cancer appears to be cured. He is convinced that horse training saved his life. "It's betting on horses that can kill ya'" he jokes.

Though different from his first career, the second is every bit as satisfying. In the meanwhile, on rare occasions that he has extra time, he pecks away at his novels in the hope that someday he may find an editor who takes in literary strays.

E-mail: wmevans@bright.net

# This Sunday Zebra
# Is A Performer

The test for Art Holst is not how good you are, but "how good can you be? "

**Art Holst still controls his game of life.**

For most of his professional life, Holst was a salesman and foundation administrator. He served his community on civic committees. Then he spent 15 years as a top official in the National Football League (NFL). Now in his 80's and retired from officiating, Holst combines both experiences as a motivational humorist lecturing on excellence in management.

He gave his first speech for free to a hometown Rotary club, as a last minute sub for the governor of Illinois. "What made me a

©2003 Lon Horwedel

humorist was that first speech," he remembers, "when the MC said, 'Here's someone who needs no introduction, because frankly I never heard of him before.' They all thought I wrote the gag line. I didn't. He was right, no one had ever listened to me, including my wife."

Holst's next speech netted him $100 and his third $250. Today he gets up to $6,000 per

**"In sports, as in life, you can't ignore criticism. Boos are part of the game."**

appearance, although he gives time freely to schools and many charitable organizations. It was his NFL experience, being on national TV week after week before millions of football viewers that made him famous. Between NFL officiating and professional speeches to management, sales and educational groups, he was on the road 150 days a year.

At the age of 57, an injury forced him to give up on-the-field officiating. Since his family claimed he traveled too much, he set up his own marketing organization.

He stays affiliated with the NFL as an officiating scout in the Midwest. Every weekend, he attends a college football game and watches, not the players or the score, but the officials. A number he scouted and recruited are officiating in the NFL today.

The hallmarks of a great official, Holst claims, are his knowledge of the game, his judgment and his loyalty to other members of the crew. An NFL official can never let fans know there is a serious dispute among them. Officials must exhibit a tough exterior to coaches and players, but develop a soft inside to respect the players and coaches, and cover for each other.

"In sports, as in life, you can't ignore criticism," says Holst. "Boos are part of the game–'that's spelled boos, not booze.'" He claims officials are at their best when the going gets tough, as in big games that are close to the final minute, and that blowouts are harder to officiate than tight games. The players get more careless and anger gets out of control easier, he explains, provoking more roughness penalties.

"It was at such a rough game in New Orleans that I was blindsided by a 300-pound lineman and lay unconscious on the field for two minutes. When I finally got up and jogged to my officiating position, 78,000 spectators applauded. Well, I officiated big games for 15 years, including three NFL championship games, four NFL division playoffs and two Super bowl games, and the only time I was ever cheered by a crowd was when I got knocked on my ass."

He believes sports are a great metaphor of life. "In the game, you can't predict a fumble or a dropped pass. In life you can't predict dramatic change. Anything can happen, so you can only prepare for it, especially retirement."

One of Art's commandments is for retirees to keep physically fit. "There is little you can do unless you're physically fit. And that takes discipline. You must do the walking, you must do the jogging and you must do the push-ups. They don't come in a bottle or a pill

box." He believes a sharper mental image and physical fitness come as a package. To keep in shape, even at his 80 plus years, he still walks two miles a day or bicycles eight to ten miles a day.

For retirees who dream of getting into sports, Holst is encouraging. Teams at every level, from high school to the pros, are always looking for volunteer help that might turn into a permanent job. You can't become a "Sunday Zebra," the name of a book Holst wrote about his NFL experiences, unless you've worked your way

*It's Never Too Late to Plant a Tree*

©2003 Lon Horwedel

up the officiating ranks for 15 or more years. But with training you can work tomorrow as a ticket taker, an usher, a scorer, a timer, a security guard, or a public address announcer at many sports.

"The big lie has been the social security mentality," he claims, "which suggests to people of 65 that they should retire. For many, that's when people are at their best, because they have a lifetime of experience learning from mistakes and an appreciation of the necessity of goals."

Goals are a major theme of Holst's, and he sometimes finishes a speech with this poem he wrote:

"As I pause to think of something that sets some men apart
It seems to me that goals in life must be the place to start.
Imagine playing football on an unmarked field of green
Not a goal line to be sought, not a goalpost to be seen.
It would be an aimless battle were there nothing to be gained
Without a thing to strive for, nor a score to be attained.
We must have purpose in our lives for the flame that
        warms the soul
Is an everlasting vision. Everyman must have his goal."

As usual, Art Holst gets a standing ovation.

E-mail: aholst33@aol.com

# They Can Spice Up Your Life

Gabe and Margaret Joseph want to add some spice to your life. No, it's not something you'll find advertised in the "Personals" column of a risqué magazine. It's a salad dressing, sold in dry spice packets under the name "Gabe's Gourmet Foods" by a husband-and-wife team, who turned a retirement hobby into a substantial business.

> **"The maitre d' said, 'If you can guess 7 of the 9 ingredients, I'll give you the recipe'. I guessed all nine."**

Gabe was a college administrator and Margaret a K-12 teacher. Joseph always had a passion for cooking and had developed a considerable local following for his vinegar and oil, sweet-and-sour dressing. "I originally made the dressing as gifts," he says. "I'd go the restaurants in Walla Walla, Washington, where we live and the surrounding areas and get their Chianti wine bottles. I'd sterilize them, fill them with the dressing, put fresh corks in the bottles, and present them to friends as gifts.

"When I started, it was only for Christmas, just once a year. Pretty soon it was twice a year, then, four times a year. I was always running out of dressing. Finally, our friends said, 'You're making so much of it, why don't you start doing it commercially?' So that's what we did."

"My recipe goes back to 1968. I worked for a finance company then, and I was on the road quite a bit. I had my wife and kids join me in Spokane for her birthday. The hotel where we stayed had the most wonderful salad. I couldn't get enough. When I asked the maitre d' for the recipe for the salad dressing, he said, 'If you can guess seven of the nine ingredients, I'll give you the recipe'. I guessed all nine.

"During the following 30 years, I kept improving the recipe until it now has 17 different ingredients. It's sweet and/or sour or neutral, blending with many different foods. It's the finest marinade for white fish, chicken, wild game, and pork. It has over 30 different uses."

Joseph claims his ability to make his "unique dressing" comes from having excellent taste buds. Whatever it is, Joseph has something special.

When Joseph took his dressing to be tested to get it licensed to sell commercially, he was asked, "At what temperature is the dressing heated?" Joseph replied, "I don't heat it at all. It would spoil the dressing."

"In that case," said the inspector, "no license."

 **"We developed a five-year plan to make the business successful. We did it in three."**

"Look," Joseph argued, "that dressing was 18 months old when I submitted it. You tested it for an additional 12 months. If it didn't spoil in 30 months, it's not going to spoil, is it?" Joseph got his license and began selling to gourmet shops in the immediate area of Walla Walla.

After Gabe's retirement as an administrator of Walla Walla Community College program at the Washington State Penitentiary in 1990, and Margaret's retirement from the local school district in 1991, the Josephs turned their hobby into a part-time business. Joseph says, "We developed a five-year plan to make the business successful. We did it in three."

At first, the Josephs made and bottled the dressing in the kitchen of the Olive Branch Restaurant in Walla Walla. That meant going to the restaurant after it closed at 10 P.M. They had to haul all their supplies and materials from their home to the restaurant and back because there was no storage available.

©2003, Jeff T. Green Photography

*It's Never Too Late to Plant a Tree*

Opportunity came in the form of a refurbished cannery that was made into a licensed, state, and federally approved kitchen, sponsored by a consortium of federal, state and local organizations in Milton Freewater, Oregon, just 13 miles from Walla Walla. All of the supplies and materials could be shipped to the kitchen. The Josephs also rented storage space.

"We sold to gourmet shops and individuals in trade shows around the North West. Most of our business was in the area of Washington and Oregon, but shops in Atlanta and Idaho bought also. When Margaret and I went on a cruise, we'd play, 'What's My Line?' Nobody ever guessed our line. We'd have a table set up to sample our dressing and took orders."

In 1998, the Josephs gave up their bottled lines and went into dry packaging, because of convenience in shipping. The spices are always fresh and they can receive a new shipment in a week or less.

When asked whether his dressing is ever compared with Paul Newman's, Gabe replies, "I'm not as rich, but I'm better looking. My picture's not on the label, and, frankly, I think my dressing is so much better. So far, I haven't heard from Paul Newman. When we quit bottling, our friends gave us bottles of Paul Newman's dressing. We still have some of those bottles."

E-mail: josephgm@wwwics.com

# Hitting the Trail with the Aging Adventurer

She doesn't look like a typical biker. If you spot her zipping along the road, near her home in Virginia, you won't see any of the familiar biker regalia. In fact, Emily Kimball has osteoporosis, wears two hearing aids, is in her 70's and runs a thriving, full-time business.

To set the record straight, Kimball rides a 21-speed bicycle, not a Harley-Davidson.

"Yes, I'm a big biker," she says, "and I do love to be outdoors. In 1993, I spent 114 days riding my bike across America. I turned 62 while riding in the rain up the going-to-the-sun highway in Glacier National Park. It wasn't the usual birthday, but it was just what I wanted to do, ride the length of the United States from the East Coast to the West Coast. "

©2003, Jay Paul

*It's Never Too Late to Plant a Tree*

True to form, 10 days before Kimball turned 71 in the summer of 2002, she celebrated her birthday by completing a 2,168-mile-hike of the Appalachian Trail, which starts in Georgia and ends in Maine. It was a hike she had begun in 1992, breaking up the strenuous journey by hiking one month each year.

"Hiking the trail, walking and carrying everything on my back, was a lot harder than riding across America," she says, "but it was worth the effort, being outside and enjoying the hike. I love nature, away from all the distractions of society. On the hikes and on my bike, there's no loud music, no talk about wars and the world's problems. You can just be in your own space."

Kimball's serious biking and hiking began after a career in a variety of professional positions, capped by 12 years as an outdoor recreation manager. When she retired, she had two main goals: to bicycle across America and to hike the Appalachian Trail. Sitting indoors and relaxing was not an option.

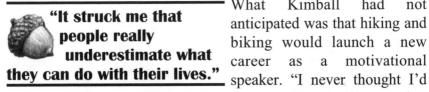

**"It struck me that people really underestimate what they can do with their lives."**

What Kimball had not anticipated was that hiking and biking would launch a new career as a motivational speaker. "I never thought I'd make my living as a speaker," she says. "It just kind of happened. It struck me that people really underestimate what they can do with their lives. I decided that I would go out there and try to share my experiences."

At first, she focused on her adventures. "I told my audiences how when I first started out on the Appalachian Trail, each year I went back to where I ended the previous summer and moved forward. I did it a month at a time. I usually had people with me on the trail, though most of them were faster than me. I met a lot of wonderful people that way."

Those speeches were well received. After a while, she started to talk about her career in outdoor recreation. Later she started talking

©2003, Jay Paul

*It's Never Too Late to Plant a Tree*

about keeping balance in one's life, creative aging and risk taking "I do enjoy influencing people's lives in a positive way and helping them to be all they can be," Kimball says.

As the focus of her speeches evolved, Kimball became more widely known for her public speaking. She now addresses conferences and meetings all over the country, has her own website, www.TheAgingAdventurer.com, and has been interviewed for her expertise by magazines such as *Family Circle*. She was also one of the seniors interviewed on *Forward In Time*, a Public Broadcasting System special on creative aging in fall, 2003.

On her web site, you can find practical advice:
- Focus on personal dreams and long-term career goals.
- Ferret out resources to make dreams happen.
- Remain determined in the face of obstacles.
- Take risks that extend and enrich one's life and work.
- Recover and regroup after failures.

"I'm getting busier all the time," Kimball says. She now books speeches far ahead of time and is excited about having the opportunity to reach more people. The hardest part, she adds, is marketing herself, so that more organizations and individuals learn about her public speaking.

"It's not easy," Kimball says. "It's a continual job. That's how I spend my time each day, but I still seem to be able to do what I want to do. I exercise every morning and I do something active every single day of the week."

In her workshops and speeches, Kimball talks to people about reaching their dreams, and explains how she achieved hers. She also addresses business groups on the subject of setting and achieving goals. One of the nicest parts of her job, she says, is hearing from people who reach their goals.

"People seem to get inspired," Kimball says. "They leave the workshops and speeches with some concrete ideas on how to move ahead. They seem energized."

She figures that when her audience sees that, despite her osteoporosis and hearing difficulties, she can get out and do things, although she's in her 70's, they become more willing to get out and reach for their dreams, too.

Now that she has achieved her goals of hiking the Appalachian Trail **"Walking and carrying everything on my back was a lot harder than riding across America."**  and riding her bike across America, Kimball isn't sure what she will do for her next adventures. "But I'll do something," she says. In the meantime, she knows she'll continue to be busy throughout the year speaking to people, young and old.

Kimball has discovered a number of parallels between the challenges of her extensive hiking and biking expeditions and the dilemmas of everyday living. In confronting each experience, she has followed the advice she gives to others:

- Be a risk taker.
- Be a vital example of creative aging.
- Be a role model to others on how to set, and reach, your highest goals.

Web site: www.theagingadventurer.com

# Her Daughters Were Having So Much Fun, It Changed Her Life

Who's that 70-something woman boating down the Amazon? Wait, I think I remember her from that 17,000-foot climb in the Himalayas. Or, was she the one on a camel in front of us on a 21-day trek across the Sahara Desert?

 **"I decided it was time to prove I could do these things on my own and survive."**

Yes, Yes, and Yes. It's Harriet Lewis, a transformed suburban Great Neck, New York homemaker, who decided at age 53 that it was time for her to start dealing with strenuous life adventures independently and then to share them with others.

"I owe it all to my daughters, Amy, Nancy and Tracy," says Lewis, now 78 and still living in Great Neck. "The whole family was athletic and competitive—tennis and skiing occupying a major portion of our lives—but we traveled in a rather deluxe manner. Then something happened. It was the 60's and 70's. The girls and their friends were backpacking around the world on five dollars a day, and I began to envy the freedom and independence they were experiencing. I felt I was missing out on something. And then there was the Women's Movement. A product of the 30's, 40's and 50's, marriage, motherhood and the expectancy that our husbands would take total care of us was the norm of the day.

"It was, I decided, my moment to change my life, to grow up, to see the world with a backpack, to trek and camp in wild exotic lands. When Dick and I had traveled together, he had always carried our passports, changed our money into foreign currency and checked us into hotels. I was a passive bystander. Now, I decided it was time to prove I could do these things on my own and survive.

©1985, Sikkim. *With Tenzing Norgay, conquerer of Mt. Everest*

*It's Never Too Late to Plant a Tree*

"Each trip I took over the succeeding years was more challenging than the year before. By now, I've probably done 30 or more trips. Because I was usually the oldest one in the group, I had to train hard for those trips, often three months in advance. I would hike the sands of Jones Beach with backpack and hiking boots for three or more hours or climb 34 flights of stairs four times in a nearby apartment building. Nancy, my middle daughter, who was living in Alaska by then, encouraged me to do these things. At times, when doubts would arise as to my abilities to handles the upcoming challenges, I'd say to her, 'Nancy, do you think I'm capable of doing something like this?' And her reply, I've never forgotten her words, was, 'But of course, you can, Mom!'

A tennis competitor at an early age (she was Number 1 ranked player in the East at 18) Nancy's life was forever changed when she went on an Outward Bound survival trip at 19. For the first time she came in contact with the natural world—mountains to be scaled, rivers to be rafted, wildernesses to be explored. From that moment on she sought new and difficult challenges endlessly. In her first summer in medical school, she put a pack on her back and trekked alone for six weeks in Alaska. On returning she announced, 'Alaska is where I'm going to practice medicine.' A family medicine physician for 20 years, she delivered over 2,000 babies. She had a deep and abiding love for Alaska, for its people, for its magnificent mountains and wild rivers.

"As for me, when I first started doing these off-beat trips—the jungles of Borneo, Patagonia, the high Atlas Mountains of Morocco, etc.—Dick didn't go with me. He was still active in the fashion industry, which required him to be in New York City. As for the trekking, he said that World War Two had given him his fill of living out of doors.

"Visiting Nancy regularly in Alaska changed that. Eager to show us an Alaska most tourists never experience, she provided us with unique experiences such as a 65-mile canoe trip on the Noatak River in the northerly Brooks Mountain Range, where we were entirely out of touch with civilization for eight days. Dick had just come down with cancer but that didn't stop him. We went anyways. In all we visited Alaska 16 times, bear watching, moose hunting, and camping on remote rivers."

In time, Harriet Lewis's explorations turned into a side business. "Thinking about these adventures and having documented all of them on film," she says, "I hit on the idea of doing a series of slide shows. You know you can only show your travel pictures to friends once or risk being a terrible bore, but by doing slide presentations of my trips, I get to relive my adventures over and over."

Lewis has been doing this for 18 years now in local libraries and for various organizations, and she finds it amusing that people follow her wherever she goes.

"The slide shows are, more or less, directed towards older women, and the audiences are generally retired people. Yes, there are some men,

**"I hit on the idea of doing a series of slide shows."**

too, but my idea is to challenge women to do things they THINK they're not capable of. I tell them, 'You don't have to cross the Sahara Desert or climb mountains. There are just so many things you imagine you can't do and you'd be amazed at what you can do.' That message runs through all my slide shows and when I talk to people. Very often someone will ask me, 'What was your favorite trip?' and I say I have no favorites. I loved them all.'"

Beyond sharing her adventures with others, Lewis has helped send a boy in Uganda through school, and she works four to five hours a week in a soup kitchen not far from her home.

She recently helped establish an elementary school in Uganda for orphans of mothers who die of AIDs and is busy collecting funds for supplies for the schoolhouse, which was built by volunteers in an impoverished village there. Lewis plans to visit the school in the near future and meet the 50 children who will attend. She is particularly pleased that most of them are girls, who rarely get an education in Uganda.

It's Never Too Late to Plant a Tree

"Meeting people I'd never met before, and doing things I'd never done before has really changed me as an individual," she says. "My value system changed. I paid more attention to the environment. I love bird watching, and I became president of The Audubon Society. And there's another part of the equation that figures in my life. It's my daughters, Amy, a successful, independent businesswoman with three children and Tracy, a psychotherapist, who probably holds the record for independent travel in the family.

Nancy's life ended on June 15, 2001, piloting her own plane with three friends, a nine-year-old boy and his parents.

In addition to being Harriet's adventurer partner—the Lewises have been married for 55 years—Dick calls himself "a perennial student." After 50 years in the fashion industry, he decided to go back to school, having missed college during the Depression years when he was growing up. So, at age 74, he graduated magna cum laude with a B.A. in history from Long Island University's C.W. Post College. The next day he went back and started working on a second baccalaureate in criminal justice. He now uses this knowledge as a volunteer in the office of Nassau County's District Attorney.

Harriet Lewis's health is excellent ("She can outrun someone half her age," says Amy Tabor, her eldest daughter), Dick Lewis, now 81, has pushed on in the face of prostate cancer and heart problems. Together they intend to keep going, still guided by daughter Nancy's memory and reassurance, "But, of course, you can."

E-mail: rclew676@aol.com

# I Have Longevity On My Side

For Clifford Matson, bedding down in his car was the only way for him to enter college.

On his own, young Matson had come to Oregon from his home in South Dakota. It was the midst of the Depression, and in order to go to college at the resident rate, living in the state for one full year was required. "I stuck it out for one year and 17 days, doing odd jobs, finding lodging wherever I could, whatever it took so I could qualify for the tuition rate of $26 a semester." Matson says with a chuckle, "Can you imagine that? $26 a semester."

It is 1998 and Matson, now age 80 and a retired dentist, is living comfortably in his home in Junction City, Oregon. His days of sleeping in the car are far behind, but his inventive mind is as alert as ever, and he loves to solve problems. He watches silverfish scuttling about in his bathroom. Not pleasant. A seasoned putterer, he wonders how to get rid of them. He's been reading a book about Neem trees, with seeds that serve as natural pesticides. The trees are native to India and Myanmar (formerly Burma), but if it works there, why not in Oregon?

**In order to go to college at the resident rate, having lived in the state for one full year was required.**

He applies a couple of drops of Neem oil to a small cork square, similar to the ones separating double-pane windows in his bathroom and waits for the next invasion. Zap! The silverfish are dead. His next target is cockroaches. Zap! Down they go.

It takes two years for the Patent Office to approve his application. In order to avoid a protracted struggle, Matson drops Neem oil as a pesticide and switches to cedar oil, which he applies to Cork-EZ, an adhesive backed piece of cork, the size of a Scrabble square.

"It works almost as well," he says, "and it smells better."

The key is marketing, and Matson is realistic enough to know that without proper investment and marketing, his invention is likely to go the way of most of the 6-million patents granted before his. So he hires a licensing agent.

"I think we're going to be able to sell in every state in the country," he says, "but right now given the economic situation, getting venture capital is tough. It's a formidable task to get something on the market."

Fortunately, Matson takes the long view. "My father lived to be 92, so I've got those genes on my side."

He also has a reservoir of curiosity that has taken him into a variety of byways.

"I graduated from the university in 1942 and went straight into the Army. Served for three years to the day overseas with the 3rd Infantry Division. When I came back, I got married right out of the service and decided to be a schoolteacher. Did that. Went back to

school, taught some more, the last year as an administrator before I returned to the University of Oregon and the School of Dentistry."

By the time Matson retired in 1982, he was ready to turn to "all the other things I wanted to do, but never had a chance to. I'm just sorry that I got to them so late in life."

Did he find the transition hard? "No, not at all. I looked forward to it. Also in **"One of the things that I did was missionary work in the mountains of Haiti."**  1982, it was a tough economic climate and young fellows coming out of dental school were having a hard time finding work. I felt it was fair to retire and give them a chance.

"No, I have no regrets," he says, "and because I didn't do something before doesn't stop me from trying. Having been a dentist all those years gives me a lot of manual dexterity.

"One of the things that I did was dental missionary work in the mountains of Haiti. That was 1985. It wasn't very long, but it was an interesting experience. I went with one other dentist under the sponsorship of the United Methodist Board of Global Missions. I've worked with senior citizen services in Junction City and around the area. And I have a big yard, and my two daughters have houses, so they ask me to help them out, and I'm glad to do that."

In the meantime, Matson is busy reading books and working with his licensing agent. "He just told me the other day that he bought 150 pounds of cork and a gallon of cedar oil and that he's meeting with a man who's interested in investing. I don't even know who the man is, just that he's interested in the project."

The fact that Matson doesn't have another invention on tap today doesn't mean that he won't have one tomorrow. And while the question wasn't put to him, he'll probably make a great spokesman for Cork-EZ, once it gets to market.

Stand by.

*It's Never Too Late to Plant a Tree*

# Because It's Not Broken Doesn't Mean It Can't Be Improved

When you've been involved with military aerospace, anti-submarine warfare and lunar landings, there are some things you can't talk about, even years later.

That's the case with Al Miller, who was employed by Loral Electronics for a decade. Except what's hard for him to explain has nothing to do with classified material. It's how his inner radar works, when it comes to sensing an opportunity.

"I'm attracted to problems, to fixing things, to making them work," says Miller. That sounds like what an engineer does, which Miller.

©2003, Thomas Hart Shelby

is. It doesn't explain what took him from being an engineer, to salesman – something many engineers are not comfortable doing – to entrepreneur, and, more recently, at his accountant's prompting, to becoming a financial planner.

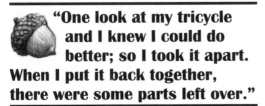

**"One look at my tricycle and I knew I could do better; so I took it apart. When I put it back together, there were some parts left over."**

"I was doing exciting things at Loral during the 1960's," he says, "but I found that I missed being with people. When sales reps called on me, I found it was appealing, something I could do. "I went from engineering to sales because I realized that for me there is more to life than oscilloscopes and electrons. So I joined a manufacturer's representative company selling electronic components, called R.T. Reid Associates, and one my first clients turned out to be Loral. After a few years there, I joined with two others in buying out the company and we renamed it Technical Marketing Group (TMG)."

"We did well with offices in New York and New Jersey for 26 years, but I became restless for another change, so I told my partners that I wanted out, and we negotiated a buyout. At the peak of my earnings, I might add.

"So there I was, financially secure, but ready for something else. Aha, recycling old electronic equipment and extracting gold, silver and other precious metals—that's what I would do. However, after six or seven months of recycling, all my wife could see was the house getting loaded with junk. And she didn't like what she saw.

"Come to think of it, many years before, my tinkering with things got me in hot water with another close female relative—my mother. I was maybe five, and she bought me a tricycle. One look at the tricycle, and I knew I could do better; so I took it apart. When I put it back together, there were some parts left over. 'That's it,' she said, 'no more bicycles for you.' Well, we moved, and after awhile, she relented and bought me a two-wheeler. Okay, you're right, I took it apart. Only this time when I put it together, it was improved.

"In the case of my wife and the recycling, my accountant, Bill, came to the rescue. I was moving up to my 60$^{th}$ birthday. He suggested that I go into investment planning with emphasis on seniors. He even had clients whom he was willing to refer to me. What I found appealing was the opportunity to work with people in a different way than in engineering, to help them plan and solve their problems. The other day I got a call from a man who had just lost his wife. He was distraught and needed to talk. I felt good that he called me for support. Part of it is financial; part of it is just trying to give some guidance, but most of it's people.

"So far, I've done well in sensing opportunities. I think this is another one." Miller sees his various transitions as evolutionary, one building on the other, just like life. "The subtlety here is that I'm the one pushing myself into new areas. In the case of financial planning, it is working for me, because I am, once again, solving problems (like a true engineer), but the problems this time are related directly to people, as compared with business or engineering. Let me give you an example of what I find gratifying."

"One of my accountant's clients came to us a few years ago to ask for help in retiring. He had a good career in banking, was 39, **"When people come to an investment counselor or financial planner, they really lay themselves bare."** and married with two young children. He also was legally deaf, but not from birth. He wanted to help other deaf people cope with their disease. With Bill's help, we set him up with annuities that enabled him and his family to live comfortably, not extravagantly, to pursue the service work he wants to do."

Miller makes no pretext that all of this can be done "abracadabra."

"Once I decided to become a financial advisor, I knew it had to be taken seriously, and realized I would have to become a Certified Financial Planner (CFP), the recognized credential in the field. It's a three-year college program, which is why I hesitated in the first place; after all, recycling doesn't take much training, and doesn't require initials after your name. Anyhow, I took a deep breath and went back to school at C.W. Post in Long Island, New York. In June 2003, I graduated with the college certificate for a CFP. The next hurdle is the national test in November."

Once he has his CFP, where does Miller go next?

"I'm still building my business, and there are a lot of prospects out there. But I'm keeping in mind what I learned from my engineering work – try to focus on a few accounts and get to know them in depth. That way I can understand their needs and better serve them. I discovered from the outset that the sale is more than just walking in the door and walking out with the order. That's what I'm trying to do now, getting to know the families.

"When people come to an investment counselor or financial planner, they really lay themselves bare. And the way government regulations keep changing, it's very difficult to come up with a 'once and for all' plan. What's required is maintenance. And as I go along I can see myself concentrating on maintenance with my clients. Keeping them up to speed and doing the same for myself."

With a son just graduated from Cornell and two children from a first marriage further along in their careers, Miller sees no need to get off his present-day bicycle. He's convinced that all it requires is a careful shifting of the gears. Nor has he given up on real bicycles. In the summer of 2003, he and his wife completed a two-week bike trip through southwest France.

"It was great," he says.

E-mail: miller84@i-2000.com

# Move Over Paris, Zanesville has "Z Right Bank"

For all you seniors who've been there, done that, seen it all as you travel the world, get ready for "Muddy Miser's Cool River Café." It's on the Muskingum River, where novelist Zane Grey learned to fish and not far from where President James Monroe had breakfast. You won't find the café listed in Frommer's, but give it time.

> **Mitzel pictured in his mind's eye a vital, rejuvenated area with condominiums, a restored park, an Event Center and a vibrant nightlife.**

The café, with a seating capacity of only 48, is always packed with young people. Its walls are lined with shelves of Zane Grey books. Other memorabilia include a cancelled check to a fishing boat captain for a chartered trip, one of many in Zane Grey's career as a world-class fisherman, a career on which Muddy Miser launched him as a boy. A long bar looks out on the river, the only café for miles around with such a view.

Carl Mitzel doesn't own the café, but he had a big hand in rescuing the area from further decline and turning it into what it is today. It was early 1999 when Mitzel drove by a 38,000-square-foot building that stretched along the riverfront, not far from where the café sits today. Once the home of Zanesville Mould Company, where moulds for glass products were formed, it had become a storage facility for an embroidery company.

What outwardly was no more than a decaying building, Mitzel, in his mind's eye, pictured as a vital, rejuvenated area with condominiums, a restored park and a vibrant nightlife. All of which it has become.

Mitzel's first step was to buy the old mould building, as well as a nearby house, which became the home of his son, David, and daughter-in-law, Katherine, who had been on the drive with him that day.

**At age 85, Carl Mitzel jokes that he "could be on the National Register," but not to tell the young women who now flock to the Muddy Miser's Cool River Café.**

The deed to the building in hand, the senior Mitzel wasted no time in turning his vision into reality. The proposed condo site adjoined a junkyard and sat across from several houses, well known to the Zanesville Police Department as drug houses. From the time of the purchase of the factory until work began on the conversion in Fall, 2002, Mitzel and two of his sons purchased the drug properties, removed the tenants, and either gutted or mothballed the buildings surrounding the proposed condos. The family also purchased a nearby commercial building in disrepair and began to convert it into an event center.

In June 2003, three years after the death of his wife and two years after his heart bypass surgery, Carl Mitzel moved from his lifelong home in Cleveland into the first of ten luxury river-front condominiums that he built. The condominiums are styled in Federal architecture to match the early architectural treasures nearby.

Mitzel had been a building contractor in Cleveland for more than 50 years. With his father, he had built more than 25 churches and numerous industrial and commercial buildings in northeastern Ohio. His only venture into residential construction was a subdivision of California-style ranches in 1953, a true departure from the homes then being built in his hometown of Rocky River, a western suburb of Cleveland.

The commercial building that the Mitzels made into an Event Center was constructed in the 1890s as a shirt factory. This and several other properties the Mitzels purchased are in the Putnam

©2003, Jackie Belden Hawthorne

Historic District, which is listed on the National Register of Historic Places. Their premier purchase, the Wells-Hazlett house, a finely constructed brick house called "the finest architectural treasure in the county," sits directly across from Carl Mitzel's condo. Constructed in 1808, it also has the distinction of having had its owners host President James Monroe for breakfast in 1817.

At age 85, Carl Mitzel jokes that he "could be on the National Register," but cautions those who know his age not to tell the young women who now flock to the Muddy Miser's Cool River Café next to the condominiums.

"I have realized the best dream possible for a man my age," states Carl. "I live across the street from one son, Ward, who moved from Cincinnati last August, and two blocks from David. I'm leaving a legacy by improving this district. And I'm enjoying the best view of any home in Southeastern Ohio."

Part of his view is downtown, part, the river, and part, the park that his septuagenarian neighbors Bart and Kate Hagemeyer have re-created from the ruins of an earlier park that had become a junkyard. But that is another story of courage, energy, and commitment to resuscitating a dying community through the creation of Restoration Park on the site of the old Spangler Park.

Carl Mitzel's dream has helped encourage other dreamers on each side of the condos: the Hagemeyers with their park and John Starner, a former schoolteacher, who opened Muddy Miser's. The district is now referred to by the name "Z Right Bank" since it is on the right bank of the Muskingum River as it flows southward to the Ohio River at Marietta. As the letterhead of the stationery for the Mitzels' company, Z Right Bank Limited, reads, "Paris has Z Left Bank, and Zanesville has Z Right Bank. *Vive la différence!*"

# Job Satisfaction
# Can Last A Lifetime

I'm Dick Sarns and over the years, my wife, Norma, and I have been able to share our good fortune with others. In one respect, though, we've been stingy. I'm talking about not taking proper vacations from our business.

We're both in our 70's now, and by "proper vacations," I mean anything more than two weeks at a time. Maybe it has to do with growing up as a kid during the Depression. I don't know. I'm not a psychologist. Anyhow, when our 50$^{th}$ anniversary rolled around in 2002, we shot the works and booked a two-month 24,000-mile cruise in the South Pacific Ocean. The cruise was terrific, and maybe we'll do more travel of that kind in the future.

The surprise on the cruise was the insight it provided me into the kinds of businesses

**"What kind of wake-up call does the senior generation need to get off the couch?"**

I've been in. Don't smirk. I really had been determined to keep my mind off work, and I wasn't being sneaky. Let me explain.

I'm an engineer and I've been with health and fitness companies my entire professional life, so I may be something of a fitness nut. Early each morning I'd be up on deck to get the juices flowing. The only reason Norma wasn't with me is that she had childhood polio and has had to contend with limited physical mobility. Not that it's stopped her in other ways. She's been at my side, day in and day out.

Anyhow, back to the ship. Out of 250 people on board, maybe four or five other early birds were on deck, usually younger women. Same scene when I'd work out in the gym; four or five younger women. Nice company, but where were my contemporaries? Given the advances in medical science, the relationship between fitness and aging, I wonder what kind of wake-up call the senior generation needs to get its citizens off the couch and away from the dinner table. If you don't fall in that category, good for you.

I'll back up a bit. In 1967, when Dr. Christian Barnard of South Africa performed the first human heart transplant, he used the Sarns Model 2000 heart-lung machine, which my company, Sarns, Inc. developed and produced. A dependable heart-lung machine was a huge leap forward. Nevertheless, in those days, if the patient made it through the miracle of not breathing and not pumping his or her own blood, while a heart-lung machine sustained life, the follow-up procedure, invariably, was bed rest and more rest.

Since then, we've learned the importance of *getting out of bed* as soon as feasible. I'm talking about the indisputable value of restoring function promptly. Of course, you don't need anything as drastic as open-heart surgery in order to profit from regular, appropriate exercise. What distressed me aboard ship was the

©2003 Lon Horwedel

realization that wide segments of society are still so slow in embracing demonstrated methods leading to wellness and longer life.

**"When Dr. Christian Barnard performed the first human heart transplant, he used the Sarns Model 2000 heart-lung machine."**

What has this got to do with my not retiring? First of all, I love what I'm doing. Yes, like most people I know, I've had my share of setbacks and disappointments. But what matters is that work has never been drudgery. As I look back I see a logical progression from making toys in my dad's shop and selling them door-to-door to founding Sarns, Inc. and then NuStep, Inc.

At Sarns, we developed and manufactured innovative life support products used in open-heart surgery. It was a major step in enabling physicians and healthcare professionals to extend life. After I sold my company to 3M and helped grow that division at 3M, I started NuStep, Inc. Again, the objective was to develop and manufacture healthcare products that would extend and improve life. What we've come up with is an effective, safe, low-impact exerciser designed and developed by exercise physiologists, ergonomic specialists, and health professionals working with everyday people. To me, it's a natural evolution.

In all of this, I've had two advantages: (1) Parents who gave me a strong work ethic and taught me the importance of having a vision and building on it. (2) A loving wife who raised tough questions early in our marriage. Here's an example.

"What are our long-range plans for the future?" she asked. "What are our personal goals? What do we want to accomplish in life?"

Asking tough questions was something Norma knew how to do. She was a teacher in a school provided by the University of Michigan Hospital for youngsters who were long-term patients. Our connection with healthcare came early in our marriage. Still, my first professional encounter with doctors had me scared stiff.

I was gong to school at night and we were invited to a party for "people from work" at the University of Michigan Hospital, where Norma worked. Most of her colleagues were married to doctors, and frankly, I wasn't looking forward to it. I was worried that I wouldn't fit in, that I would be the odd man out. Pretty soon we were all gabbing away. The doctors were researching an array of surgical procedures that would require, for the most part, devices that didn't exist yet. There was no such thing as "biomedical engineering" as we know it today. Doctors would actually go to the hardware stores looking for tools that could be adapted to surgery.

Here was the opportunity that meshed with our goals. Not only was the need obvious, I knew that I had the skills and ability to do the job. Norma and I had decided we wanted to form a business and make useful products we could be proud of. Because of my interests and work experience, we focused on developing electro-mechanical products with high value added. That was the seed that germinated into Sarns, Inc.

Today, we believe that NuStep is poised for the next horizon in healthcare with emphasis on physical therapy and rehabilitation. The post-World War Two "baby boom" generation has crossed the 55-year-old line, and its views of fitness and longevity are different than a generation or two previous. Our younger son, Steven, who is an exercise physiologist, is Vice-President of Marketing and Sales. Our other son, David, went in a different direction and is Chief Operating Office for Rockefeller and Company in New York.

Finally, the cooperative relationship between physicians and engineers is far more efficient than it had been, which is a positive development. I don't know if the sky's the limit, but I'm convinced we're on the right road, and we have no intention of stopping.

Web Site: www.nustep.com.

# Retirement In Full Bloom

David Sayer has yet to meet a daylily he doesn't love.

He first fell in love when he worked at a garden center to help pay his college tuition. His grandfather had been a florist, but growing up he wanted to be a mechanical engineer, so he was a bit surprised when he found himself tending daylilies, hosta and orchids–and liking it.

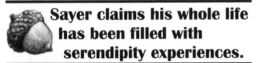

**Sayer claims his whole life has been filled with serendipity experiences.**

Following a four-year stint in the Navy, he worked in the engineering departments of such insurance companies as Continental, Kemper and Home, checking property and casualty risk exposures. When he retired at 55, he did consulting work for Nationwide Insurance and other independent inspection agencies. This was fine except for the frequent travel and overnights away from home.

In 1992, he attended an Ameriflora show. Just before its season closing day, he asked one of the exhibitors what he intended to do with his greenhouse.

"Wanna buy it?" the sales manager asked.

Sayer, who claims his whole life has been filled with serendipity experiences, impulsively said, "Sure!" He made an offer, the salesman accepted, and they finalized the closeout deal for $10,000. A few days later, a truck delivered a 500 square feet superstructure of aluminum and glass to his 1/3-acre home lot, and Sayer was suddenly a full time greenhouse constructor and gardener.

Getting his wife to agree to turn their backyard into a horticultural labyrinth was not a problem. "Now that I think of it," said Sayer, "I knew Barbara was the gal for me when, on one of our first dates, we visited a garden and she bent down and pulled up a weed growing near one of the plants."

Diving into propagating perennial plants may have started out as a lark, but it's not a retirement project for the financially meek. Even before he started, Sayer had to hire an architect and petition for zoning and building permits. Then, using his engineering skills and experiences working on construction sites as a teenager, Sayer spent three months personally reconstructing the greenhouse, which, he admits, is still a work in progress ten years later. While Sayer does not regard greenhouse gardening as a wealth- building enterprise, he always manages to break even or better, he says.

He is constantly improving the heating automation, the humidification, ventilation and fertilization as new cultivars are introduced.

Orchids, for example, have three climates – warm, medium and cool. So a greenhouse is an expensive assembly plant. It requires a dependable heating system, fans for air circulation, water-misting

*It's Never Too Late to Plant a Tree*

apparatuses, gauges, hundreds of special pots, and pounds of fertilizer and materials for pest control and monitoring. It needs daily testing for bugs and, most importantly, like watching a boiler on a ship, checking to keep the heat below 85 degrees F and above 50 degrees F. When the outside temperature soars above or below those goalpost ranges, Sayer explains, you crank up the expensive indoor heating or air conditioning units. Like a farmer, you check the weather report daily and do a lot of praying.

Sayer thinks greenhouse gardening is the greatest retirement activity there is. You don't have to leave home, you're on your own

**New hybrids can be patented and Sayer has a few plants that he intends to register in the future.**

schedule, you rarely need to mow your lawn, it's a hobby at which both spouses can work, and you can increase your disposable income modestly. Sayer specializes in daylilies, hostas and orchids and has over 500 plants covering every foot of the Sayer front yard, back yard and greenhouse space. On weekends, his plants and flora are highlights of the local community garden tour.

A real gardening hobbyist must love plants, but you've also got to like people.

Sayer and Barbara are members of a variety of daylily, hosta and orchid societies and, according to the Sayers, members are fun and a little crazy. On a recent Father's Day, his sons purchased bales of broken containers of manure from a local garden center. Then they delivered all of this on Sayer's driveway, which resulted in a pile 10 feet wide, 40 feet long and three feet high. It was a Father's Day gift that kept on giving. Sayer was able to make use of every inch of the natural fertilizer and, in a few days, all his plants burst into lush growth. "I don't mind being dumped on," brags Sayer. Here is a hobby that benefits from the special relationship between plant and animal nutrients.

Vacations are almost always tied in with gardening activities. David and Barbara travel around the country visiting auctions on society bus tours or on their own.

Acquiring new varieties of hosta, daylilies and orchids is a must. They speak more Latin than you'll hear anywhere outside the Vatican. At local events, they often pack their RV and sell their private stock off the back. The Sayers find themselves being teachers and advisers, and they both have qualified as garden and flower contest judges.

If you're lucky at crossing or hybridizing cultivars—crosses that sometimes can take years to bloom—you can make a small fortune from daylily hybrids. It is not uncommon, at auction, to fetch from $100 to $500 for each plant. The most popular new plants can also be produced in the thousands from tissue culture, a genetic-engineering process known as TC, which allows mass distribution at auctions, or at garden centers or major retailers like K Mart, Home Depot and Wal Mart.

If you want to sell plants from your own backyard, you can personalize your plants with your own names – and garden customers love the personal touch in plants as much as art lovers seek out original paintings.

New hybrids can be registered, and Sayer has a few plants that he intends to register in the future.

To get started, there's a great deal of information in libraries and now on the Internet. Sayer highly recommends joining the various garden societies that help put members in contact with people who want to share their knowledge.

David and Barbara Sayer don't think of themselves as unique. They believe there are thousands of retired seniors just like them involved in greenhouse gardening. What is important is that they're happy. They wake up every day knowing there are hundreds of living plants just outside their window waiting for their affectionate care. That's why with other retirees, the Sayers never tire of giving a salute of "Hosta La Vista, baby!"

E-mail: surfer@iwaynet.net

# The Man Who Knows Noodles

One look at James "Gillie" Stalder, and you know that he's always worked with his hands. For 43 of his 87 years he was an old-style printing press operator. What's not visible is a string of blue ribbons that Stalder has won for his noodles, homemade pies, chilies and picnic main dishes.

If you're interested in a first-hand sampling of Gillie's wares, take a trip to Nelsonville in Appalachian Ohio, a village of 5,000 people where he lives, in old coal-mining country, and in another era, in bootlegging country. And if you go to an American Legion picnic, you're in for a treat. As an alternative, try Kroger's in Nelsonville or Lancaster or Seamens in Athens, and ask for "Gillie's Noodles."

How did it all start?

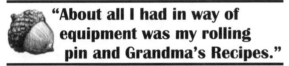

**"About all I had in way of equipment was my rolling pin and Grandma's Recipes."**

"I love to cook," he says, "and Mother was a great cook. We lived on a farm and she used to can, and she was especially good on the noodles. On Sundays, she made the best chicken and noodles. I would help out while I was still a kid, maybe 11, but I never planned to sell the stuff and have a company called 'Gillie's Home Bakery.'

"When I came back from the service in 1945, I'd been in the Army for almost four years. I'd go round to some of the senior citizen dinners and the fish fries the Legion had just about every Friday night, and I'd do the noodles. Afterwards, if there were some left over, I'd sell them or give them away.

"But that was something I was doing on the side. When I got out of the service, I went back to my regular job at the McBee Company, running a rotary letterpress. Were we ever busy! Factory worked three shifts round the clock. Must have turned out millions of tickets for the Long Island Railroad. I still found time for my

*It's Never Too Late to Plant a Tree*

cooking, but it was only after my wife died that I began to think about cooking as a business, got kind of bored being by myself.

**"Are those noodles as good as Grandma's? And I said, 'No, but they're pretty good noodles.'"**

"Anyhow, one day after I'd been cooking at one of those picnics, a fellow from the Health Department came around. He told me the state says to make this legal, I ought to have a license. Well, in those days, there wasn't so much of what you'd call red tape, so I paid $10 for a farm license. Still have it. About all I had in way of equipment was my rolling pin and grandma's recipes, and that's how 'Gillie's Home Bakery' got started.

"With one thing and another, I had a tough time keeping up with demand, and I was doing some catering on the side. But my printing job at McBee was my bread and butter, and I wasn't going to give that up. I got that job in 1936. That was during the Depression and getting a job then was real tough. Hamburger was 25 cents for two pounds in the store, but a lot of people didn't have that quarter. My sister worked at McBee and that gave me an "in." I was hired and made 30 cents an hour, 40 hours a week. That was $12 a week. Pretty good pay in those days. I finally got a raise to $15. That was a big deal."

Where does the "Gillie" come from? That's from his middle name, Gilbert, which no one calls him. As for the "James," Stalder claims there are people in the area who don't even know that's his first name. One way or another in a wide radius of Nelsonville, you're not likely to find too many people who don't know Gillie Stalder. In addition to his culinary achievements, Stalder has been active in veterans' and civic organizations.

"Our Legion post had a pact with Ohio University, which is about 10, 15 miles away in Athens, to usher football and basketball games, so me and my Legion buddies did that for maybe 50 years. I was District Commander of my 40 and 8 group for quite awhile. That name, 40 and 8, comes from World War One, when they used to send 8 horses up to the front in a big boxcar and come back with 40 prisoners of war. Well, I've been a member of the 40 and 8 group here in Athens since I was discharged, and I'm still active. One of our big projects is to help 'burned-out' families. We donate to a children's welfare fund and help girls become nurses and that sort of thing. We got a plaque last year, showing that our 40 and 8 group helped more girls get through school to become nurses than any other 40 to 8 group in Ohio."

While he doesn't make a big deal of it, Stalder did cancer counseling for many years at O'Bleness Memorial Hospital in Athens, being a cancer survivor, himself. He also continued to cook and serve dinners at different functions. Meanwhile, "Gillie's Home Bakery" business kept moving along at a good pace.

"I sold maybe 100 packages a week, and at the farmers' markets, I'd sell 50, 100 packages there. They seem to like those old-fashioned country noodles.

"Yep, it made me a little extra money, some spending money, but it was more important to get out and meet people and that sort of things. Get to talk, maybe see people I haven't seen in awhile. I don't owe anybody anything. Little bit I got is all mine. I lost my wife 25 years ago, never re-married. It would have been 35 years that we were married. Been in the same house for 50 years. My three kids are all grown and married with kids of their own, two in California, one in Florida, all with good jobs. Sent all three of them through college. Good kids, and they treat me good."

In 2002, Stalder sold his business and started to spend more time with his daughter in Florida, and son and daughter in California. "Just became more than I wanted at this part of my life," explains.

Wherever he is, though, he keeps cooking, still using grandma's recipes, which are still doing the trick for him.

A little while ago, Gillie says, a friend asked, "Are those noodles as good as Grandma's? And I answered him, 'No, but they're pretty good noodles.'"

# Seniors To the Front

Decisions. Decisions. Decisions. Decisions.

For starters, here are four puzzlers

"My husband and I are at a stage when many of our friends and relatives have moved to Florida or Arizona. But we have kids and grandkids up here and don't want to give up theater and music and museums. The bottom line is, we'd prefer to stay where we are. How can we?"

"Sometimes I'd like to be able to *Do Something* about the way seniors are ripped off or discriminated against because of our age. I'm not a wild-eyed activist. Still, I'd like to know that I'm not helpless."

"I have a will, and my financial and personal affairs are in pretty good order. Still, there are a lot of unknowns, and I'm not sure in an emergency that family will be available. Where's my support going to come from?"

"I do a lot of volunteer work, but it's not the same as a regular job. Not that I'd like to go back to a 9 to 5 routine. It's just that earning some extra money wouldn't hurt, and I do miss the camaraderie of where I used to work.?"

Here's how others have tackled these problems.

1. *Don't want to move.* In Beacon Hill, Boston, you can find a "virtual retirement community," that brings necessary services to you. *Moving Forward By Staying Put.*

2.  *A remedy for helplessness.* There are other seniors out there who've mastered the techniques of lobbying to legislators who can act on their behalf. *Learn, Then Act!*

3.  *Pretty well set, but...* Life is unpredictable. Emergencies and crises don't give advance notice, but there are prudent steps to help you sleep better at night. *Now Is The Time To Know...*

4.  *Not retired, but not on the commuter schedule, either.* Here's an idea—well, it's not just an idea—it's an economically sound business practice. From *The Corporate World: A Case of Win-Win.*

*It's Never Too Late To Plant A Tree* is not a "how-to" book, per se. However, it's full of practical examples of what others have done. Find just one that can be replicated, and you'll have performed a great service. For others and for yourself.

# From the Corporate World: A Case of Win-Win

If you've been the boss for almost 40 years and thinking of stepping back, only to find yourself on the factory floor weekends, there has to be a better way. Especially when you've pressed your wife into service to help fill orders. Well, Jess A. Bell of Bonne Bell, Inc., a leading cosmetics manufacturer, finally found a way.

"Demand was so strong," he says, "it was either farming the work out, something I didn't want to do, or finding an alternative, which I did. I figured that retirees have a wealth of experience and a high work ethic. So I passed the word in Lakewood, Ohio and through local churches and neighborhood organizations of other communities that we were looking for part-time production workers. The response was immediate. Right off the bat, we signed up 13 workers. Within weeks, we had 60 retired teachers, nuns,

©2003, Jackie Belden Hawthorne

*Seniors to the Front*

nurses, and homemakers on board. That was in 1997. Today, we have well over 100 seniors and a waiting list. You'd be surprised at how many seniors, even super-seniors, welcome the extra income, not to mention a sense of self-worth."

During two four-hour shifts, 7:30 a.m. to 11:30 a.m. and 12:00 noon to 4 p.m., Monday through Friday, the seniors operate three machines that can "blister pack" Lip Smackers, Lip Lix and other cosmetics that pre-teen and teen-aged girls use all over the world.

The most senior member of the group is Evelyn Cicerchi, who has been with the program since 1998 and is a Never Retire figure of some consequence.

Mrs. Cicerchi is 92, a great-grandmother, who owned a drapery business for forty-plus years before selling it and going to work for the new owner. That didn't pan out, so in her late 80s she left. Seven weeks of "idleness" was more than she could handle, which brought her to Bonne Bell.

"I love working here," she says. "Everyone is so nice. I pack, label and make boxes five mornings a week. Why do I do it? The people are wonderful and I can use the extra spending money for 'fun things.'"

**"Everyone is so nice. I pack, label and make boxes five mornings a week. The people are wonderful." Evelyn Cicerchi, 92.**

Neither is Mrs.Cicerchi a "stay-at-home." Recently she went to Las Vegas with a male friend, and when she visits one of her sons, who lives in Corning, New York, she drops in at a local casino. "I do enjoy it," she says. Her other son lives in Ohio.

Enjoying what she does and remaining active is a key to her continuing vitality. At 92 she has her own apartment and lives independently. She drives to work each weekday morning, arriving at 6:45 A.M. to walk the treadmill for a mile and a half in Bonne Bell's exercise room before heading to the blister pack machine at

*It's Never Too Late to Plant a Tree*

©2003, Jackie Belden Hawthorne

7:30 for her four hour shift. For a time bursitis interfered with her exercise routine, but she got through that.

"We have arrangements for the seniors to sit and work," Bob Wotsch, the program supervisor says, "but Evelyn prefers to stand most of the time. She's absolutely amazing. Looks at least 20 years younger than she is, and acts even younger than that. I think some of the 'younger' workers envy her because she's so enthusiastic and energetic. She may miss one day a month because of illness."

As for continuing at Bonne Bell, she says, "I plan to keep going till I'm at least 100. My grandmother lived to 100 and died in her sleep, so I've got the genes going for me. After I'm 100, I'll see."

The program has been so successful that the company relocated earlier this year from its Georgian-style Lakewood headquarters to its main manufacturing center in Westlake, about 10 miles away.

"It was strictly an operations move," Bell says, "and it's great, because now everything is under one roof. Besides, we anticipate the number of workers will soon increase on each shift, since the new space can accommodate them. Fortunately, we believe our waiting list will be able to handle the load."

The retirees play host to monthly birthday celebrations and social events. Turnover among them is rare. Bell attributes the program's success to its members having dedicated work areas of their own. Their areas are separate from younger employees who work elsewhere in the manufacturing area. The company also provides a van to and from its Lakewood offices for those who need transportation to Westlake

"Our idea was to provide retirees with useful, productive work and to pay them for what they do. So, it's not just a 'do-good' effort," says Bell. "We rely on these workers and what they consistently do for our company. No one can do it faster or better than this group of workers. It's exceeded our expectations."

In addition to the pay, the company offers a number annual paid vacation days and discounts on Bonne Bell products to their seniors.

Jess Bell was born in Salinas, Kansas in 1n 1925. Two years later the family moved to

**"You'd be surprised at how many seniors, even super-seniors, welcome the extra income, not to mention a sense of self-worth."**

Cleveland where his father, Jesse Grover Bell, founded Bonne Bell. Jess served in the U.S. Army for three years during World War Two. Following his discharge in 1946, he joined the firm, but as an Army Reserve Office, he was recalled to active duty, when the Korean War broke out in 1950. Three years later, he rejoined Bonne Bell.

The success of Bonne Bell's Retirees' Production-Line Program has sent out ripples to other parts of the country.

"It's really gratifying that other companies are beginning to recognize the value of our senior citizens as a necessary resource, as something that needs to be rewarded," Bell says. "We have more than 33-million Americans over age 65, and they can bring a lot of muscle to the workplace. That percentage is going to rise over the next 20 years. It would be a mistake to neglect the contribution they can make."

Bell has been an innovator before. Twenty-five years ago, he was a prime mover behind the creation of corporate fitness and wellness programs across the country. Considered novel at the time, these programs are now common. He has received international recognition for his contribution to physical fitness and sports participation by American women.

Bell is a believer in practicing what he preaches. At the company's main offices in Lakewood, employees can take part in jazzercise class and use an array of exercise equipment. Those who work at the company's production facility in Westlake can use its exercise room and outdoor fitness track.

"What it comes down to," he says, "is that you can do well, by doing right. Seniors have profited, not just monetarily, but in the way they feel about themselves. For us, it's like re-opening a mine that has been shut down, and discovering that it still has a lot of gold in it. It's strictly a win-win situation, the best kind there is."

Web site: www.bonnebell.com

# Learn, Then Act!

Remember the saying about a team of dogs pulling a sled, "If you're not in the lead, the view never changes."

Dorothy Epstein didn't coin the phrase, but for the greater part of her life, she's been out front, and her view has kept changing. Welfare worker. Labor leader. Wartime Relief Agency manager. Business executive. Now as she approaches her 90th birthday, Epstein is still out front, this time helping train seniors to represent themselves more effectively. "I've always embraced social issues," she says, "women's rights, civil rights, you name it. I was always a leader."

In 1989, at the age of 76, Epstein retired as president of Synergy Vitamins and turned her attention to senior issues. She joined a Senior Center and in short order became president. Next she got involved with the Joint Public Affairs Committee (JPAC) of the Jewish Association for Social Action (JASA).

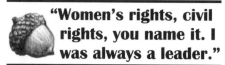 **"Women's rights, civil rights, you name it. I was always a leader."**

"JPAC organizes bus trips to Albany every year to lobby the Governor and the Legislature, and I joined in," she says. "Groups of five or seven seniors would visit the chair of every committee with jurisdiction over senior affairs, as well as other influential legislators. And you know what I found? In a typical group, one or two would speak; the others would stand around or raise points that weren't relevant. Right then, I knew we had to do better, and the only way to do better was to train our members on what to do and how to do it."

From that seed came the Institute for Senior Action, with Epstein taking the lead

"After seeing how our groups performed or didn't perform in Albany, I went back to JPAC," Epstein recalls. "I said, 'We ought to have a school where we train seniors to work more effectively. The passion is there. They have the knowledge in many cases, but they have to hone it so they make their presentations more useful.' There was a lot of enthusiasm for the idea, and of course, some skeptics who said, 'We tried classes and it didn't work.' Well, I told them that was then and now was now. It took a year to get the Institute off the ground, but in 1994 we got underway."

"You'd be amazed at how much there was to teach and to learn," she says. "I'll give you an example. There's a 95-year-old man, who's currently a member of the Institute for Senior Action. He worked for the Social Security Administration back in 1935 when it was first created, but some years ago, before the Institute started, this man went door to door in his community, telling seniors how Social Security operated and how they could benefit from it. They just didn't know, and there was no one to tell them."

Since 1994, the Institute has moved ahead with a twice a year, 10-week training program, covering topics such as Budgets and Legislative Processes; Senior Entitlements; Working Intergenerationally; Fundraising Fundamentals; Techniques of Social Action; How To Run An Effective Meeting; Writing Skills and Techniques; Conflict Resolution. By the end of 2002, the Institute had graduated its 17th class, making more than 400 people who had gone through the program.

> **"We ought to have a school where we train seniors to work more effectively."**

"And the people who teach the classes!" Epstein says. "They come from all walks of life. Experts in their fields: gerontologists, attorneys, legislators, social workers, business executives, professors and media figures like Brian Lehrer of Public Broadcasting and Gail Collins of *The New York Times*. All *pro bono*, without charge.

"What's equally remarkable is the mix of students in the classes. They differ ethnically, where they come from, their educations, their degree of affluence. But despite those differences, there's very

*It's Never Too Late to Plant a Tree*

little friction. It's a wonderful example of how people from different backgrounds can work together for a common good. Over 200 community or advocacy organizations have sent students to our classes. Not only are we training people of my generation, we're now training a second generation of seniors."

She points with pride to some of the Institute's achievements: obtaining Access-A-Ride, a low-cost bus service for older or disabled senior citizens, who may not be able to use public transportation; affordable banking; lights in poorly lit neighborhoods; securing $16.2-million in new funds for aging services from the NYC government. The list goes on.

Epstein has no plans to expand beyond New York City or to go national, but she says, "Other senior organizations have looked at what we've done and set up programs of their own. We've published a *Tool Kit* to help them."

What it all comes down, Epstein says is "Learn, Then Act," which is the Institute's slogan.

Learning, then acting is what Epstein has done since graduating from Hunter College in 1933. "It was the Depression. There were no jobs available and more than two million unemployed in New York City alone. I ended up with lawyers, would-be doctors, scientists and social workers in the Department of Welfare, because it was the one place that was hiring. I helped build the American Federation of State, County, and Municipal Employees (AFSCME), the largest public employee and health care workers union in the United States. I was the first woman state president in 1942. I was Labor Management Director for Russian War Relief during World War Two. When I was 59, I went into private industry in health foods and started a natural vitamin company with a group of men—I was the only woman—and became president of the Synergy Plus division.

While her days of demonstrating and walking the picket lines may be over, Epstein still has a full agenda.

"Our minds can produce a great deal which is very useful. I'm using mine, and I know a lot of people, who are using theirs. There are so many seniors with accrued knowledge and experience whose value has not been utilized. One of the most underestimated factors in our society is accepting a generation that's getting older and succeeding generations that will continue to get older. I'm going to help gain that acceptance."

E-mail: jpac@jasa.org

# Moving Forward
# By Staying Put

"Virtual retirement community" is not a computer game or a TV show. As J. Atwood "Woody" Ives will tell you, it's a real place in Boston, called Beacon Hill Village (BHV), with 150 members, aged 64 to 92.

This is his story and these are his words.

I'm the president of BHV, but Judith Willett, our Executive Director, makes the place run. I discovered a long time ago in the corporate world that delegating the job to the right person is a key to success, and that's what I did.

To set the record straight, BHV is less about "Retirement" and more about "Wellness" in its broadest sense—social, cultural

©2003, Dina Rudick

stimulation and physical fitness. Our members want to have fun as well as feel secure, as they grow older in their own homes. They want all this to happen in a familiar neighborhood, among younger friends with a range of diverse people, places and activities that the city offers.

**"If you're serious about being a true 'community,' everyone must be included."**

Call it serendipity that I got involved. In 1998, when I began thinking about stepping down as CEO of Eastern Enterprises, a New York Stock Exchange energy and utilities conglomerate, my wife, Elizabeth, and I bought a house on Beacon Hill. Retirement was still a couple of years away, but since we both had numerous Boston-based activities, it made sense not to continue commuting from Lexington.

Talking to our new neighbors, I discovered a group that was committed to staying in their homes on the Hill as they grew older, and was in the process of organizing to do just that. I became intrigued and joined the group. Some months later, I was offered the presidency of BHV, and I accepted.

The first thing we did was to register as a non-profit corporation with the purpose of replicating what upscale retirement communities do for their residents. Working with BHV's founding Board, we developed a budget and a marketing plan. We organized a fund-raising drive, hired staff, signed up members at $500 a year for individuals and $600 for households. In addition, thanks to some foundation money, we're able to offer reduced membership fees to residents who are financially pressed. My view is that if you're serious about being a true "community," everyone must be included.

Essentially, what BHV provides is the kind of service that a close relative who lives nearby could. We offer peace of mind and continuity of community. Our message is, Join with us and we'll give you access to lots of things, and discounts for many needed services. That way, we live longer. We live happier.

That's all well and good, but very often, we may need support. We've learned that for a spouse who is a health care provider, anxiety and strain can take a terrible toll. So much so that their life spans may be shortened by 30 to 40 percent. But there are alternatives. For example, Alzheimer Day Care Centers or home health aides can give the spouse relief for eight to ten hours a day to re-invigorate themselves. We can help point our members in the right direction, which brings me to another key element in our program.

I talked about the importance of delegating. Another key to achieving one's goals is enlisting first-class strategic partners. BHV did, by recruiting three major Boston institutions to its team. The first, Massachusetts General Hospital (MGH), provides our members access to MGH Senior Health, a clinical practice offering health care and wellness programs for those over 60. The second, Rogerson Communities, backed by three decades of experience managing elder housing in the Greater Boston area, generously provides BHV office space, bookkeeping and marketing support, advice for the Board, and informational sessions on topics such as long-term health insurance for members.

HouseWorks, the third leg of this support platform, offers a full menu of concierge services including transportation, grocery shopping, skilled handymen, and up to 24-hour home health care—all of it at a discount to BHV members.

Less than a year old, BHV already offers a range of services similar to those found in quality retirement communi-

> **"The virtual retirement community is consistent with the over-whelming desire to remain at home as we age."**

ties. Member activities have included trips to the Peabody/Essex and the Lowell Textile museums; a twilight dinner cruise up the Charles River to an outdoor rendition of Shakespeare's "As You Like It"; health club membership discounts; Tai Chi classes and walking groups; presentations by nationally known health professionals such as Doctors Herbert Benson and Kenneth

Minaker; small group discussions with Boston luminaries in the arts and journalism; and professional advice on everything from computer use to nutrition.

Those of us at BHV are confident that we're on the right path. The virtual retirement community not only addresses a growing national problem, it's consistent with the overwhelming desire to remain at home with familiar surroundings as we age. As outside validation, the Harvard Business School's Community Action Program became intrigued by the BHV model and got involved early on. Since then, inquiries about BHV have come from as nearby as Cambridge, Massachusetts and as far away as California.

Personally, my life is as full as ever. I'm active in a multiplicity of cultural, philanthropic and for-profit board tasks, such as the Boston Museum of Fine Arts, United Way, WGBH (a PBS station), Keyspan Corporation, and Massachusetts Financial Services, in addition to BHV. I've always had a blend of the two. The difference is that now there's less emphasis on the for-profit portion. Also, Elizabeth and I are able to stretch our weekends to three, maybe four days on Cape Cod, where we've had a house for some years.

Finally, just remember that, as we get older, we continue to grow new brain cells, provided we actively stimulate our minds. It's a myth that we're just atrophying. A while ago, BHV made up some canvas bags imprinted:

> Beacon Hill Village
> A virtual retirement community.

Not all our members were happy with the "retirement" part. And, as I think about it, they may be right. How about:

> Beacon Hill Village
> The Community of Tomorrow

Web site: www.beaconhillvillage.org
E-mail: bhvillage@aol.com

# Now Is The Time To Know, "What Would You Do If...?"

Question: What is the single most important time in your life to plan ahead?

Answer: In one word... Now!

**"Whom could we call on in an emergency? What services are available, and how could I get to them on short notice, if the need arose?"**

Listen to Ray Josephs, a renowned expert on time management. Still unstoppable at 91, Josephs' wife, Hanny, suffers from macular degeneration, an eye affliction. As they thought about her condition, Josephs realized there was a gap in their life planning. Yes, he has a will; his financial, business and personal affairs are in good order. But he realized there's an unknowable future that he did not want to leave purely to chance.

"Hanny and I have been married for 62 years," he says. "We never had children and have limited family to step in, if we have a medical or other crisis. I had to ask myself some questions. 'Whom could we call on in an emergency? What services are available, and how could I get to them on short notice, if the need arose?' It's not a matter of money. I've been fortunate that way, but where would the support come from?"

Having made his reputation in public relations and as a self-help guru who has sold millions of copies of "How to Gain an Extra Hour Every Day" and "How to Make Money From Your Ideas," in 27 languages plus other books, Josephs was not willing to just wonder rather than act.

The result is an enhanced "on demand" service, called Senior Source, a New York-based comprehensive management program that specializes in planning, coordinating and providing elder care

services that foster independent living at home. It provides the types of solutions Josephs was seeking, if and when needed, and opened a new and personally rewarding mission to which he devotes a considerable chunk of his carefully scheduled time.

None of this happened overnight. Without a professional background in healthcare management, Josephs went to work, when he recognized the need. He reviewed professional care systems already in place through the Internet and through contacts built up over more than 50 years in public relations and writing.

"I was public relations counsel for United Jewish Appeal (UJA) Federation-New York for 30 years," he explains, "and now I'm a volunteer member of its Community Cabinet. UJA is the nation's largest city net of 130 agencies that provide health, family, senior services, and a wide variety of support services for people in need. What I found was an uncentralized coordination of services among the providers and a lack of user-applicable information on the part of those who might need their services.

*It's Never Too Late to Plant a Tree*

"So, I went to Bonnie Shevins, an executive at UJA-Federation who, by coincidence, also was exploring new models of prospective member agency services for New York's expanding senior population. She referred me to Stuart Kaplan, CEO of SelfHelp Community Services, an affiliated agency.

Josephs encouraged SelfHelp to utilize its existing social service and homecare programs to allow a new range of clients, such as himself and his wife, to create options for developing comprehensive care plans before they actually needed them. Then, Josephs took the crucial next step. He drafted a seven-page proposal to SelfHelp, outlining a program that gives him and others a One-Stop Resource for possible needs in the years ahead.

"One of the first lessons in public relations," Josephs says, "is to put yourself in the other person's shoes. That's what I did, when I wrote this proposal, and it worked."

SelfHelp was so impressed and enthusiastic, it (a) accepted Josephs' proposal for him and his wife (b) designated Senior Source as the vehicle for delivering its services to others for modest fees. Its roster includes:

Companionship; Escorting to appointments; Housekeeping; Custodial care; Financial management; Advocacy for benefits and entitlement and help with applications for

> **"Private organizations charge two to three times what SelfHelp does. I see it as a case of doing well, by doing right."**

concrete services; Collaboration with physicians and hospital personnel during the acute phases of illness and hospitalization to ensure a smooth transition from hospital to home; Home care; Assessment and referral for alternate care; Skilled nursing; Rehabilitation. In short, "an extended Family of Last Resort."

A leading not-for-profit geriatric and home care agency in the New York metropolitan area, SelfHelp Community Services currently serves more than 20,000 elderly and/or chronically ill individuals and their families. Its comprehensive network of services includes individual case management, court-appointed guardianship, counseling, meals-on-wheels, home care, housekeeping and emergency assistance services.

Senior Source cites the types of worries it encounters.

From a very busy working couple: "We travel, have full time jobs, three kids, mortgages, and aging parents who live far away. We worry that we can't get there when they need us. How can we make sure they get help when they need it?"

From a retired couple: "We love being independent, but we're getting older and can't manage everything ourselves anymore. Where can we turn for help?"

Josephs says, "We're looking at a growth market with this segment of our population. As more people live longer, they may need these services. I think it will be an important addition for SelfHelp, which has been around for over half a century. Private organizations charge two to three times what SelfHelp does. I see it as a case of doing well, by doing right." And he points to the reaction of CEO Kaplan.

"Stuart has been an enthusiastic supporter of this effort. He realizes that seniors may not require all that Senior Source offers. But, he makes the analogy with automobile insurance. It's something to have, in case you ever need it. You hope you never do, but if you do, Senior Source is in place, ready to do the job."

Earlier this year, the New York State Department of the Aging recognized Josephs with its Senior "Achievement Is Ageless" award with a plaque and a handshake from the mother of Governor George Pataki.

"There's still so much to do," Josephs says, busy as ever in his well-ordered apartment overlooking the United Nations in New York City.

"I'm helping promote the Access-Benefit program at the Senior Centers of New York. Volunteers, like myself, help seniors access

39 agencies in New York and act as their advocate. Their services are often a jumble for the ordinary senior. Senior Centers are making it easier for them to access existing service. Getting the information is the first step, but only the first step. It doesn't do the job. It's a tough world out there. It's so complicated, you don't know where to turn. You have to have support."

Far from being depressed by all of these "What If's?" Josephs remains energized.

"I revised 'How To Gain an Extra Hour Every Day,' in the 1990's, because so much has changed. But the basic premise of personal time management remains: Plan ahead and follow your plan. You'll accomplish your goals with far fewer worries. And achieve your objectives more easily."

The Josephs continue to travel here and abroad, without having to worry too much about, "What would we do if..."

For further information: SelfHelp Community Services, Inc. 520 Eighth Avenue, New York, NY 10018 (Tel.) 800/935-3701; (Fax) 212/290-8039

# A Personal After Word

*It's Never Too Late To Plant A Tree* has been both a
moving and uplifting experience. Especially when it
came to talking with someone in her or his 90's. As of
this writing, mid-2003, both of us are 78, not too shabby for two
working men. But Bud Reid, Ora Anderson, Evelyn Cicerchi,
Frances Petit, Ned Putzell, Jack Chilton, Roland Sharer, Dorothy
Epstein, Ray Josephs, are all 90 and up. Wow! And most of them
had to make time to squeeze us in for interviews.

In the course of writing this book, we've met a fascinating array of
people. Most were strangers. Fewer than a dozen of those profiled
had been known to one or the other of us previously. The
remainder, the vast majority, we encountered for the first time.

The decades are great dividers, physically, psychologically and
actuarially. Remember what it was like crossing from your 20's
into your 30's? And phrases like the "Big Four-Oh" or the "Big
Five-Oh." Friends, every decade is BIG.

In terms of content, the stories of the women and men in *It's Never
Too Late To Plant A Tree* are more dissimilar than alike. Former
CEO's and blue collar workers. What they share, as you can see, is
a determination to move forward, not to dwell on past glories or the
chagrin of failure, but to take life in stride to the best of their
abilities.

As must be obvious, these profiles provide no more than glimpses
into their lives. Just think of trying to compress the essentials of
*your* life into a thousand words, give or take a couple of hundred
words. How can a writer, in a sentence or a paragraph, sum up the
continuation of life after losing a spouse of half a century? And to
recount the trauma of losing a child? How? In two cases, Saul
Bennett and Harriet Lewis, never able to forget, preserved the love
and memory of that child in the work they did and continue to do.

*323*

When we started on this journey, we were energized by the prospect of gathering stories of those who chose not to go into conventional retirements, but to keep putting one foot in front of the other.

"Boy, what a terrific idea," we said to each other, as we assembled the profiles. Better yet, outside reaction was so positive as to give us a sense of increased pride and pleasure as we come to a close.

Because we've signed off on this book doesn't mean we're finished. To the contrary, we invite you to nominate yourself or someone you know—friend, relative, business associate—for our next book. Yes, we really believe that *It's Never Too Late*...

Good luck. God Speed and let us hear from you.

> University Sports Press
> P.O. Box 2315
> Athens, OH 45701

> Mel Helitzer & Morrie Helitzer

# Acknowledgments

It's taken a small army of foresters to plant this book. To find the 62 award winners, we searched all over the United States and Canada. And we are grateful to the hundreds of people and sources whose help was invaluable. Any omissions are inadvertent.

Friends, relatives and associates: Robert Althoff, Philip Basse, Bill Brickner, Jack Ellis, Bezhad and Harriet Fakhery, Irwin "Sonny" Fox, Leona Green, Deborah Helitzer, Vivienne Hylton, Paul "Jake" Jacobson, Michael Johnson, D. Warren Kaufman, Mark Kaufman, William Lavelle, Dale Leslie, David Mitzel, Tom Murphy, Richard Nostrant, Robert Orben, Carol Poll, Sandra Porter, Norman Rebin, Edward See, David Sklar, Carol Ann Smith, Jerry Sloan, Karen Stalder, Virginia Tooper, Al and Margaret Topping, Linea Warmke, Igor Webb, Kenneth Wong, and Wayne Zirkin.

From colleges and universities: Michael Bugeja, Iowa State University; John Boal, University of Michigan; Robert Glidden, president of Ohio University; Mary Geraghty Kenyon, University of Iowa; Diana Knott, Ohio University; Dale R. Leslie, University of Michigan; Michael Real, Ohio University; Fred Talbott, Vanderbilt University; and Peter J. Titlebaum, University of Dayton.

Communication and media companies: George A. Becker Public Relations; Barbara Chessser, Meyer Resource Group; Tom Ciesielka, TC Public Relations; Mary Conway Communications; Robyn Gunn, Silver Lake Publishing; Scott Lorenz, Westwind Communications; Martha Popolski, Morelink Public Relations; Sue Porter, E.W. Scripps Media; radio station KWXY, Palm Springs; Mark A. Staples, Augsburg Fortress; Sue Reddy Silverman Public Relations; and Martta Rose, Rubenstein Communications.

Publications and reporters:*The Albuquerque Tribune; Cincinnati 50 Plus Weekly;* Betsy Butler, *Columbus For Business First Magazine*; Nick Claussen, *The* Athens News; free lancer Leslie Jimenez; Tom Lavis, *The Johnstown Tribune-Democrat; Palm Desert Magazine;* Bill Pfeiffer, *The Columbus Dispatch;* Rita Price, The *Columbus Dispatch*; Danielle R. Tabor*, The OU Post; The New York Times;* Joan Slattery Wall, *Ohio Today Magazine*; and Larry Walsh, *The Pittsburgh Post Gazette.*

Retirement and recreational communities: June Hussey, The Fountains; Guy Lombardo, National Ski Patrol of Summit Mountain; Judy O'Brien, The Fountains at Boca Ciega Bay; Barbara Printz, Pacific Regent; and Becky Schulte, LifeSphere.

Photographic and art team: David Ahnthulz, Judy and Don Asman, Joe Clark, Brian Day, Janet Doan, Ocean Eiler, Terry E. Eiler, John Ewing, Rich-Joseph Facun, Lee Ferris, Michael J. Gallegos, Jeff T. Green, Joe Gonzalez, Barbara Sue Haines, Jackie Belden Hawthorne, Adrienne Helitzer, Irene Helitzer, Lon Horwedel, Eric Jennings, Helen Jones, Marilyn Kutin, Tammy Lechner, Richard Marjan, Brad Martin, Albert T. Parker, Chris Pietsch, Walt Ratterman, Brian Ray, Kevin Rivoli, Stephanie Schmidt, Dirk Shadd, Thomas Hart Shelby, Allison Shelley, Mia Song, Jeanie Adams-Smith, Bruce Strong, Richard Tsong-Taatarii, Greg Undeen, William Walsh, Jackie Winch and The Athens Photographic Project.

Public service organizations: Jon D. Moor, The Carter Center; Mark A. Staples, Lutheran Seminary at Philadelphia; Beacon Hill Village; Institute for Senior Action; Muskingum County Community Foundation; SelfHelp Community Services, Inc.; and The United Jewish Appeal of New York.

From proud children: Julie Garner, Nancy Stalder Haramy, Edna Kaplan, Susan Nielsen, Dan Snyders, and Amy Tabor.

Public relations: Susannah Greenberg

Proofreader: Lowell VerHeul

# Author Bios

## Mel Helitzer

If Mel Helitzer weren't one of this book's authors, he could have been profiled himself, as a senior who has led an inspiring and admirable career. For 30 years, Helitzer was a nationally respected advertising and public relations executive in New York. He received numerous industry awards, including two Clio statues for advertising, four *Advertising Age* awards for outstanding commercials and the Edward L. Bernays award for "the most outstanding public relations of the year." In 1956 he was a speechwriter for Presidential candidate Adlai Stevenson, and for 12 years he wrote humor material for a number of famous entertainers.

In 1979 after he sold his agency and retired, he was invited to join the faculty of the Scripps School of Journalism at Ohio University. Within a few years, the student body named him a distinguished "University Professor," and college alumni named him one of the professors who most influenced their professional careers. A major speakers bureau selected him as one of the 100 most popular public speakers in the country. He is the author of seven books and one Broadway-bound musical. Two of his books, *Comedy Writing Secrets* and *The Dream Job: Sports Publicity, Promotion and Marketing* became national best sellers.

E-mail: helitzer@ohio.edu

# Morrie Helitzer

Morrie Helitzer is still trying to figure it out. Because his high school principal warned him that a Depression-era kid had to study something that would provide a living, he took a degree in electrical engineering. World War Two and the U.S. Navy opened the path to what he really wanted to be, a reporter, first in Madison, Wisconsin, then Chicago. From there, across the Atlantic, as a freshly-minted foreign correspondent in Berlin during the blockade; Vienna; Yugoslavia; Paris. Then back to the United States. No Great American Novel, but a one-hour Kraft TV Playhouse production of *Dateline:Vienna*. Next stop: a year of free-lancing in India, then a real job in New York with ABC, followed by four years as a foreign correspondent in London and Germany.

A return ticket to the United States and a one-year fellowship. Time to switch gears. Seventeen years with McGraw-Hill, learning book and newsletter publishing. Meanwhile, Franklin Watts published his young people's book, *The Cold War*. Now for the entrepreneurial leap. He became a consultant, established a book imprint for Battelle Memorial Institute, and launched two magazines, learning as he went. Next move? Who knows? When it comes to planting trees, Helitzer's shovel is always ready.

E-mail: NewDuBois@aol.com

# Other Books By Mel Helitzer

## COMEDY WRITING SECRETS

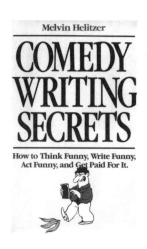

If you long to make people laugh, this book reveals all the tricks of the humorists field. It teaches the practicalities of a sense of humor, the basics of comedy writing and the avenues by which you can turn your comedic talent into a well-paying pursuit. Published by Writer's Digest Books, Cincinnati, Ohio $16.99. Nearly 100,000 copies sold since 1987.

## OH, JACKIE! - HER FATHER'S STORY

For thousands of Broadway theater lovers tired of earsplitting, hard pounding dance musicals, *Oh, Jackie*! is a critically praised production with lyrical award winning music you can remember and words you can sing on your way out of the theater, all wound around a heartwarming story of the special secret that existed when a scandalous father helped turn Jackie Kennedy, America's most unforgettable daughter, into an international icon of style, beauty and grace. Book includes CD cast album. Published in 2003 by University Sports Press, $19.95.

## THE DREAM JOB: SPORTS PUBLICITY, PROMOTION AND MARKETING

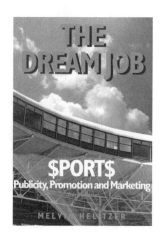

Designed for sports management professionals and interns, the book has been reviewed as "one of the most important texts published in sports administration." In addition to basic publicity techniques, it also includes primary responsibilities of sports pr managers, how to get guests books on broadcast interview programs, how to plan fundraising events and crisis management solutions. Published by University Sports Press, $29.95. Now in its 3rd edition, it has sold nearly 50,000 copies since 1993.

The Golden Acorn stained glass trophy, designed by Jackie Winch, is awarded to each senior in the book